Exposing the Maya

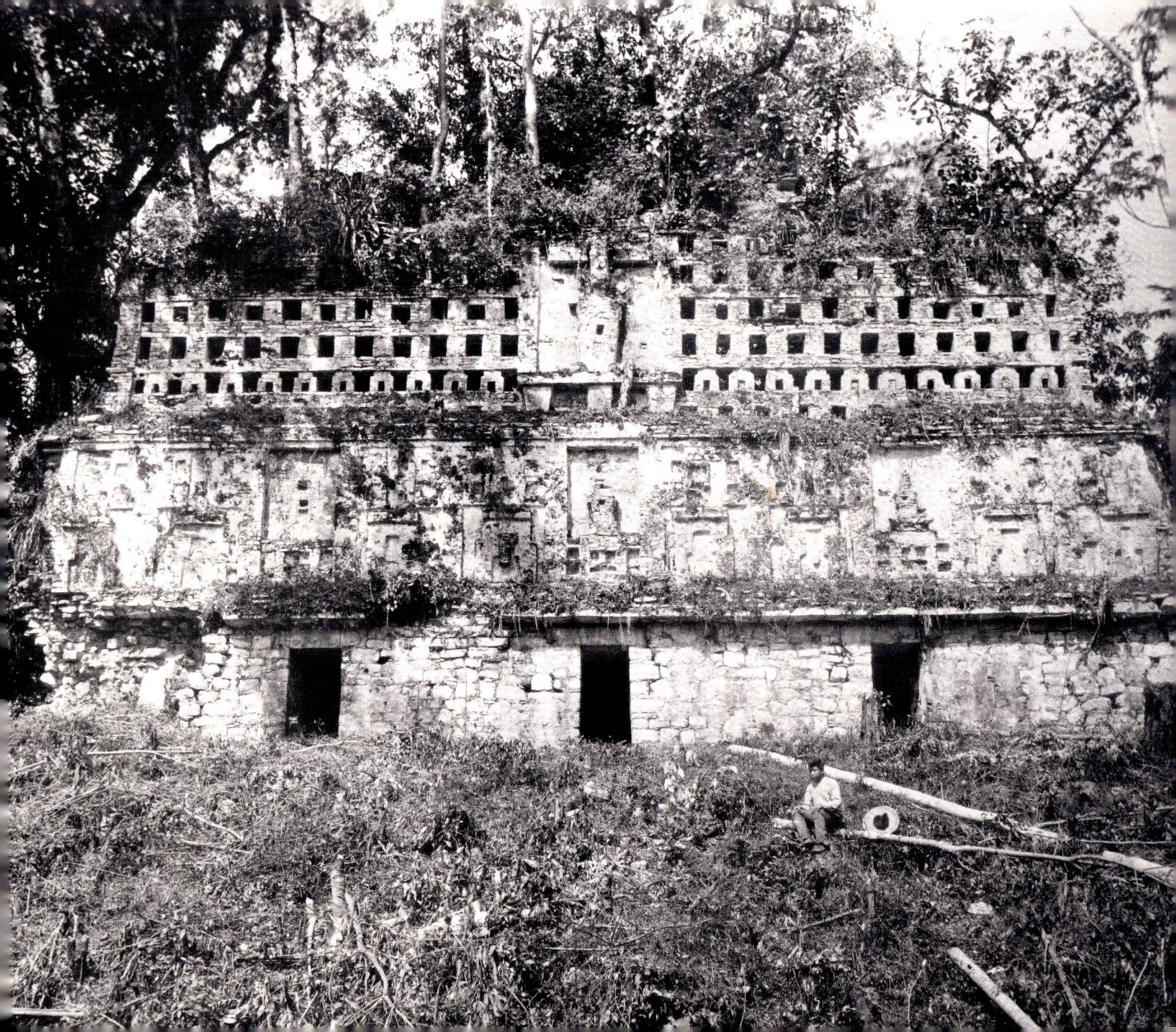

EXPOSING THE MAYA

Early Archaeological Photography in the Americas

Katia Sainson
John W. Hessler

D Giles Limited

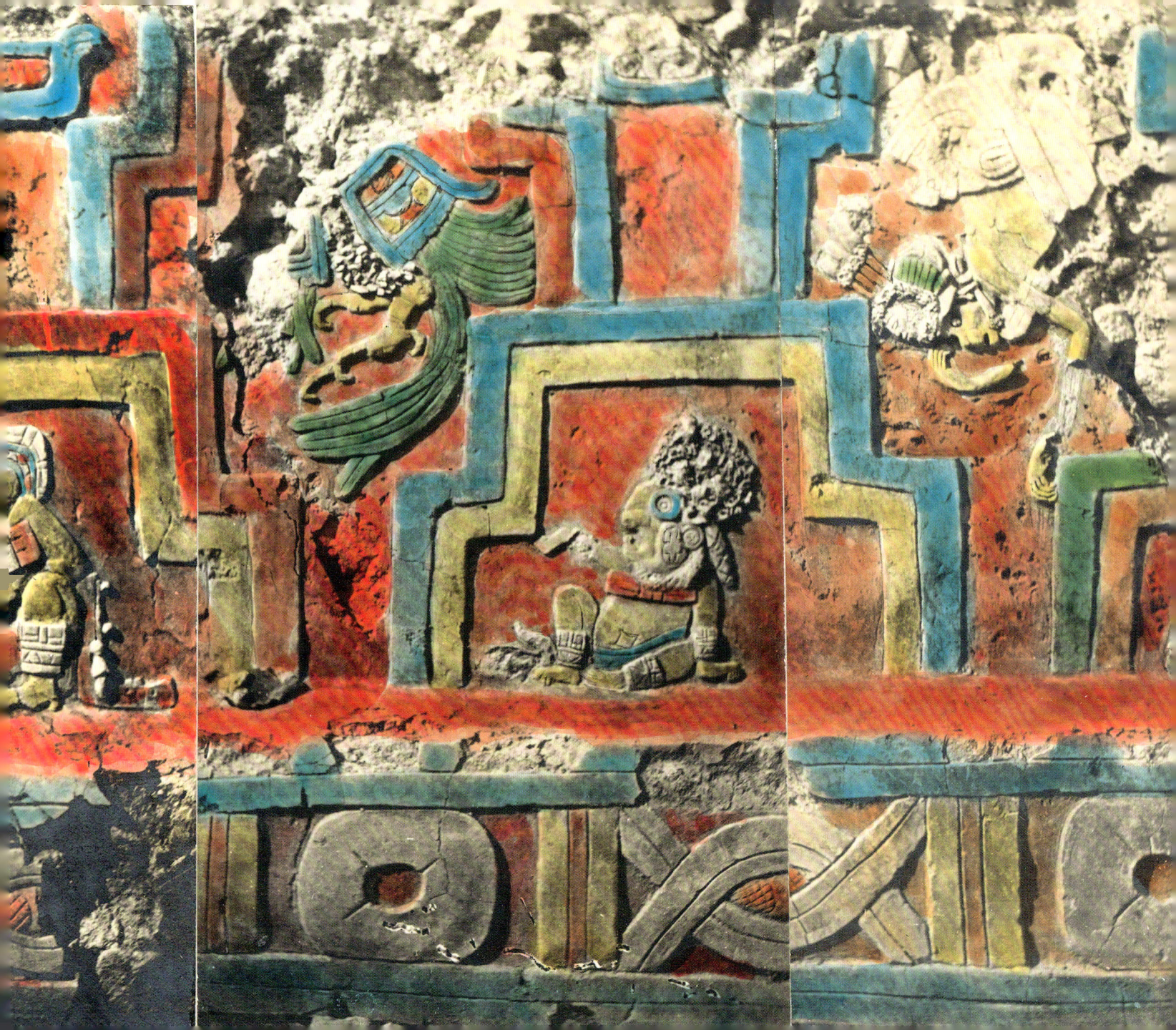

© 2022 Katia Sainson and John W. Hessler

The right of Katia Sainson and John W. Hessler to be identified as the authors of the work has been asserted in accordance with the Copyright, Designs and Patents Act 1988 (as amended).

First published in 2022 by GILES

An imprint of D Giles Limited
66 High Street,
Lewes, BN7 1XG, UK
gilesltd.com

ISBN Hardcover: 978-1-913875-24-4

All rights reserved

No part of the contents of this book may be reproduced, stored in a retrieval system, or transmitted in any form or by any means, electronic, mechanical, photocopying, recording, or otherwise, without the written permission of the authors and D Giles Limited.

Copy-edited and proofread by Sarah Kane
Designed by Alfonso Iacurci
Produced by GILES, an imprint of D Giles Limited
Printed and bound in China

Front cover: "Deity side" of Stela 11, Yaxchilán. Detail of Fig. 82.

Back cover: Engraving by Agostino Aglio of the 1824 *Ancient Mexico* exhibition of New World antiquities at the Egyptian Hall, Piccadilly, London, organized by William Bullock. Detail of Fig. 7.

Frontispiece: Structure 33, Yaxchilán. Detail of Fig. 80.

Preface	7
Exposing the Maya	9
The Photographers	
Désiré Charnay	29
Alice and Augustus Le Plongeon	63
Teobert Maler	87
Alfred Maudslay	121
Adela Breton	147
Notes	166
Bibliography	170
Index	173
Photo Credits	176

In Memory of Jay I. Kislak
Collector & Philanthropist

Preface

This work grew out of one of the authors' obsession with the *Biologia Centrali-Americana* (1879–1915), a series of beautifully produced fascicules, conceived of and edited by two of the most creative naturalists of the late nineteenth and early twentieth centuries, F. Ducane Godman and Osbert Salvin. The sixty-three volumes, mostly dedicated to zoology and botany, also contain photographs by Alfred Maudslay and drawings by Annie Hunter, of the great ruined cities of Central America. In this encyclopedia archaeology was illustrated like natural history.

The other author came to the subject through her translation of the travels of Brasseur de Bourbourg, that great manuscript hunter, who searched, found and preserved many of the early manuscripts of great importance to historians of the ancient Americas, like the Popol Vuh.

Our researches came together in the archive of Alfred Maudslay preserved at the British Library and so painstakingly examined by the archaeologist, Ian Graham. It is his work that truly inspired ours.

Works like this always need support and we would like to thank the Kislak Family Foundation for their generous grant to support the publication. We would also like to thank John Mease, and Geannine Callaghan at the Towson University Foundation, as well Chris Chulos, Paula Zyne and Lauren Rowe, from Towson University for their help in making this book possible.

Many archivists and librarians helped track down documents and suggested photographs for the book including Alessandro Pezzati of the Penn Museum of the University of Pennsylvania, Lisa Graves from the Bristol Museum and Art Gallery and Katherine Meyers Satriano of the Peabody Museum of Archaeology and Ethnology. Lastly, our sincere thanks to Adrienne Lundgren, of the Library of Congress, for many discussions about early photography, and whose obsession with nineteenth-century processes is contagious.

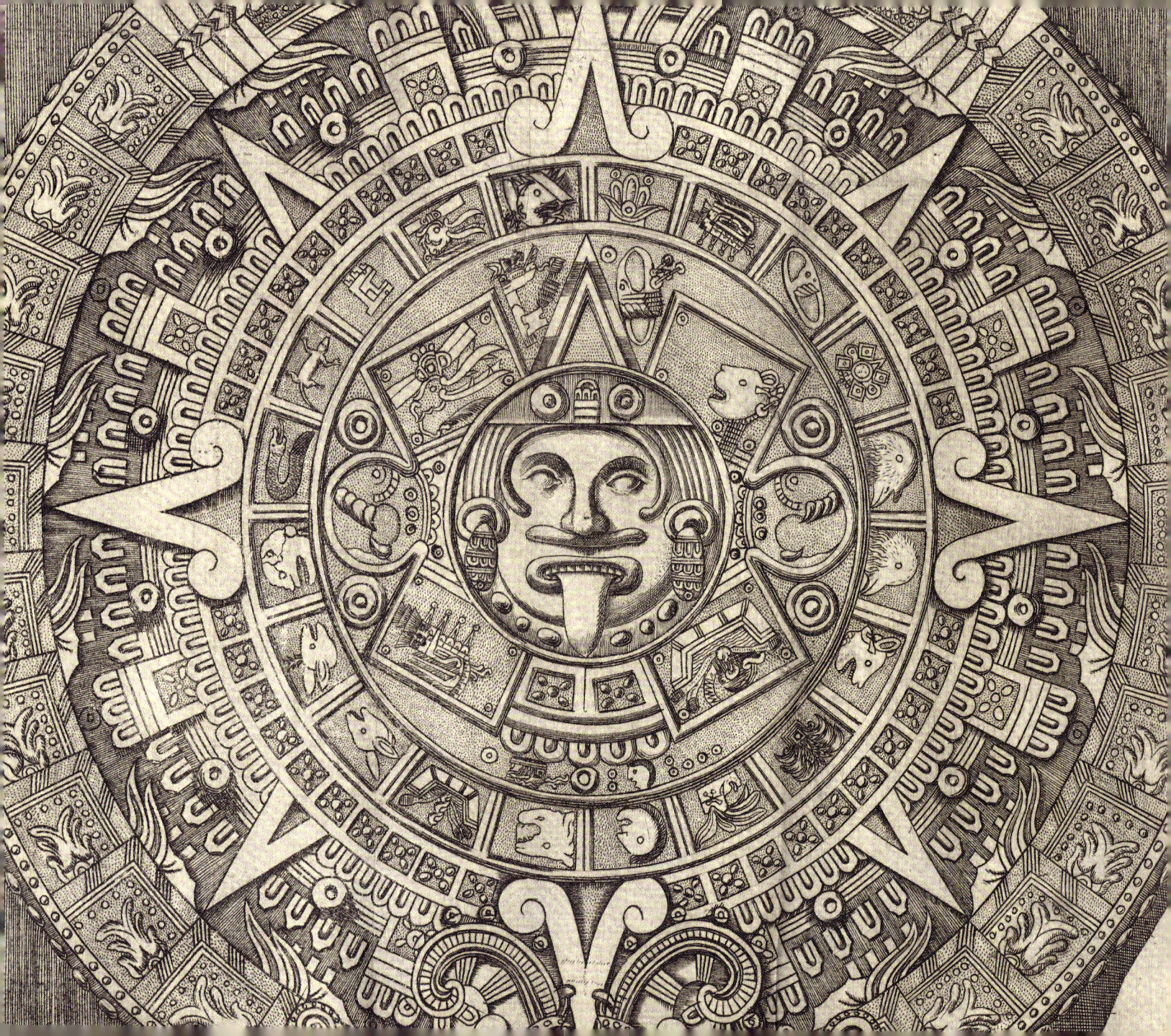

Exposing the Maya

Early Archaeological Photography in the Americas

A photograph of landscape is merely an amusing toy, [however] one of early architecture is a precious historical document; and [...] this architecture should be taken, not merely when it presents itself under picturesque general forms, but stone by stone, and sculpture by sculpture.[1]

John Ruskin

On July 3, 1839, at a meeting of the Academy of Sciences in Paris, François Arago, head of the astronomical observatory in Paris, made a dramatic announcement: a chemical process had been invented that would, for the first time, using a lens and a box camera, deposit a realistic image of the world on a polished metal plate. Arago proclaimed that the daguerreotype, one of the first stable photographic processes, was a revolutionary technique that could be used to faithfully copy the mysterious hieroglyphs inscribed and sculpted in low relief on the recently discovered ancient Egyptian monuments of Thebes, Memphis, and Karnak. Arago went on to imagine that this new technology, which could accurately reproduce complex epigraphy, would allow scholars to unlock the mysteries of ancient civilizations whose languages were unreadable and whose histories were lost to the ravages of time.

From that date in 1839, the science and technology of photography quickly evolved. Those early daguerreotypes were unique images on silver-plated copper sheets that could not be duplicated. Soon to follow were calotypes—William Henry Fox Talbot's negative-positive process on paper—and then the wet-collodion glass-negative process, which "ruled"[2] from 1851 up until the advent of the gelatin dry plate in the 1880s.

Developments in this "miraculous"[3] technology coincided with the emergence of a modern, more empirically based form of archaeology. The antiquarians and curiosity-seeking collectors in pursuit of rare antiquities at the start of the nineteenth century would yield, by the 1920s, to an increasingly academic field, with missions sponsored by national governments or scholarly institutions often serving as the handmaidens of a politics of imperialism.

When Arago proclaimed the technological breakthrough in 1839, he stressed that, by translating light into images, daguerreotypes would preserve for posterity structures that might one day fall victim to vandalism or the decay of time. In France and Great Britain, travel, discovery, and industrialization brought a new-found appreciation of local cultural patrimony and a desire to survey and restore monuments of the past. In writing about the photographer Édouard Baldus, who took part in what was called the Mission Héliographique in 1851—a state-funded undertaking to document vestiges of the past throughout French territory—Barry Bergdoll points out that "the photograph was both an irrefutable historical record and a powerful instrument in the Sisyphean battle against the ravages of time on these monuments which so many saw as repositories of historical memory."[4] Further afield, the growing ease of travel, along with European colonial and mercantile expansion, facilitated the exploration of a growing number of ancient ruins. Ernest Lacan, the editor of France's leading photography journal *La Lumière*, wrote that photography was "precious" for archaeology, making ancient ruins "immortal"—even if "time, revolutions, terrestrial convulsions can destroy every last stone, they henceforth live in our photo albums."[5] Photography became a tool of conservationists and scholars as well as trophy hunters, who used the new technique to document ruins and create a record for posterity. This same group also often simultaneously contributed to the despoiling of sites, as they shipped back artifacts that became showpieces for the museums of London, Paris, Berlin, or New York.

A camera, Arago explained, worked faster than any artist could and was also, most importantly, a faithful reporter that could be relied upon to provide accurate images. Unlike illustrations that were "incapable of grasping" the true spirit of ruins, because the artist's pen was "capricious," the camera was on the side of "precision" and "reality" and left no place for "fantasy or falsification."[6] French commentators extolling the virtues of photography regularly compared it to a *procès verbal*—an official report with the authority of a legal document—thereby underlining the new technology's objectivity and veracity. Photography was the indisputably reliable witness, the means to an unmediated truth. In an article on the use of photography as a tool in archaeology, published in the 1879 issue of the *Bulletin de la Société archéologique, scientifique et littéraire du vendômois*, Paul Martellière asserts that archaeology, like any science, "must categorically banish any form of whimsy."[7] He maintains that archaeological illustration should not be merely ornamental. Images, which go beyond the written word in communicating information about archaeological remains, "must be as dry and precise as a *procès verbal*, and the only way to ensure this is to use photography. […] A camera is not a poet, it never has poor eyesight. It has no imagination. It simply records what is."[8]

Arago's 1839 statement about the application of photography in archaeology proved amazingly prescient and, by 1860, Europeans would be familiar with the wonders of ancient sites in Greece, Egypt, Assyria, Jerusalem, and Palestine found in the photographs of Joseph-Philibert Girault de Prangey, Jean-Baptiste-Louis Gros, Maxime Du Camp, Auguste Salzmann, and Francis Frith. By experimenting with various forms and processes of the newly developed method of visualization, these early expeditionary photographers pushed the study of ancient cultures, their lost languages, their art and their architecture forward, becoming the true founders of today's scientific field.

As was the case for the civilizations of the Middle East, Egypt, and Greece, the nineteenth century marked the European exploration of the great Indigenous civilizations of Central America. Before the development of photography, the dissemination of images of the great cities of the Aztec and Maya were confined to sketches, paintings, and engravings. Alexander von Humboldt's popular accounts of his expeditions in Mexico and South America in the years between 1799 and 1804 ushered in an era of Western fascination with the Americas and its teeming jungles, most of which had been cut off to travelers and scholars during the centuries of Spanish rule beginning in the early sixteenth century. One of Humboldt's books—the *Vues des Cordillères, et monumens des peuples indigènes de l'Amérique* (1810)—was filled with colored lithographs and engravings that not only revealed flora and fauna but also gave the reader tantalizing hints regarding the ancient history and archaeology of the region, with its images of artifacts and pages from the Dresden Codex, one of the four known surviving books written in the hieroglyphic language of the Maya.

Printing a selection of pages from the Dresden Codex spurred interest in Maya writing, one of the first mentions of which is found in *The Decades of the New World* (1511–30) by the Italian humanist Peter Martyr d'Anghiera. Martyr writes that the books had "letters very different from ours: dice, hooks, loops, strips and other figures, written in a line as we do, they greatly resemble Egyptian forms."[9] Even though Martyr speculated that these strange forms contained the history of kings, the proof that the hieroglyphs provided historical information would not be grasped by historians until the middle of the twentieth century, when the Maya writing system was re-deciphered through the efforts of linguists and archaeologists aided by the work of earlier photographers.

Predating Humboldt's books, we have the first illustrations of a Mesoamerican archaeological site, Xochicalco, in José Antonio Alzate y Ramírez's *Descripción de las antiguedades de Xochicalco* (1791). Whether it was because of his apparently "feeble painting skills,"[10] or perhaps because of what Jules Janin called the "capricious pen" of the artist, in one of those images Alzate replaced the reliefs on the Temple of the Feathered Serpent with "Mexica glyphs from the tribute list known as the Matrícula de Tributos taken arbitrarily from the *Historia de la Nueva España* by Cardinal Lorenzana (1770)"[11] while, in another reimagining, he took an image seemingly inspired by a relief in the church of San Hipólito in Mexico City and presented it as a relief from the same site.[12] These drawings were later the basis of copper-plate engravings for the publication by Pietro Marquez, *Due antichi monumenti di architettura messicana*, published in 1804.

In the midst of excavations related to urban renewal projects undertaken in Mexico City in 1790, a sculpture of Coatlicue and the Sun Stone, also known as the Calendar Stone, later featured in Humboldt's book, were brought to light. Antonio de León y Gama, "a leading member of the group of *criollo* intellectuals"[13] active in Mexico at that time, featured images of both of these finds in his *Descripción histórica y cronológica de las dos piedras*, with illustrations by Francisco Agüera.[14] Invoking the growing interest in Europe for the archaeological past, León y Gama wrote of his determination "to publish the description of both stones, in order to throw some light on ancient literature, so much encouraged in other countries, and which, our Catholic Monarch Charles III [...] being King of Naples, promoted in the celebrated Museum, which at an immense expense, he founded at Portici, from the excavations he commanded to be made in discovery of the ancient cities of Herculaneum and Pompeii; buried for so many ages under the ashes, stones, and lava thrown out by the eruptions of Vesuvius."[15] His stated mission was to elevate the ancient civilizations of his region, which he deemed equally worthy of study and preservation: "I was induced to make known to the literary world a part of the great knowledge which the Indians of America possessed in the arts and sciences whilst heathens; that it may be shown how falsely they have been calumnied

FIG. 1 José Antonio de Alzate y Ramírez, *Descripción de las antiguedades de Xochicalco* (Mexico City: Don Felipe de Zúñiga y Ontiveros, 1791).

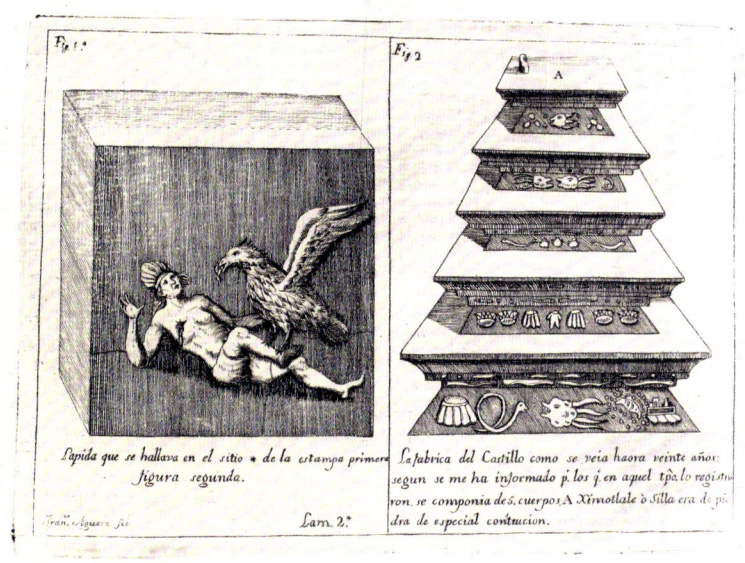

FIG. 2 The copperplate engravings of reliefs from Xochicalco, in Pietro Marquez, *Due antichi monumenti di architettura messicana* (Rome: Il Salomoni, 1804), are based on drawings by José Antonio de Alzate y Ramírez.

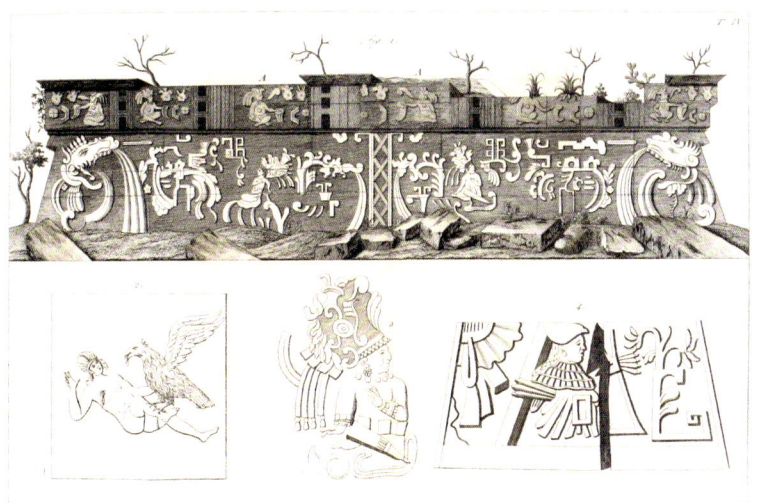

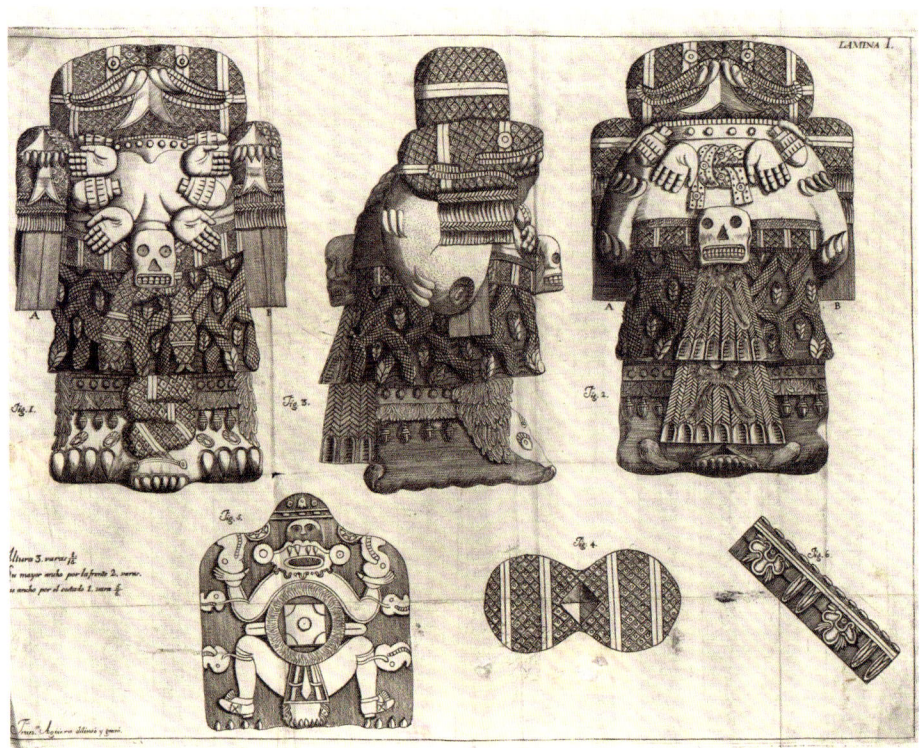

FIG. 3 Various views of the colossal statue of the Aztec mother goddess Coatlicue, in Antonio de León y Gama, *Descripción histórica y cronológica de las dos piedras que con ocasión del nuevo empedrado que se está formando en la plaza principal de México, se hallaron en ella el año de 1790* (Mexico City: Don F. de Zúñiga y Ontiveros, 1792).

as irrational or foolish by our enemies." Like his European counterparts, León y Gama understood the importance of capturing these precious vestiges in images, emphasizing the importance of the illustrations that were made under his own watchful eye before "rustic and childish people" could do damage to the figures or in case "by any accident it should be demolished, or the contemplated disposal of it, take place."[16] Despite the enthusiasm of a handful of scholars, neither of these eighteenth-century texts was available to a wider public inside or outside of Mexico.

Also at the end of the eighteenth century, in 1786, an artillery captain, Don Antonio del Río, made the first excavations at the ancient site of Palenque, which had been explored in the previous year by José Antonio Calderón. Del Río, who was accompanied by "a fairly competent artist named Ricardo Almendáriz,"[17] wrote a report, which was dutifully sent off to Spain where it was "swallowed up in the archives."[18] A copy, which managed to make its way from Mexico to Guatemala, was eventually published in London in 1822 as *Description of the Ruins of an Ancient City*, with illustrations that were "copies of copies" of the originals. These line lithographs by the "incredible, flamboyant" Jean Frédéric Maximilien, Comte de Waldeck, which constituted "the very first published depictions of Maya writing carved on stone," launched a frenzied interest in Palenque and continued to fuel the nascent field of Americanists in Europe.[19]

Another important mission that helped draw attention to the area's archaeological past was the one led by Guillermo Dupaix in 1807, on which he was accompanied by the draughtsman José Luciano Castañeda, who "made a series of rather stiff and

FIG. 4   Front view of the Sun Stone, in León y Gama, *Descripción histórica y cronológica de las dos piedras.*

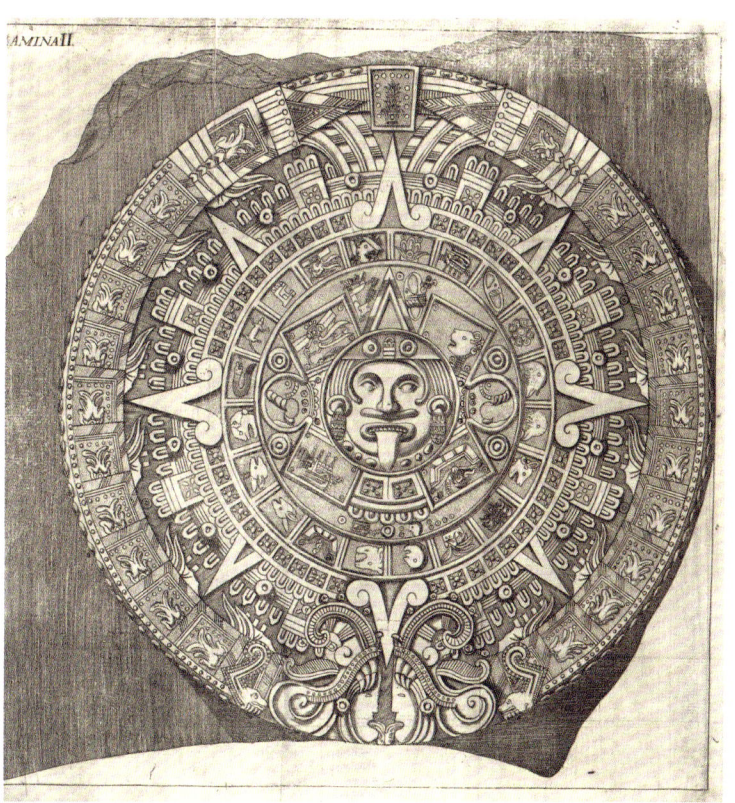

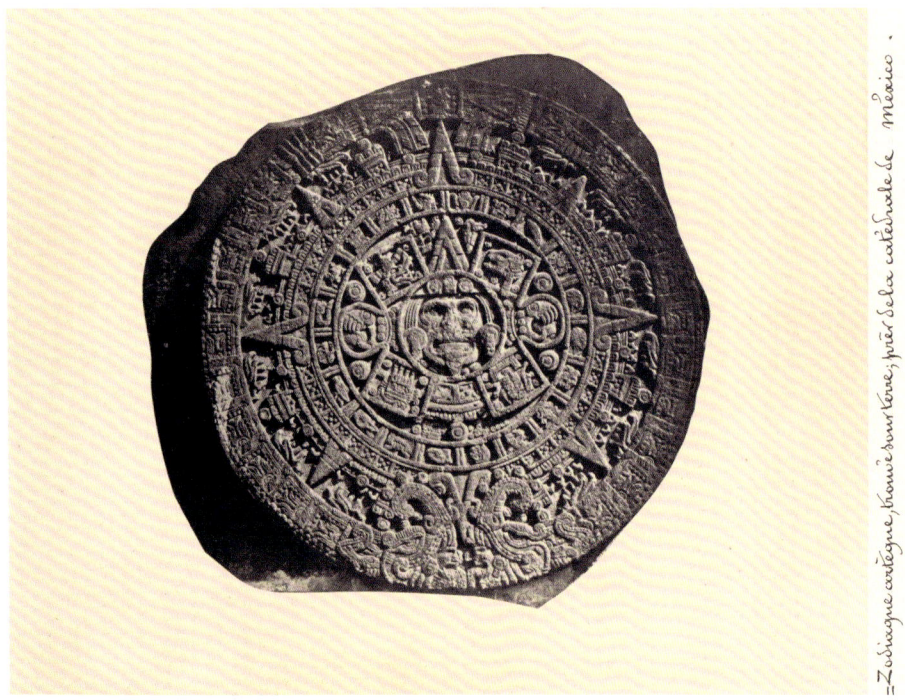

FIG. 5 Désiré Charnay's photograph of the Calendar Stone, published in *Cités et ruines américaines: Mitla, Palenqué, Izamal, Chichén Itzá, Uxmal* (Paris: Gide / A. Morel et Cie, 1862–63).

crude drawings which missed entirely the spirit of the place."²⁰ That said, Dupaix, who had been commissioned by Charles IV of Spain to provide an inventory and evaluation of the archaeological sites of what was then known as New Spain, recognized the primacy of images over words in his undertaking: "The technique of delineating the artifacts is necessary, as an image satisfies more than the most prolific of descriptions."²¹ Dupaix's report, along with Castañeda's drawings, would only be published twenty-seven years later but formed the basis of two foundational publications in the field. First was the monumental series *The Antiquities of Mexico*, with illustrations by the Italian Agostino Aglio, the first volumes of which were published in 1829 and 1830 by Edward King, Viscount of Kingsborough, "an Irish nobleman obsessed with the notion that the ancient Hebrews had populated the New World."²² The second work, which reproduced the entirety of the material from Dupaix's report, was published in France by Jean-Henri Baradère in the "luxuriously produced" *Antiquités mexicaines*

FIG. 6 Frontispiece from Jean-Henri Baradère, *Antiquités mexicaines* (Paris: Jules Didot, 1834). The caption translates as "Scholarly research will dissipate the clouds that envelop Mexican monuments and will reveal to future generations the history of the past."

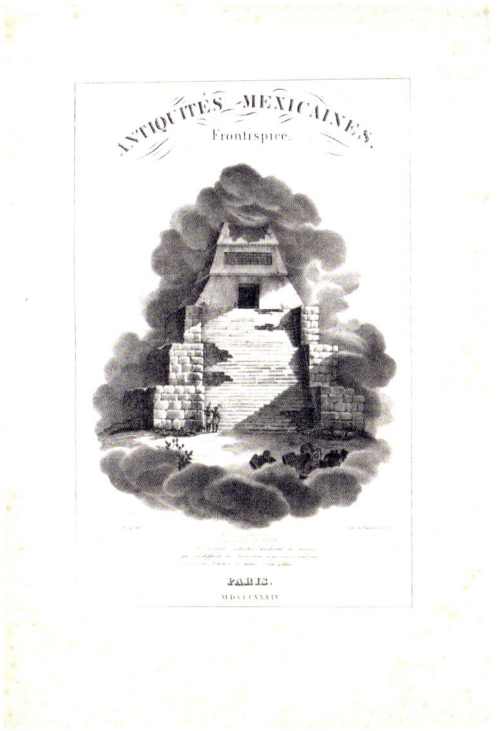

FIG. 7 Engraving by Agostino Aglio of the 1824 *Ancient Mexico* exhibition of New World antiquities at the Egyptian Hall, Piccadilly, London, organized by William Bullock.

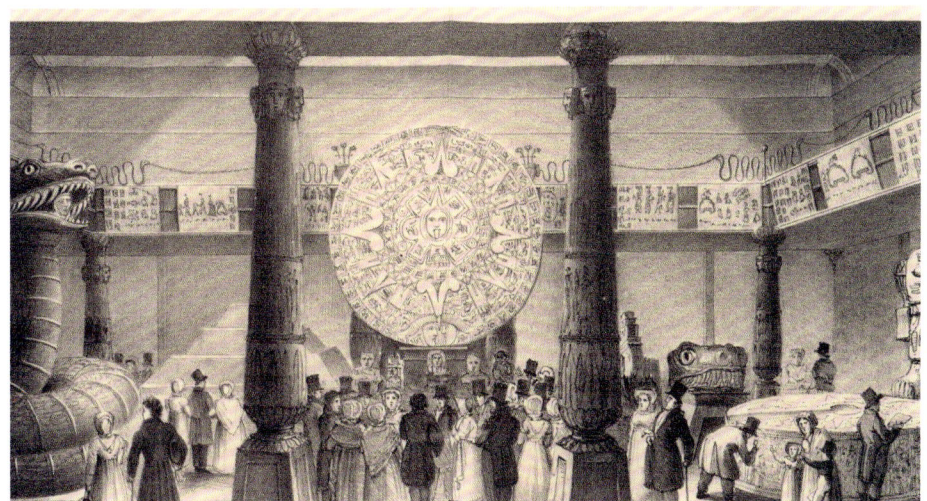

(1834), "the most comprehensive visual and written account to date of Mexico's ancient monumental architecture and sculpture."²³

Humboldt's own *Vues des Cordillères* (Views of the Cordilleras), published in 1810, was, as previously mentioned, a groundbreaking book, which included thirty-two plates related to Mexico, five of which were directly tied to the archaeological sites Cholula, El Tajín, Xochicalco, and Mitla. Having only visited the first of these sites, he reproduced the drawings of Alzate and Marquez to illustrate the vestiges. He also included a plate that he incorrectly identified as a "relief from Oaxaca" but that was in fact a relief from Building A of the palace complex of Palenque.²⁴ Despite these dubious illustrations, Humboldt's books on his travels in South America and Mexico "met with such success among the intelligentsia of the day that from them arose a renewed desire to become acquainted with things Mexican, and this not only in France, but in England and Germany as well."²⁵

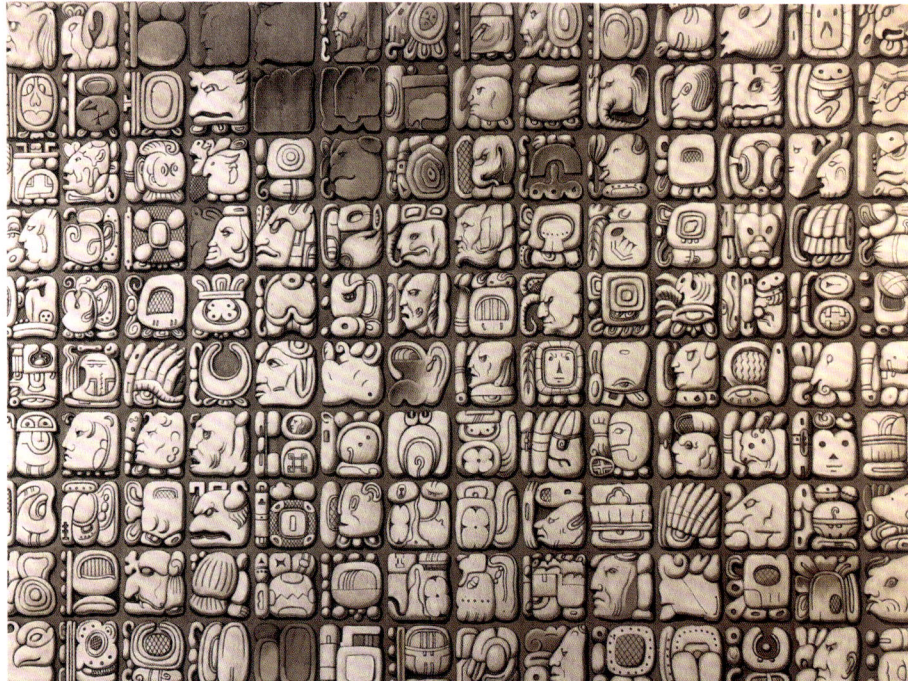

FIG. 8   Jean Frédéric Maximilien de Waldeck's drawing of glyphs from the Temple of the Inscriptions, Palenque, in Abbé Brasseur de Bourbourg, *Monuments anciens du Mexique: Palenqué et autres ruines de l'ancienne civilisation du Mexique* (Paris: Arthus Bertrand, 1866).

FIG. 9   Waldeck's illustration of a panel from the Temple of the Cross in Palenque, in Brasseur de Bourbourg, *Monuments anciens du Mexique*. The figure is one that Waldeck associated with Vishnu, due to the flowing liquid that is visible in the image.

FIG. 10   Another of Waldeck's drawings of a panel from the Temple of the Cross in Palenque, in Brasseur de Bourbourg, *Monuments anciens du Mexique*. Waldeck associated this figure with the Hindu god Brahma, the creator god with his visible breath of life.

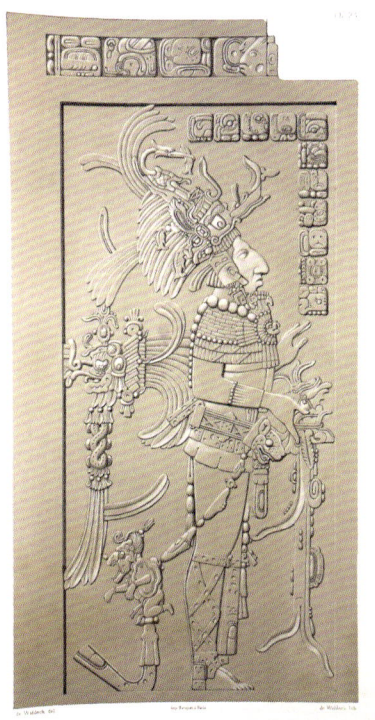 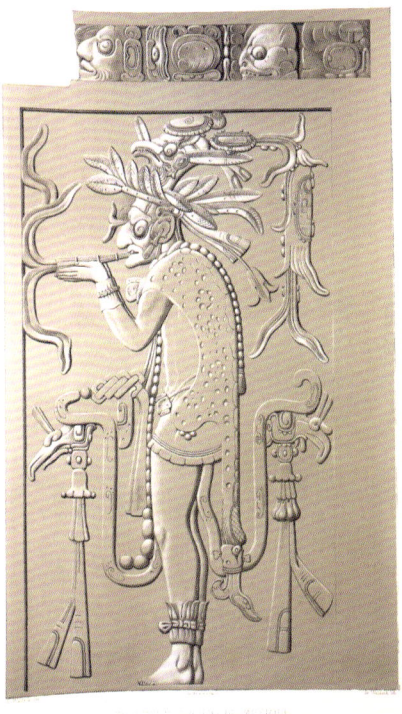

One such European intellectual was the previously mentioned Jean Frédéric Maximilien, Comte de Waldeck, who, taken by the images he had seen in Kingsborough's volumes as well as in Humboldt's work, made his way to Mexico and eventually to Palenque and Uxmal, where he explored and drew the ruins starting in 1832. The images that were published in 1838, in his *Voyage pittoresque et archéologique dans la province d'Yucatan (Amérique Centrale) pendant les années 1834 et 1836*, and in 1866 in a work entitled *Monuments anciens du Mexique: Palenqué et autres ruines de l'ancienne civilisation du Mexique*, which in part illustrated his theories linking Mexican to Asian and Egyptian cultures, have been judged as "fanciful in the extreme."[26] Despite their high degree of inaccuracy, his drawings nevertheless played a part "in the general flow of interest towards the Maya remains."[27] His renderings of glyphs, which included elephant heads and cuneiform script, showed the extent to which illustrations of Maya writing went unchecked until photography captured them and released them from the subjective interpretation of the illustrator.

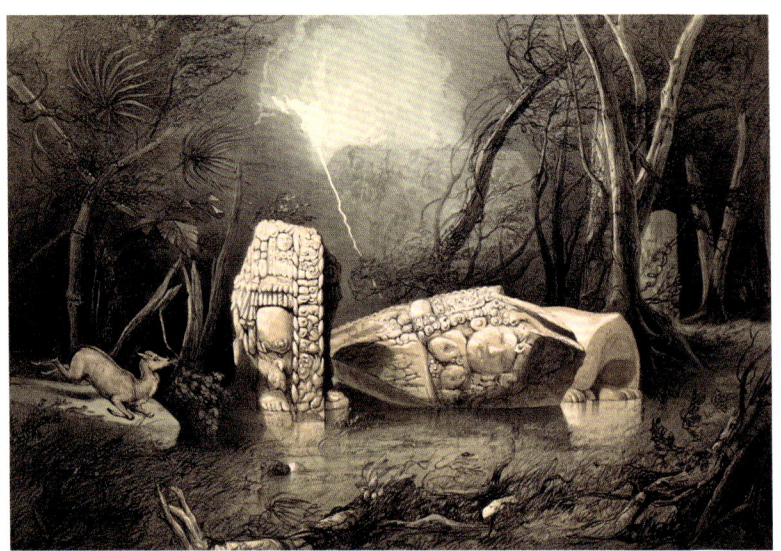

FIG. 11 Frederick Catherwood's "Broken Idol at Copan," in *Views of Ancient Monuments in Central America, Chiapas and Yucatan* (New York: Bartlett and Welford, 1844).

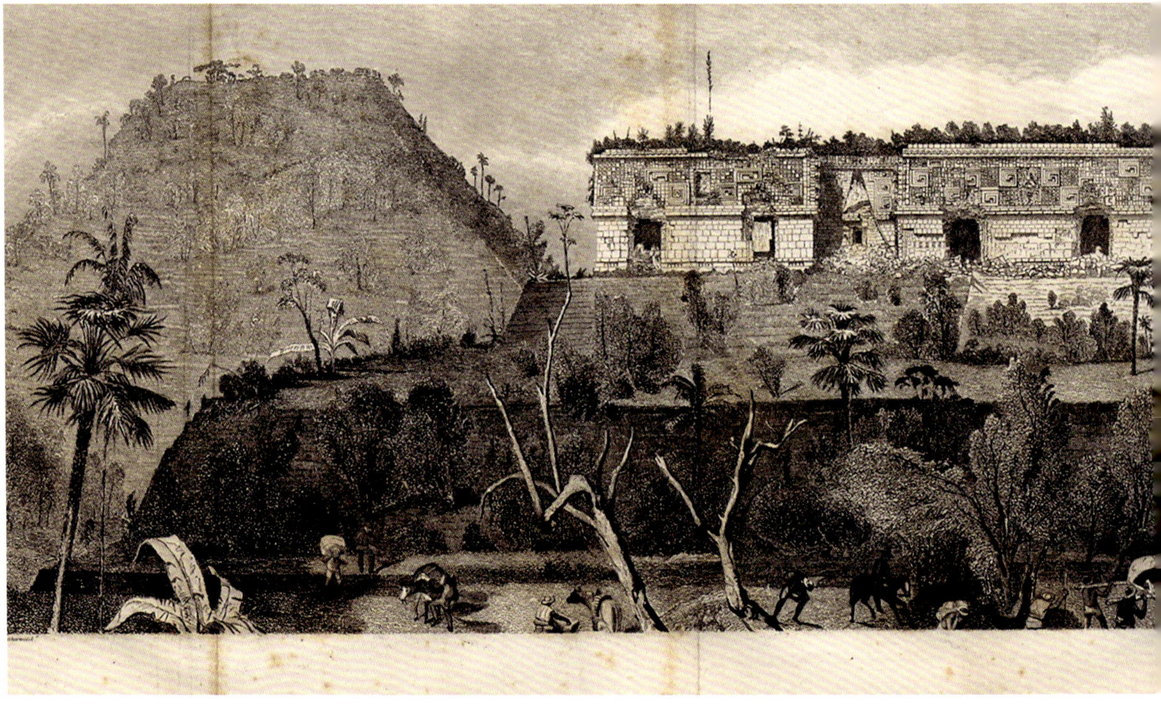

Early Archaeological Photography in the Americas

More than any other publication, however, the work that first introduced Maya civilization to a broad European audience was John Lloyd Stephens's *Incidents of Travel in Central America, Chiapas and Yucatán* (1841) and the later *Incidents of Travel in Yucatan* (1843), with its painstakingly drawn illustrations based on field drawings by Frederick Catherwood.

The accuracy of Catherwood's drawings came through his use of the camera lucida. The device, invented by William Hyde Wollaston in 1807, had been used by illustrators for many years as it allowed the projection of an image onto paper, which could then be traced. Catherwood's images were admired for their level of detail and documentary exactitude, but also for capturing "the Sublime and the Picturesque" that was the hallmark of the Romantic movement's obsession with ruins.[28] An image such as *Broken Idol at Copán*, with its "impenetrable jungle, ruined buildings and monuments, lightning

FIG. 12 Catherwood's "Casa del Gobernador, Uxmal," in John L. Stephens, *Incidents of Travel in Yucatan* (New York: Harper & Brothers, 1843).

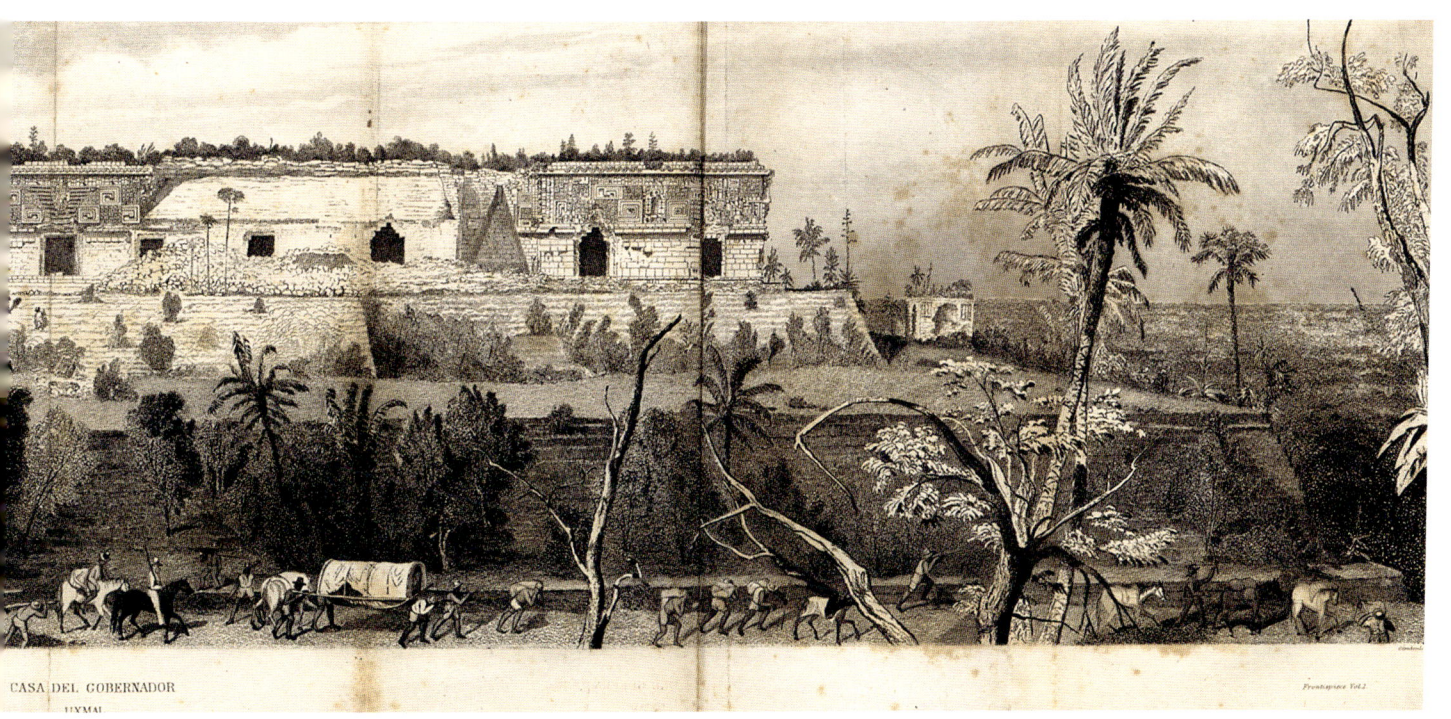

strike, and dramatic lighting,"²⁹ is as much a marvel for its precise rendering of a Maya stela as it is a study in exoticism.

Thus, before the development of photography, the dissemination of images of the great cities of the Aztec and Maya were confined to sketches and engravings, like those found in books by Kingsborough and Humboldt, and by artists like Waldeck and Catherwood. During the 1850s Baron Gros brought back images of the Acropolis, Du Camp captured Karnak and the Sphinx, and Salzmann returned with views of the Holy Land. From the earliest days of daguerreotypes, cameras were present in Mexico and being used for portraiture as well as for capturing vestiges of the pre-Columbian past. Stephens and Catherwood took daguerreotype images while in Yucatán, although unfortunately none survive.³⁰ One of the rare extant images of that

FIG. 13 Louis Prélier's daguerreotype of the Aztec Calendar Stone, 1840.

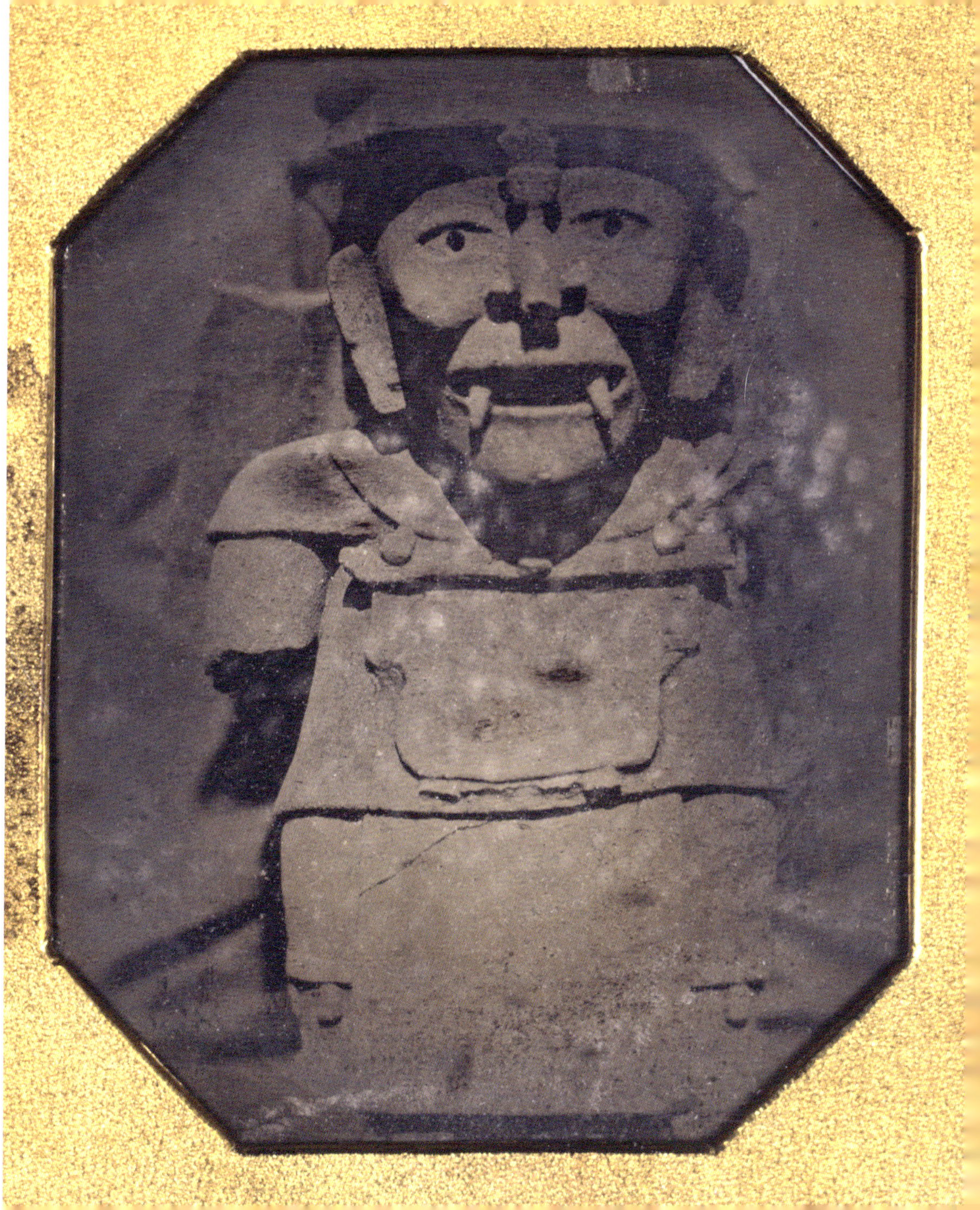

FIG. 14 Emanuel von Friedrichsthal's daguerreotype of a figure from Mayapan, 1840–41.

period is the daguerreotype of the so-called Aztec Calendar, still embedded in the wall of the Cathedral of Mexico City, that has been dated to ca. 1839.[31] The earliest known photograph of a Maya artifact, a Postclassic censer, was taken by Emanuel von Friedrichsthal, who traveled in Mexico and through the Yucatán in 1840.[32]

It was not until 1861, however, that the French archaeologist and explorer Désiré Charnay published the first photographs of the ruins of ancient Mexico that would be available to a wide audience. Charnay was using a laborious technique in which glass plates were sensitized with silver salts through the use of collodion, a process that was known as collodion or wet-plate photography. It was a major improvement over methods like the daguerreotype in that it allowed for a significantly shorter exposure time for capturing an image and enabled prints to be mechanically reproduced. However, field photographers had to carry heavy equipment and chemicals over treacherous roads and needed to have a nearby darkroom, which for expeditionary photographers of archaeological sites often meant a dark chamber in the ruins.[33] Charnay's prints, which "arguably remain the best photographs of these buildings ever published,"[34] ushered in a new era in the study of the archaeology of the Americas, when all of Europe could see with their own eyes the true nature, size, and complexity of the ancient cities of the Aztecs and the Maya.

The subjects of this book—Désiré Charnay, Alice and Augustus Le Plongeon, Teobert Maler, Alfred Maudslay, and Adela Breton—all worked during the golden age of expeditionary photography, from the 1850s into the first decade of the 1900s. They were not only travelers, explorers, and archaeologists, but also groundbreaking photographers and illustrators, each with his or her own technique, aesthetic, and agenda. And yet the major works of these Mesoamericanists are for the most part unknown outside the realm of specialists. These photographers labored under trying, if not dangerous conditions, in far-away jungles during periods of revolution and uprisings, while struggling to master an evolving and imperfect photographic technology. Each of them played a role in attempting to preserve for posterity the vestiges of the great civilizations of the Americas that were as awe-inspiring and enigmatic as those of Greece, Egypt, or Jerusalem.

The photographers in this collection grappled with the question of the meaning of sculpted stones bearing the carved remains of a language to which the key had been lost. In the spirit of Arago, the photographers of Mesoamerican sites were seeking to help scholars—who could not travel to the field—break the code of the lost language of Maya hieroglyphs. And although decipherment would not be achieved until the 1960s, it was in large part through these early photographs that the hieroglyphs of these ancient sites were finally decrypted. The exuberantly extravagant sculptures often represent a cosmos inhabited by shape-shifting creatures like plumed snakes and elaborately masked gods in scenes of sacrifice, dance, self-mutilation, and captivity—expressed in an iconography that these pioneering photographers sought if not to understand, then at least to render in readable images.

The opacity that resulted from the inability to "read" the ancient Maya sites allowed for speculation of all sorts as to the origins of the peoples of the Americas, along with their art and iconography. The works of Humboldt, Waldeck, and the great manuscript hunter Charles Étienne Brasseur de Bourbourg, all theorized a connection between the Maya people and Scandinavian, Phoenician, Egyptian, or Asian civilizations. Each of the photographers in this collection interrogated the stones they captured in their images for hints to their source, and their conclusions range across the interpretive spectrum, from the scientific to the mystical.

From Charnay to Maudslay we see the evolution of photographic processes from the extremely unpredictable wet collodion to more stable dry plates and the use of innovative techniques like stereography, the first 3D photographic technique. We also find attempts to render color in this period of black-and-white photography. These early photographers all struggled with the processes, as well as the logistics of transporting equipment and keeping ample supplies of chemicals. We get a glimpse of how the photographers of this time worked—wrapped in a certain mystery, to the point that they sometimes gave the impression of being, as one practitioner wrote, "in a secret pact with the devil."[35]

These photographers were active during archaeology's coming of age in the mid-nineteenth century, before it became a field dominated by a professional class of trained archaeologists.[36] Archaeology during this period was still largely a private undertaking, although sometimes partly aided by government or institutional support. Charnay received funding from the French Ministry of Public Education, as well as from the wealthy American tobacconist Pierre Lorillard, who was also one of the patrons of the Le Plongeons. Maudslay and Breton were largely self-funded but had institutional ties to, for example, the Peabody Museum, in Cambridge, Massachusetts, which provided financial support to Teobert Maler as well. Despite such ties, these were all individual archaeological pursuits in which there "was something very personal, even heroic."[37]

Raymond de Verninac Saint-Maur, who directed the operation to move Egypt's Luxor Obelisk, which now stands in the Place de la Concorde in Paris, wrote in his *Voyage de Luxor* (1835), "Antiquity is a garden that belongs by natural right to those who cultivate and harvest its fruits."[38] Like many of their contemporaries in the field, some of the photographer-archaeologists featured in this book operated often as preservationists but sometimes more like looters—in some cases embracing Verninac Saint-Maur's belief that, by dint of their excavations and scholarly interest in the vestiges, they as Europeans had the right to "harvest" material that would be preserved and studied in great museums in European capitals and in the United States. Charnay argued that France, "which is the head and the light of the world, [should] take possession of these precious [Mexican] monuments and provide the space that they deserve in our museums." And he made the claim that "the absence of any documentation on the origins of the American people creates a great void in the history of humanity."[39] The Le Plongeons bitterly contested Mexico's "absurd law, which forbids the removal of any of the ruins or part of the ruins," since it scuttled their plans to send the unearthed statue that they dubbed the Chacmool from Chichén Itzá to Philadelphia. Alongside the non-obtrusive techniques of capturing images on glass plates and wrapping monuments to create plaster casts, Alfred Maudslay also sent back objects ripped from the sites that he visited, such as lintels from Yaxchilán, which are now on display in the British Museum.

Typically for expeditionary photographers of their age, the photographers in this collection took a wide variety of shots, including scenes of daily life, portraits, as well as city and landscape views, but they are best remembered for their images of archaeological sites. These photographers worked to give a sense of the whole, but also of the fragment and the detail, providing images of inscriptions, sculptures, and architectural features. The Le Plongeons methodically photographed close-ups of façades, Maudslay and Maler provided meticulous studies of stelae, Charnay and Breton captured the fragile vestiges before the decay of the structure or color went any further. Their photographs sometimes included human figures—the photographers themselves or the workers they employed—who posed either to provide a sense of scale or, in the case of Indigenous workers, perhaps also to enhance the exotic nature of the surroundings in which they were working.

As photography came to be integrated into everyday archaeological practice and was used to document digs, it became a purely utilitarian tool. Photographs were meant to document and illustrate findings, as well as provide a corpus of images for the use of other scholars. These images also started to act, in the words of one scholar, "as visual time machines,"[40] with the ability to transport the viewer to another time and place. Although the photographs in this book are primarily documentary in nature, there are often aesthetic qualities to the pictures that go beyond the utilitarian and give a sense of the photographer's ability to frame and compose.

The images selected for inclusion in this book are combined with the photographers' own words, extracted from their published writings, journals, and letters to offer insights into their methods, provide context for their images, and capture the sometimes tough realities of fieldwork among the Mesoamerican ruins. Désiré Charnay, Alice and Augustus Le Plongeon, Teobert Maler, Alfred Maudslay, and Adela Breton can be taken individually, but it is also possible to appreciate the interplay of contrasting ambitions and expertise between these artists who were sometimes collaborators and sometimes rivals, who trod the same ground and pictured the same sites.

Beyond their individual objectives and eccentricities, they provided the raw visual evidence of discovery to scholars in the comfortable libraries of European cities and American universities, while at the same time translating the vestiges of distant civilizations into a visual form that would engage the wider public's imagination. They created what, in many cases, is now the sole evidence of ancient inscriptions, buildings, and façades that have since degraded or disappeared. Whatever their motives, for us today these photographers, who exposed ancient Mesoamerica, provided a record of the past that inspired and aided the growth of archaeology of the Americas and the rebirth of its most ancient languages and cultures.

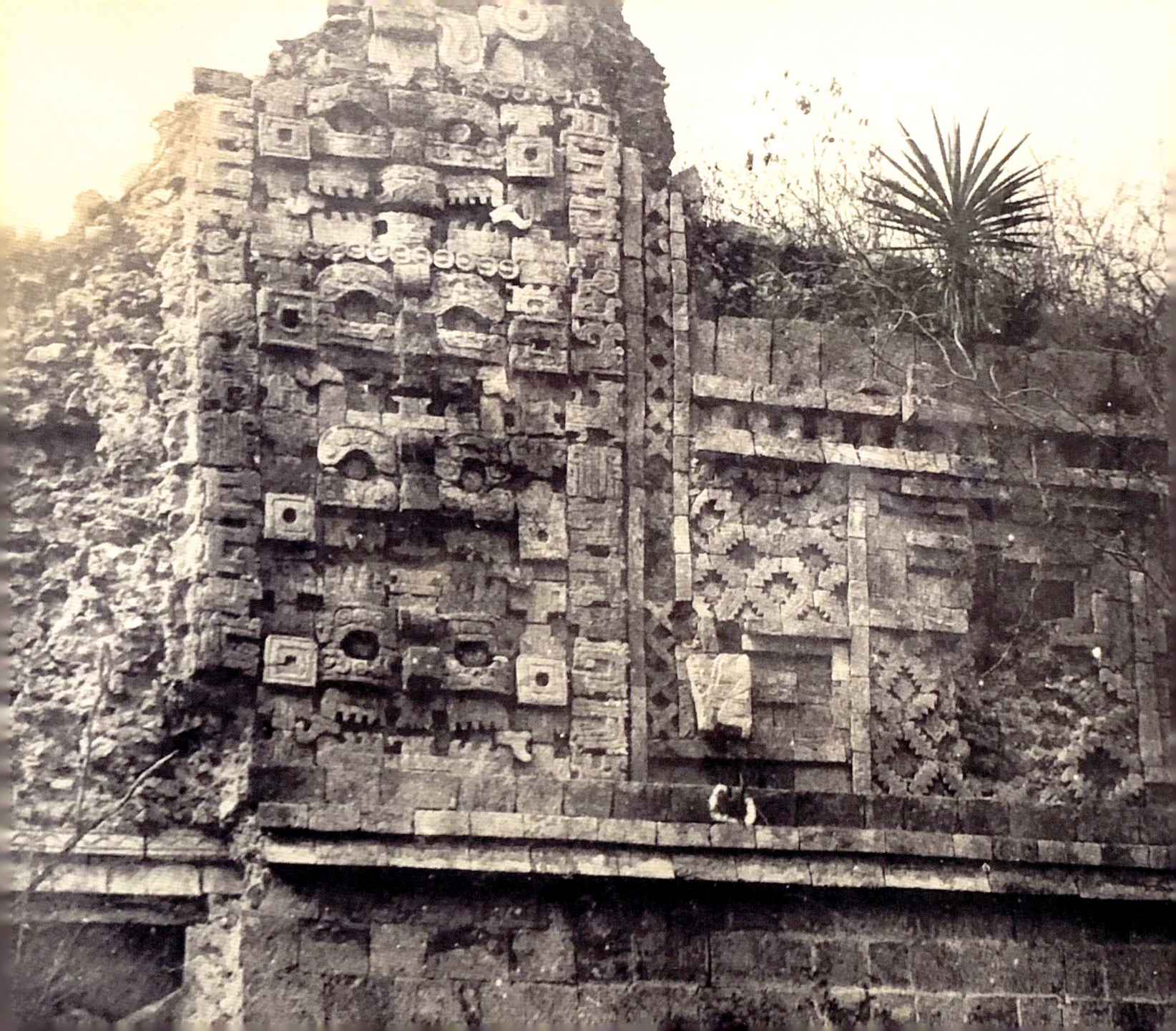

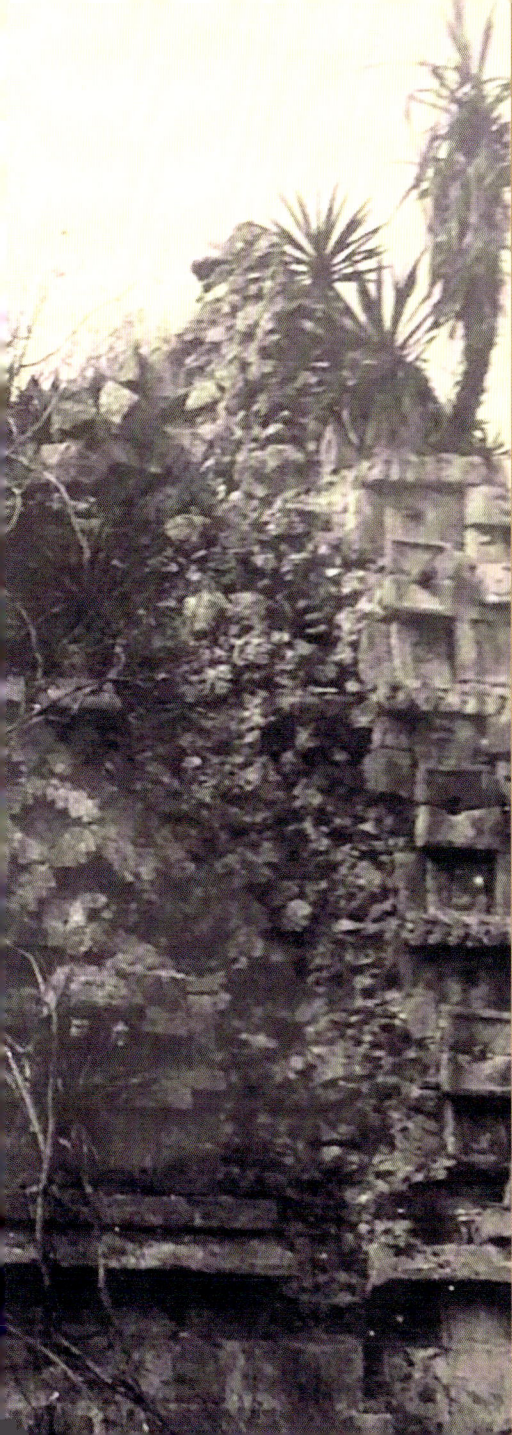

Désiré Charnay
(1828–1915)

The first person to create a photographic record of Mesoamerican archaeological sites was Désiré Charnay, who captured his earliest images of Mexican ruins in 1857. Although he made subsequent trips to the country in 1880 and 1886, his greatest contribution to the history of photography and Mesoamerican archaeology was no doubt the album that resulted from his travels across a war-torn Mexico between 1857 and 1860, in which he presented the first images of American sites to gain a wide audience and introduced uninitiated Europeans to this ancient society, whose history was largely unknown.

During that first trip, Charnay, whose mission was in part subsidized by the French Ministry of Public Education, traveled through regions in the throes of violent rebellions and civil war. He also struggled against photographic technology that he found just as bedeviling as any armed forces. His travel notes report encounters with soldiers and government officials, who destroyed his plates, confiscated his materials, or questioned his sanity for his interest in these old stone monuments. More often than not, those around him were mystified by his glass plates that, he complained, "didn't speak to their eyes."

Charnay's first photographic album—published along with his narrative of this trip under the title *Cités et ruines américaines: Mitla, Palenqué, Izamal, Chichen-Itza, Uxmal* (American Cities and Ruins)—provides an account of the unpredictable practice of photography in the early years of the wet-collodion process, which involved coating a glass plate in a light-sensitive emulsion. Unlike the daguerreotype, this process allowed for unlimited copies to be made of an image, but had its own set of challenges since, once dried, the coated plate quickly lost sensitivity. This meant that the negative had to be prepared just prior to exposure and processed immediately. Charnay's travelogue offers a backstory for his most powerful photographs and gives us a glimpse into how he captured his images on glass plates at a time when a photographer was part alchemist and part scientific master of a new technology.

"A country is a book about which any traveler can have an opinion, as long as that opinion is based in truth"[1]—from the first words in his epigraph, Charnay proclaims that his study of ancient Mexico was born of objective scientific observation. His goal was "to wipe the slate clean and start all over again with both new words and images,"[2] and the ultimate tool in pursuit of the truth was, undoubtedly, the camera. Charnay questioned why the Aztec and Maya civilizations and their ancient ruined cities had not captured the imagination of his contemporaries in Europe in the same way as the

FIG. 15   Self-portrait of Désiré Charnay on the steps of the Kabul pyramid, Izamal, 1886.

Désiré Charnay (1828–1915)

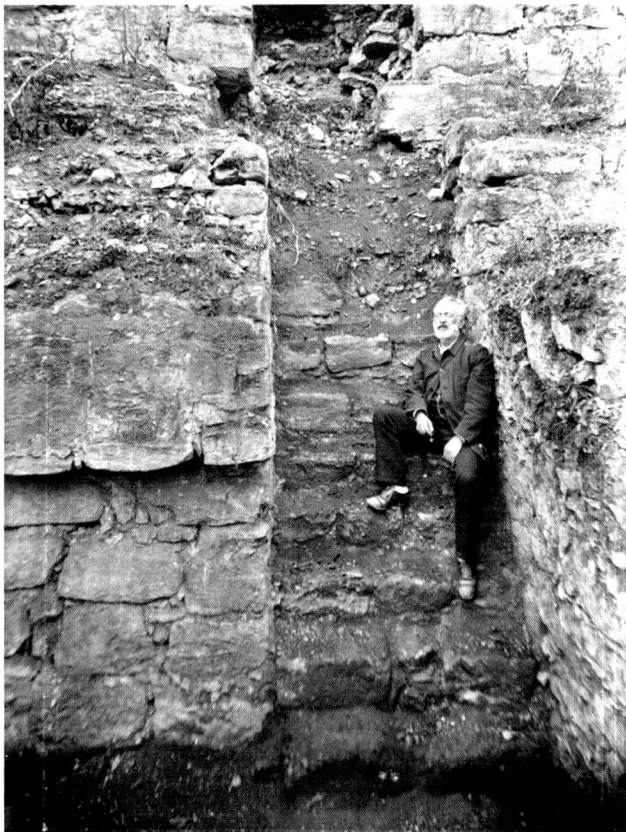

ancient cultures of Egypt and Assyria: "My only explanation for the public's indifference towards this extraordinary civilization was that it was veiled in such great uncertainty. I wanted to make sure that no one could challenge the accuracy of my work. Therefore, I relied on photography as my evidence."[3]

Charnay arrived in Vera Cruz, Mexico, in November 1857, with 1,800 kilograms of luggage and the goal of photographing the country's ancient monuments. After an extended stay in Mexico City, he traveled to Oaxaca in October 1858. The civil war, known as the War of Reform, that gripped the country from 1857 to 1860, made travel and transportation perilous.

MITLA[4]

I had been waiting in vain for my luggage to arrive for two months. I worried that transportation had become impossible due to the current state of the roads. Therefore, I decided to set to work using the resources available in Oaxaca. I made my own nitrate and gun cotton. I already had plates and one of my cameras. I was able to find ether and alcohol. To develop the images I needed iron sulfate, which is available everywhere.

    I had no luck with my first attempts. The photographs of the city's monuments came out badly. A few days later I took better ones that I would say were almost acceptable. As a result, I prepared my expedition to Mitla. [...] However, just when I was about to leave, I realized that the solutions were not working at all. For a week I performed all sorts of tests. I used old baths, then new baths. I tried a dozen different types of collodion. I used every type of developer and fixative possible. It was a lost cause. The collodion actually lost all its sensitivity. After an exposure of five minutes in the sun with a double lens all I got was a white spot.

    In a desperate attempt I mixed all the collodion I had and waited. A few days later I wanted to make another attempt and made an exposure at seven in the morning. It was good. By seven thirty—it was no longer sensitive. The next day, I had two successful outcomes without being able to have a third. The day after that, I was able to do three. Each day after that, I successfully took one more photograph than the day before—but never more. All of a sudden, the collodion only produced positives on the plates. Then the next day, it created negatives. I had no control over whether it would be one or the other. I tried in vain to find an explanation for these curious phenomena, so I leave it to more learned scholars of photography to provide an answer. I was in a precarious situation and for a while, I was sure that I was doomed to failure. I had travelled more than nine thousand kilometers with a goal of bringing back images of these fascinating unknown ruins to Europe and here I was standing before them incapable of reproducing them!

    But in the end, I bucked myself up and decided that no matter the personal cost I was determined to accomplish the work I had set out to do. Just wait! Patience is a precious gift if you are able to practice it.

FIG. 16   Exterior of the Priest's House in Mitla, Oaxaca: "I called this first ruin the *Priest's House* for the venerable priest who has lived there for the last half century. He has created a roomy and cozy retreat using the ancient structure's solid walls and adding a modern roof. [...] [It] is a muddle of courtyards and buildings, adorned in raised mosaics with extremely simple patterns. [...] There are traces of very primitive paintings with no regard for straight lines. There are crude figures of idols and ornamental patterns of winding, interlocking lines, whose meanings are now lost to us. In all of these palaces, only those few flawed paintings, which by chance were protected from the elements, have been preserved from the ravages of time. Finding such crude drawings coexisting with this refined architecture and these palaces adorned with sophisticated mosaic panels leads to the strangest conclusions." All titles of Charnay's photographs are taken from his handwritten notes in the album.

FIG. 17   South side of the Fourth Palace in Mitla (Oaxaca).

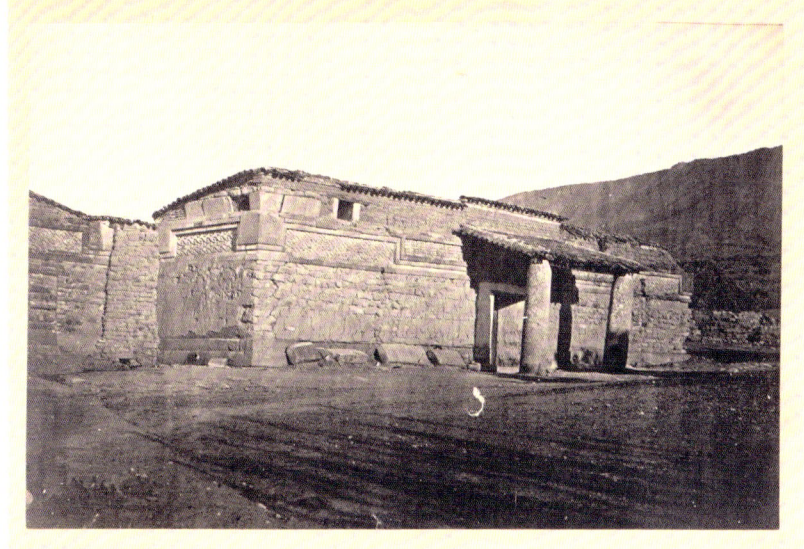

= Extérieur de la maison du Curé à Mitla. Oajaca.

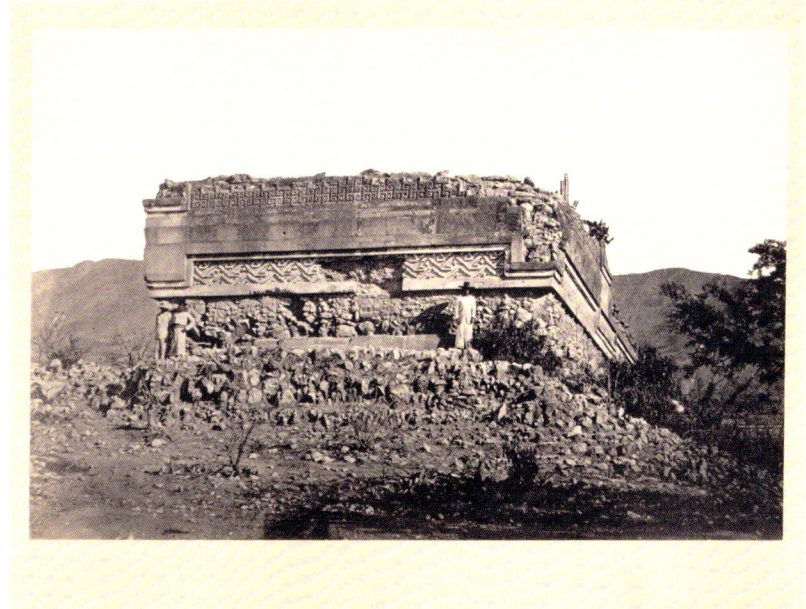

= Côté Sud du quatrième Palais de Mitla (Oajaca).

Exposing the Maya

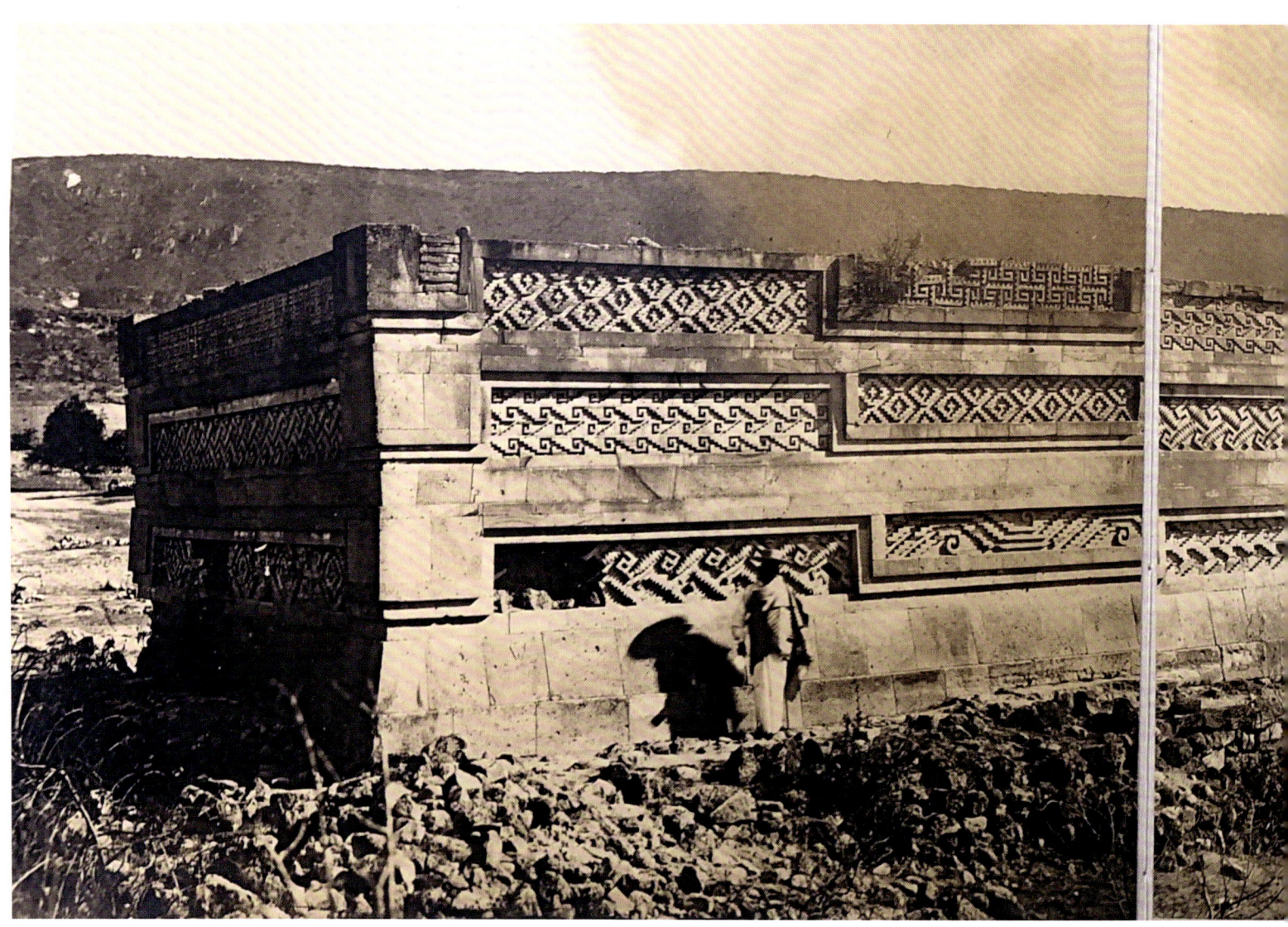

Désiré Charnay (1828–1915)

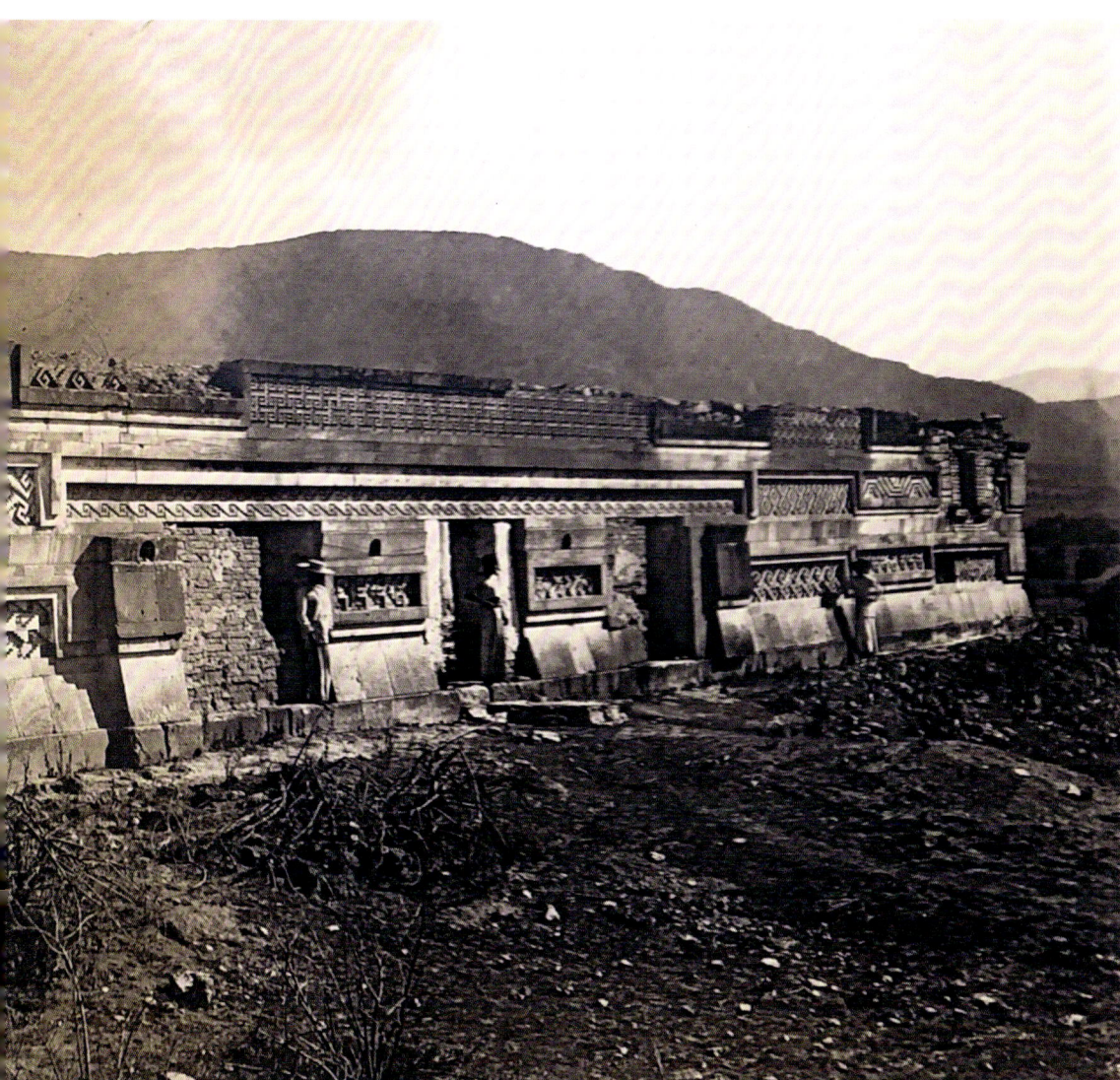

FIG. 18 The Great Palace in Mitla (Oaxaca), (left side & right side). "The Great Palace, whose roof has collapsed, is otherwise intact. It is an enormous building in the shape of the Greek letter tau. Its main façade which is south facing is the most beautiful, the most important and the best preserved of the many monuments of Mitla. It is 40 meters long with a room [...] with six monolithic columns that are fourteen feet tall [...] and three large, low doorways."

As Charnay surveyed the site, he observed that the vestiges of this past city were at the mercy not just of the elements and time, but also of the local population, who lived in the courtyards of the ruined Fourth Palace, whose walls were used to fence in their animals. Upon his return to Oaxaca, he wrote:

> Thankfully, despite the unpredictability of collodion, my reproductions of the ruins were successful. I had about twenty images that I arranged to be transported by men who carried them on their backs. As soon as I returned to Oaxaca, I varnished them. Since I had no Soehnee varnish, I created some using amber and chloroform, which did not work for me.[5] Thus, I decided to protect them temporarily with a layer of albumen—a recipe I found in Von Monckhoven's *Treatise on Photography*.
>
> Once varnished, I set the photographs to dry in the sun and turned my thoughts towards my departure. But things didn't go as planned.
>
> I went into town to pay some visits with the intention of conscientiously placing my photos in their slotted boxes as soon as I returned. Oh, Mr. Monckhoven what did you do? I came back. From a distance, the plates seemed to be perfectly clear. As I approached, to my utter disbelief everything had disappeared. The albumen's contraction had erased everything.
>
> Of course, this was a catastrophe. I had used all my chemicals and spent all my funds. I was resigned to failure. Moreover, the Liberal army, who had been routed three months earlier, had returned to the area and was now besieging the reactionary forces. The city was closed off. Moreover, I had been waiting for my luggage for 5 months with no news!
>
> It was a disastrous situation. I summoned all my strength and returned to Mitla.
>
> I could not locate my previous driver to take me there. The roads were blocked by armed gangs and no one was venturing out.
>
> I was alone, completely alone. However, I was so single-minded and galvanized that for five days I did not sleep. I spent my evenings preparing my chemicals and my plates. For a second time, I achieved my goal, and it was just in the nick of time. I had reached my limit and found it difficult to make it back to town safely. Enemy forces were already encircling the mountains. There were barricades in the streets and fires were being set.

FIG. 19   Interior of a chamber in the Great Palace, Mitla (Oaxaca): "A dark hallway leads to an interior courtyard that also has a cement floor, and whose walls, like the main façade, are covered in mosaic panels and designs of stone framework. The courtyard is square with openings onto four long, narrow rooms, covered from top to bottom in raised mosaics with a varied pattern of lines that go up to the ceiling."

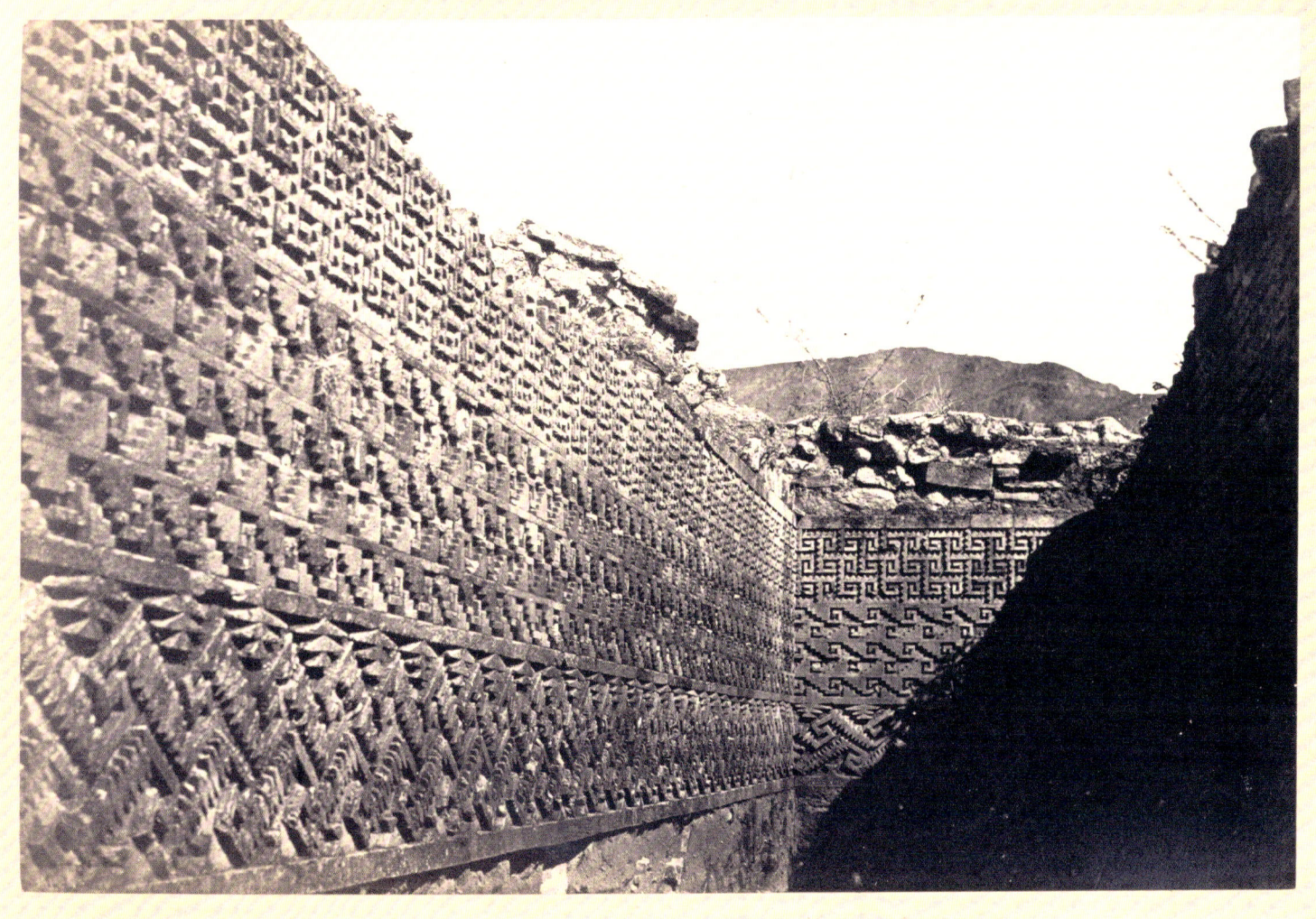

= Intérieur d'une salle du grand Palais de Mitla (Oajacca).

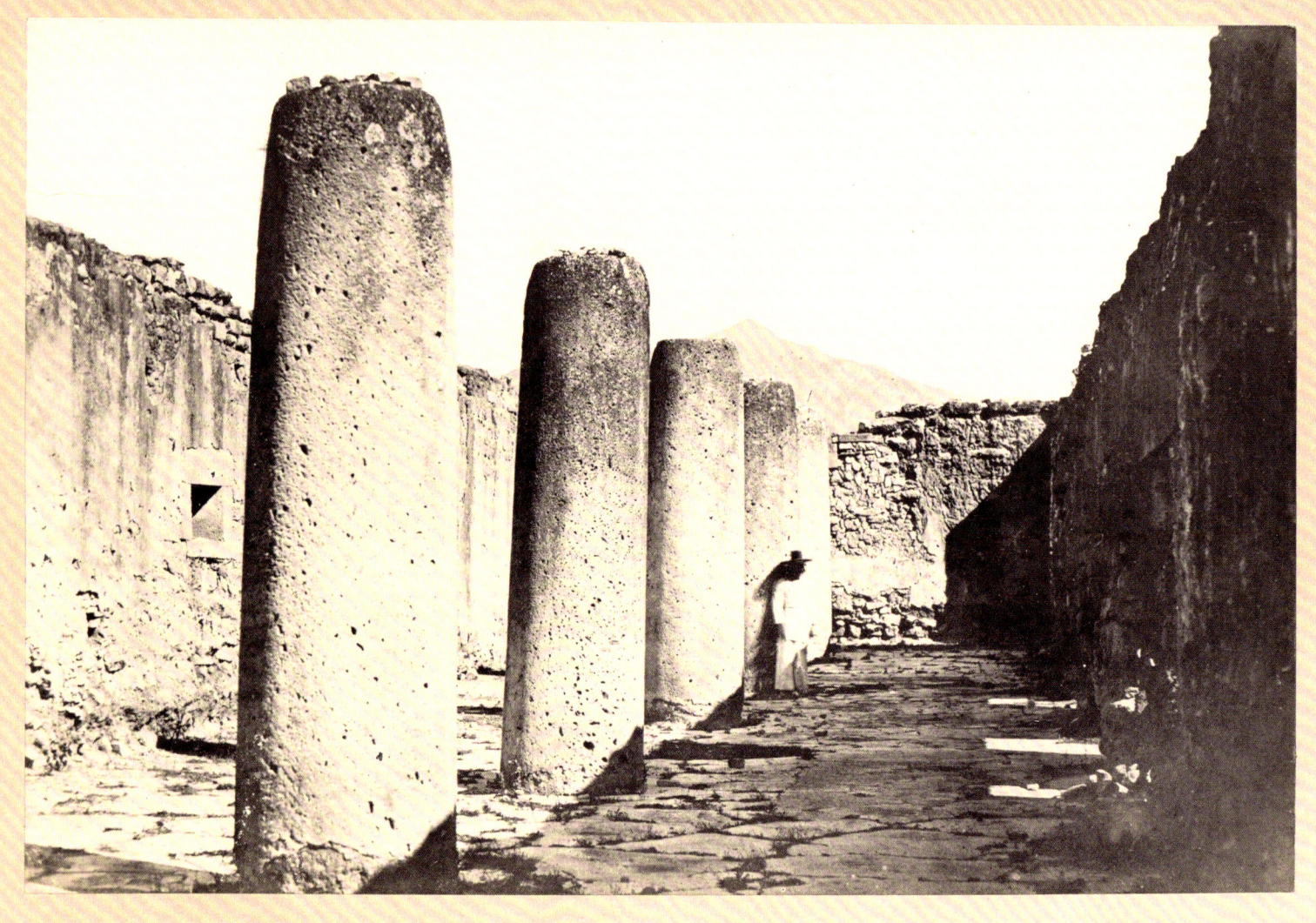

= Grand Palais de Mitla (Intérieur d'une salle) oajacca.

Désiré Charnay (1828–1915)

FIG. 21 Second Palace in Mitla (Oaxaca): "Of the standing structures in Mitla, the second palace was the most damaged. Only the door with its sculpted lintel remains standing, along with two interior columns."

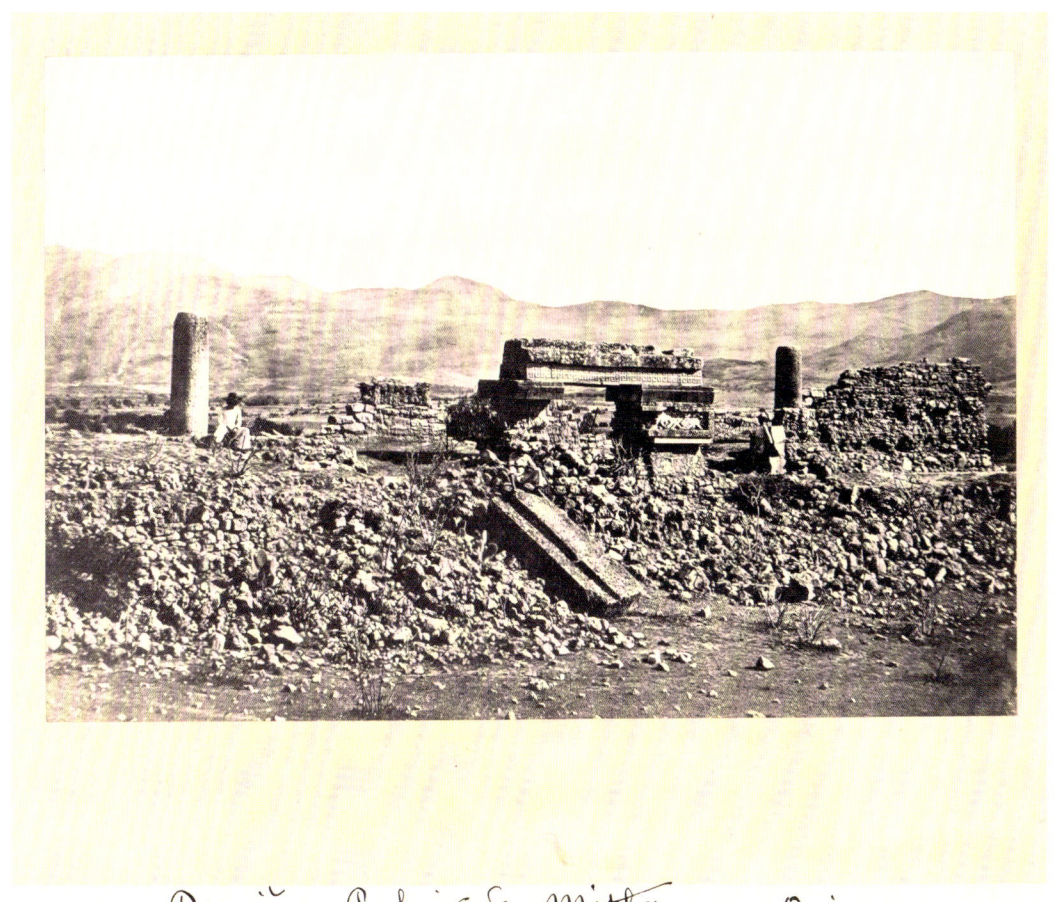

FIG. 20 Great Palace in Mitla (Interior of a chamber) Oaxaca.

Exposing the Maya

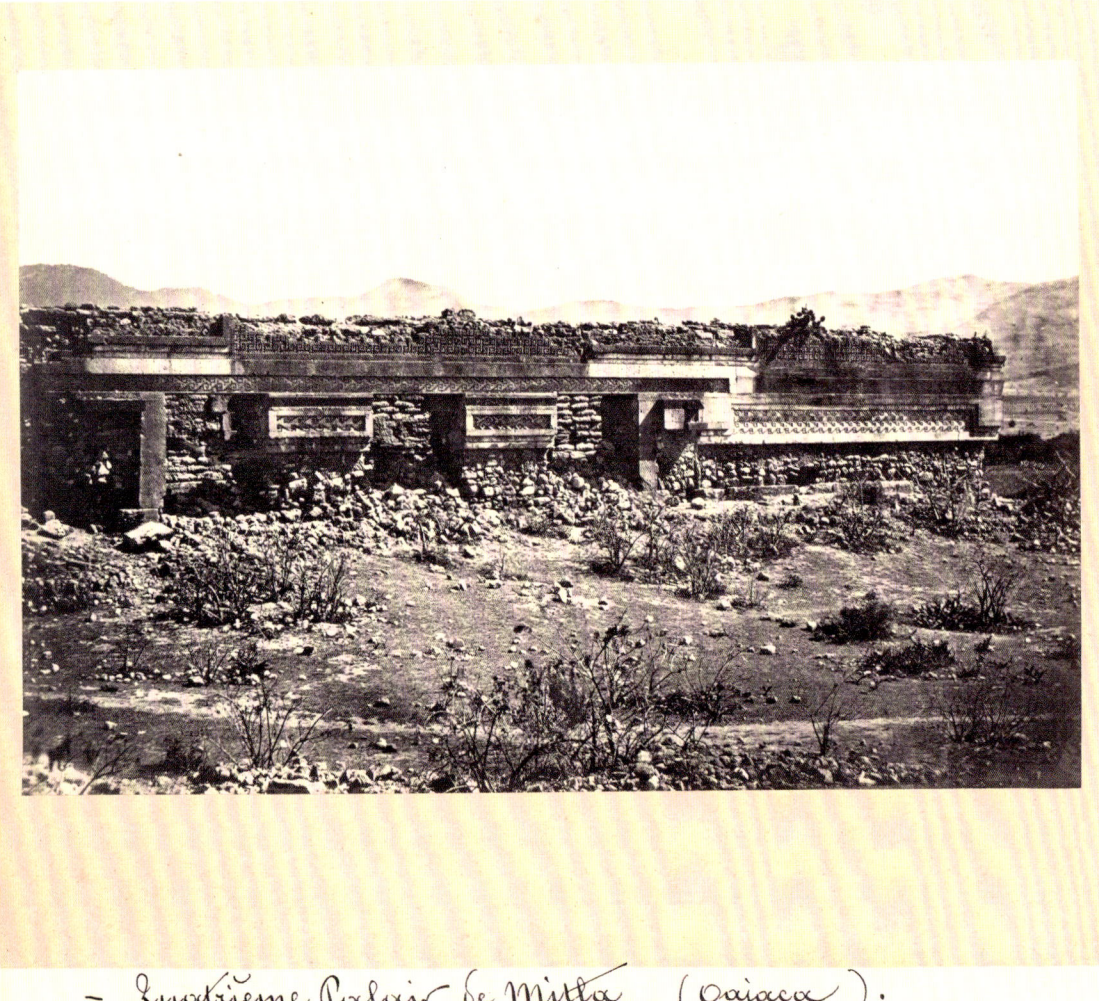

= Quatrième Palais de Mitla (Oajaca).

FIG. 22   Fourth Palace in Mitla (Oaxaca).

FIG. 23   Façade of the Fourth Palace in Mitla (Province of Oaxaca). "The fourth palace is remarkable for its oblong panels on its eastern façade. Four palaces that might well have been the largest on the site are located to the southwest of those that I reproduced in my photographs. They are partially razed to the ground and buried since their walls only reach three or four feet above the ground. Enormous foundation stones set them apart and indicate that they were significantly larger when compared with the palaces that are still standing today."

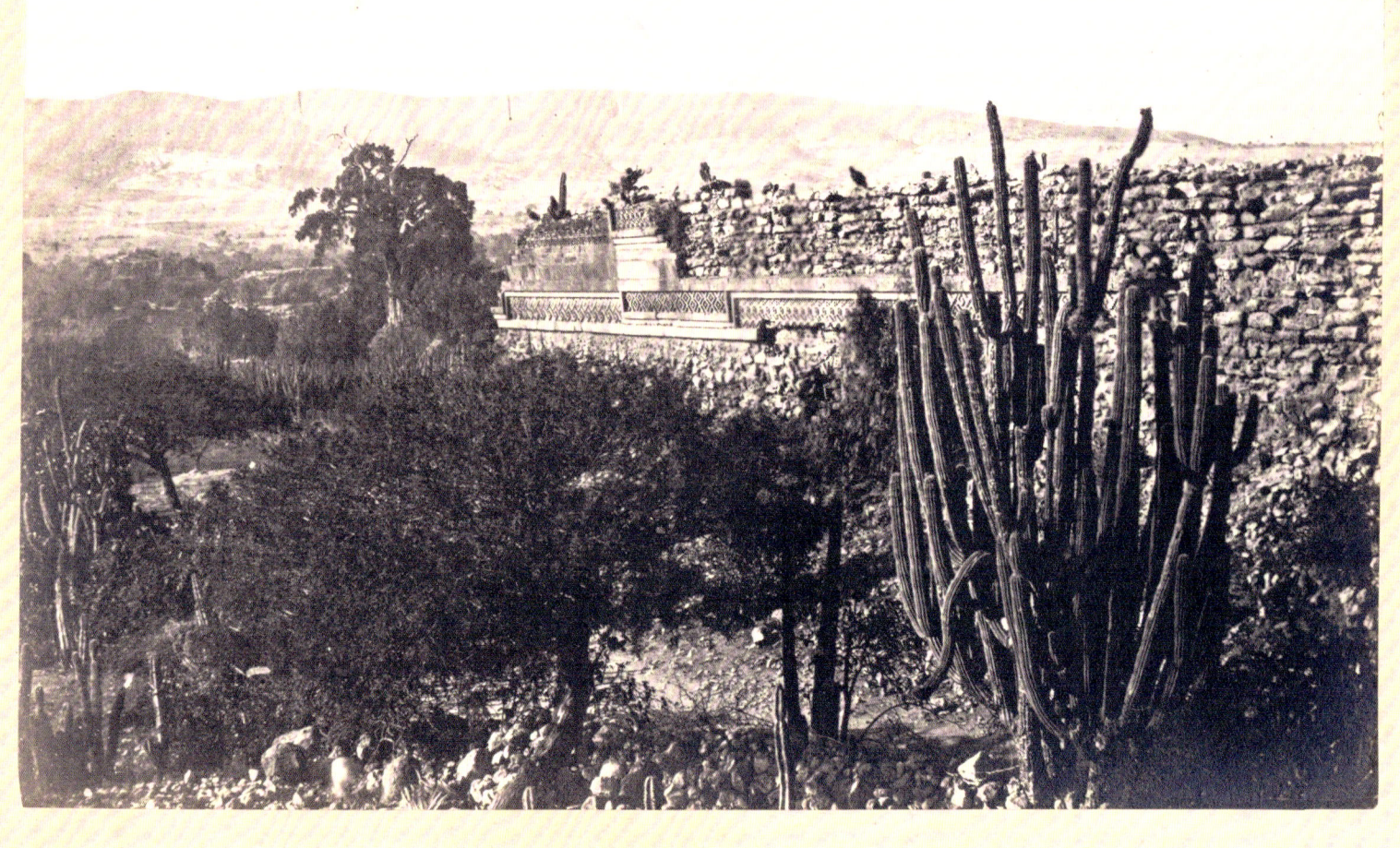

= Façade du H⁜ Palais de Mitla (Province de Oajaca).

Charnay arrived in Mérida during Easter week in 1860, from where he visited Izamal, and eventually Chichén Itzá. Before leaving for the ruins of Chichén, Charnay learned to adapt to the "vagaries of collodion" in the Yucatán, where "in April the thermometer varied between thirty-six and forty degrees Celsius and above and the heat at that point becomes unbearable."[6]

CHICHÉN ITZÁ

I washed my glass plates so that, when I arrived at my destination, they would be ready and I could avoid that difficult and bothersome task. I filled a liter of normal collodion solution ready to be sensitized and since I had noticed in my earlier attempts on 36 x 45-centimeter plates that the collodion dried on top before coating the plate completely, I mixed a solution of 110 parts alcohol to 90 parts ether and 1% silver iodide. Despite this, I had to pour it very quickly and immediately plunge the glass plate in the bath.

This dosage makes the collodion very light and delicate. Although I now know how poorly it adheres to the plates, it was the only way I could successfully achieve photos of such a size. I had no choice but to use this same recipe in all my expeditions from that time forward. Once everything was ready, I settled on a departure date. This time I must admit I was more anxious. The ruins were remote. I was travelling alone.

Charnay arrived at the ruins of Chichén during a period of great unrest in the region, with 45 men—a dozen with axes, to cut down trees and clear the monuments—as well as a few soldiers and a local priest, of whom he wrote: "The good fellow couldn't understand that, in the name of arts and science, no less, I had left my homeland and crossed the Ocean—el mar! The very idea made him tremble with emotion. And all this merely to draw ruins that the inhabitants of this country know nothing about."

We had to clear a passage using machetes. This was no easy task. We were torn at by sticker bushes and covered in garrapatas [ticks] that are types of lice that, like those insects, dig into the skin and are difficult to remove. I moved my things into one of the palace's perfectly preserved rooms. Guards were placed further away, so that they could warn us in case of any surprise attacks and the Indians set to work.

FIG. 24 Main façade of the Nuns' Palace in Chichén Itzá, Yucatán. "The guide led us directly to the Nuns' Palace, Chichén Itzá's largest monument, whose main façade I have reproduced in the album. […] Carved like a Chinese case, the Nuns' Palace, with its wealth of sculptures, is the crown jewel of Chichén. The palace door, with its inscription above it, also has decorative stone pinnacles that are reminiscent of the eaves of Chinese or Japanese buildings. Above the doorway is a magnificent medallion that represents a chief wearing a feather diadem."

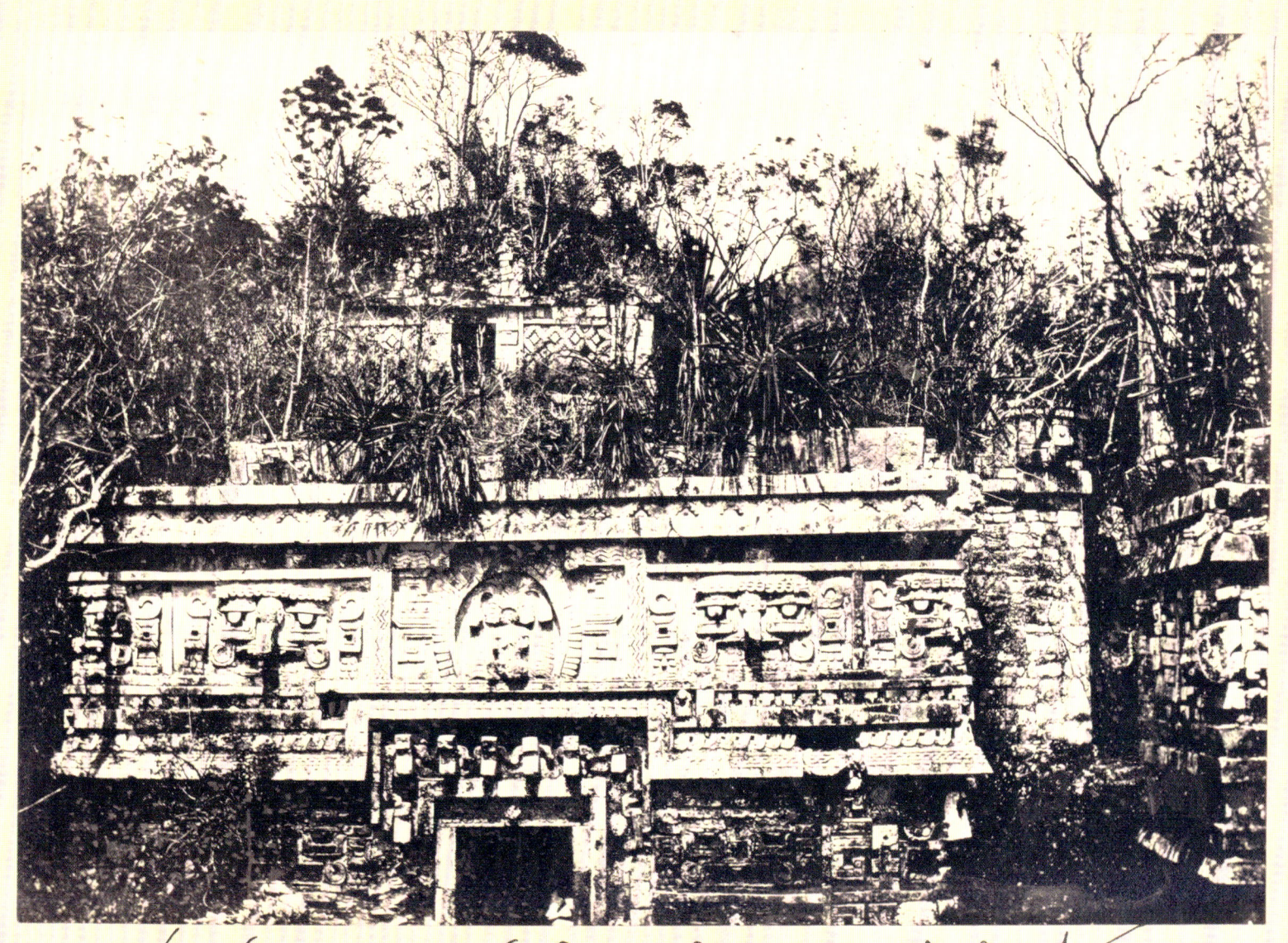

Façade principale du Palais des Nonnes, à Chichen-Itza. Yucatan.

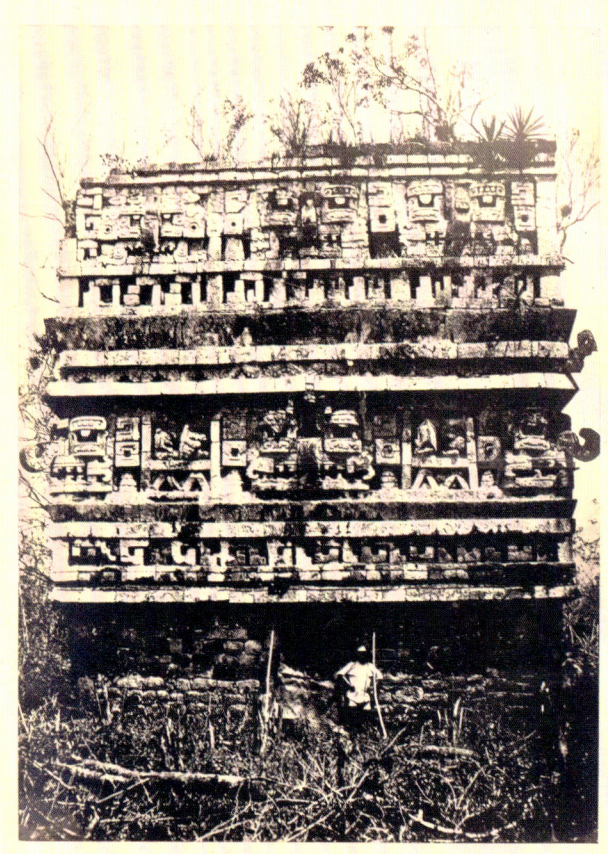

FIG. 25 Left wing of the Nuns' Palace in Chichén Itzá, in Yucatán: "The great frieze that wraps around the palace is composed of many giant heads representing idols, each with noses that are themselves in the shape of perfectly executed figures. Each head is separated by mosaic panels in the form of crosses – a pattern that is quite common in the Yucatan."

FIG. 26   Nuns' Palace in Chichén Itzá (right wing), Yucatán.

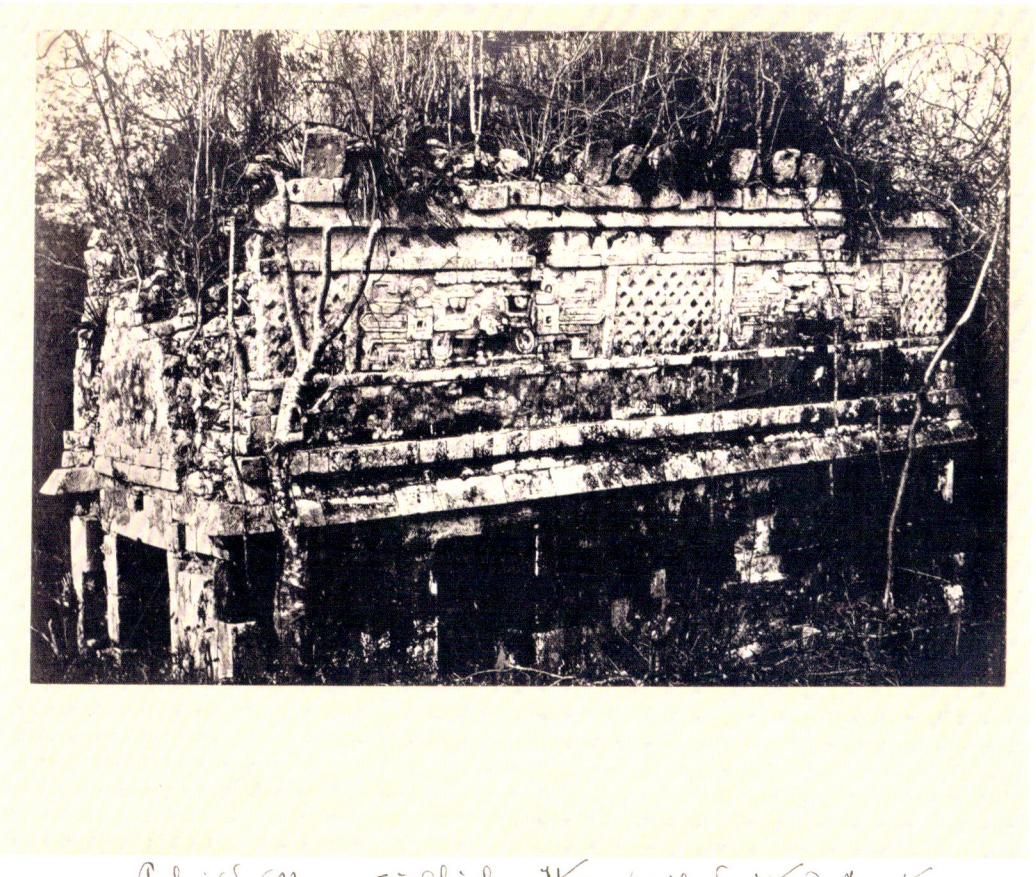

Once my darkroom was organized, I took a test photo. My fine companions were all astonished by this instrument and the phenomenon of the dark box. Once the subject was obtained, they all wanted to admire the reversed image on the frosted glass, and they seemed to be confounded by the whole thing.

The current owner of the hacienda and ruins lives in Merida. He offered to sell me his property and the ruins for 2,000 piasters. That is a paltry sum but alas I am not rich. The ruins are too remote to take advantage of its many precious features. Abandoned to the ravages of time, exposed to the barbaric acts of certain travelers, these magnificent ruins are degraded with each passing day. In a few centuries, not a single stone will be standing to remind men of the existence of these extinct civilizations. [...]

A week had passed and each morning I was asked to make haste. My companions were all eager to return to the comforts of home and the ruins did not speak to them at all. As far as I was concerned, time flew. Despite being overwhelmed by fatigue, with sunburnt arms and face, I was oblivious to my physical being in this all-consuming climate. Each night, it was a pleasure to stretch out in my hammock, which was hung from the trees that grew inside the ruined structures. We lit a fire to keep the tigers away and ate our evening meal. I was fully enjoying life, without looking towards the past or worrying about the future.

On the eighth day, I finished my work and hurriedly prepared my departure. I arrived in Citaz where the authorities of the small village demanded to see the views that they had heard from the *padre* were extraordinary. I did as I was told

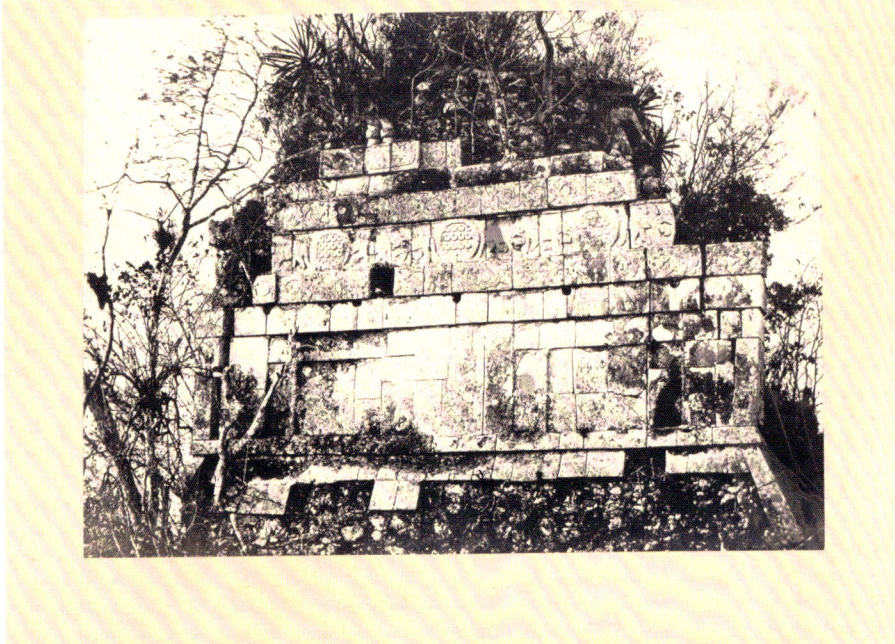

FIG. 27 Tiger bas-relief, forming part of the Ball Court (in Chichén Itzá) Yucatán.

FIG. 28 The Chichan-Chob or the Prison in Chichén Itzá, Yucatán: "The building known by the natives as *La Carcel* [The Prison] for reasons that have never been established, is a perfectly preserved structure."

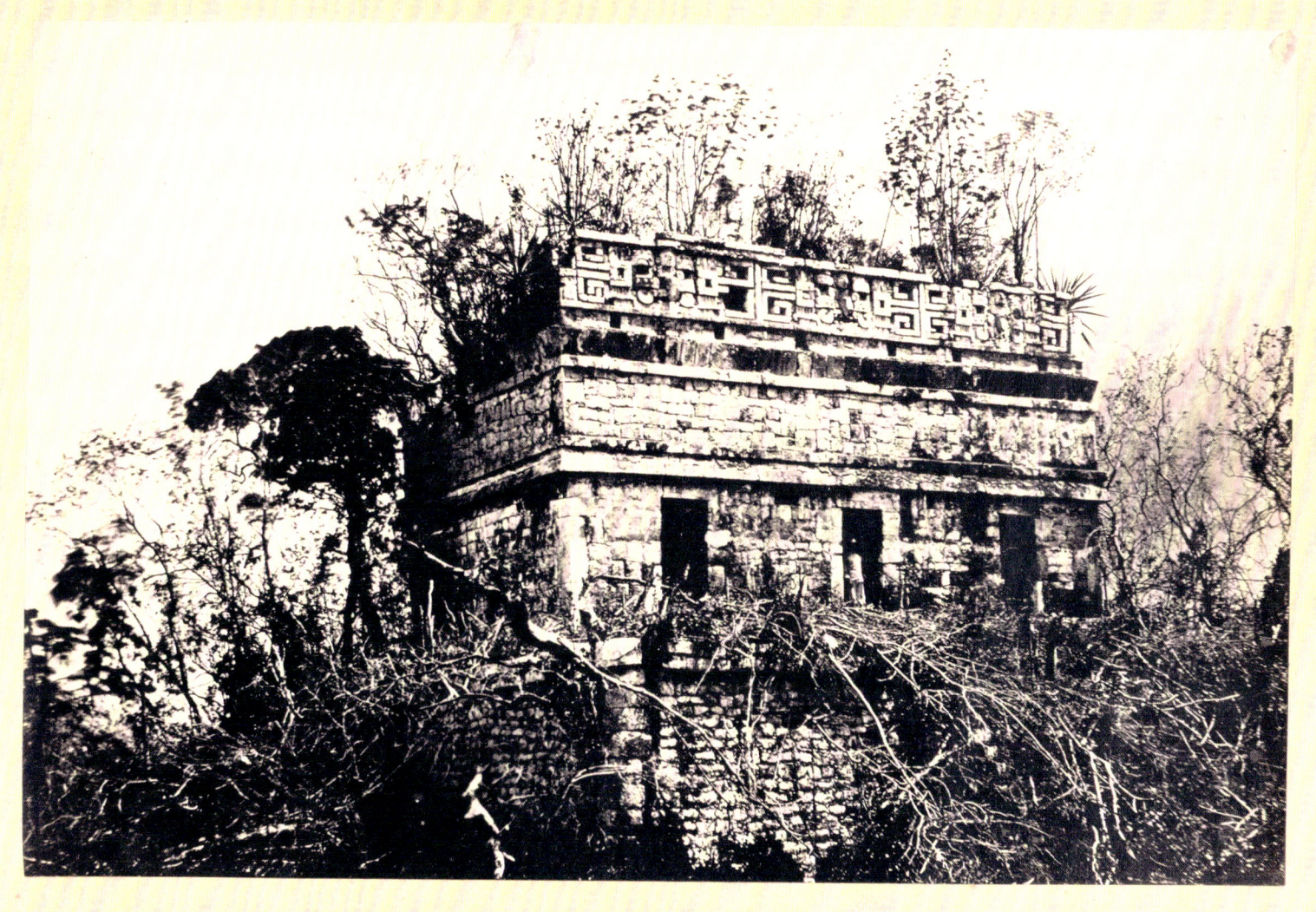

= Le Chichan-Chob ou la Prison à Chichen-Itza . Yucatan.

but they were sorely disappointed. They thought that I was playing a joke on them. Those negatives didn't speak to their eyes, which knew nothing of the mysteries of photography. They thanked me, nevertheless. Apparently, they were convinced that the treasures that I was transporting had no artistic value at all.

UXMAL

From Chichén Itzá, Charnay returned to Mérida, from where he set out for Uxmal.[7]

I had my equipment and belongings immediately sent to the ruins and the next day I set myself up in a chamber in the southern wing of the Nuns' Palace. Using mats and blankets I created a completely light-tight darkroom. I used a table I brought from the hacienda for my baths and chemicals. Two Indians were entrusted with the sole task of getting me water using earthenware jars. Four others were there to help me in my work. They held up a white cloth as a canopy above my camera so that the box would not get too hot. They also opened the door of my darkroom for me and then hermetically sealed it, as soon as I had entered. For three days, forty more Indians were put to work clearing the monuments of the surrounding thickets and vegetation that had overgrown them. Antonio acted as my reserve officer and never left my side. He held up a light for me while those four Indians held another cloth over my head to prevent rubble from the ceiling from falling onto my coat of collodion, while I was developing the photos.

I confronted countless challenges while working in Uxmal. I dealt with excessive heat, decomposing chemicals, and all sorts of mishaps, which almost compromised the whole expedition. Add to all that sleepless nights, and you will begin to get an idea of my situation.

I had set myself up in the Nuns' Palace and slept in one of the inside chambers of the south wing. I felt my energy dwindle. Because I was perspiring tremendously, work was draining. You will understand what I mean, when I tell you that I was drinking something like twelve liters of liquid a day—wine or alcohol mixed with water.

I needed as many as two or three attempts for each reproduction. Other images, which were quite good, were lost due to unexpected mishaps or sometimes due to

FIG. 29   Façade of the north wing of the Nuns' Palace in Uxmal: "One can only admire the fertile imagination of those who brought together such an abundance of ornamentation in a single palace and in such a way that, despite some recurring patterns, each façade is very different from the others."

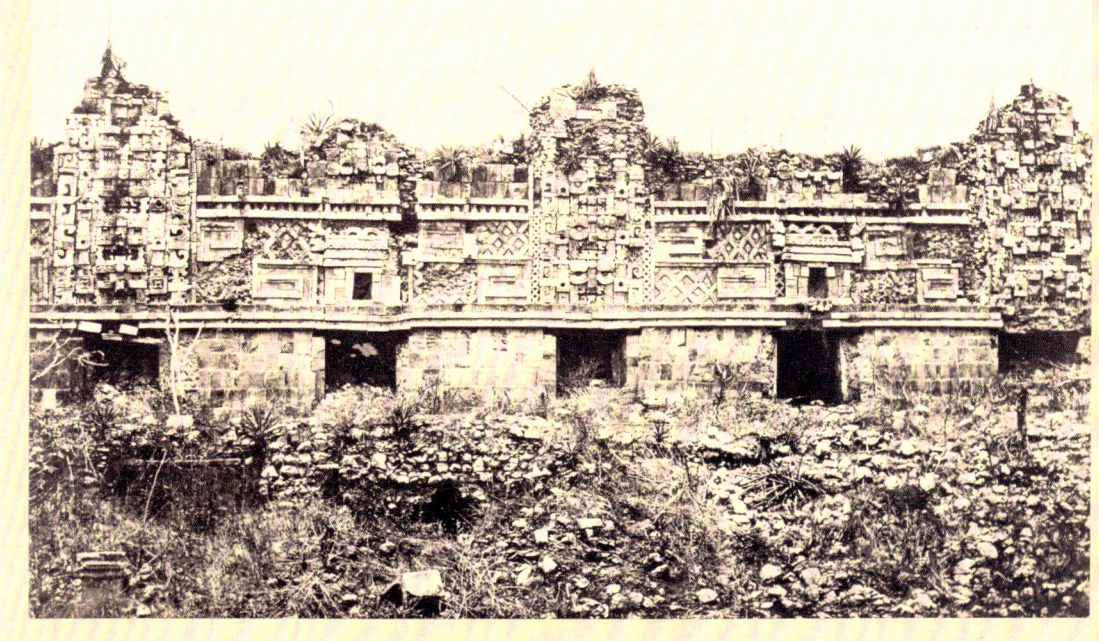

= Façade de l'aile nord du Palais des Nonnes à Uxmal.

the uncontrollable curiosity of the Indians, who despite my express instructions, handled the photos I had finished and had set out to dry outside. In this regard I had the following setback that almost compromised the reproduction of the most beautiful of the palaces on the site—the Governor's House. I kept it for last because I wanted to give it my undivided attention. The palace sits atop a pyramid, and I had to build a twelve-foot-high platform made of dry-stone on the esplanade across from it so that I could set up my apparatus at the same level as the building. My

Exposing the Maya

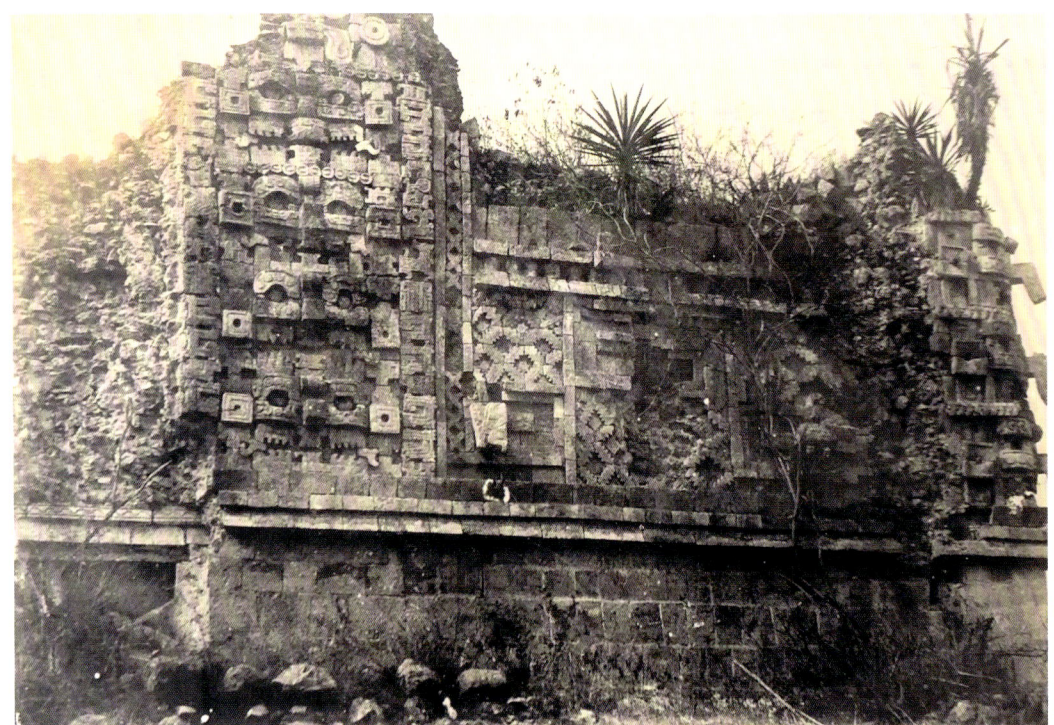

FIG. 30   Detail of the north façade of the Nuns' Palace, Uxmal: Charnay photographed the north façade with its "enormous frieze, which seems to be the culmination of Indian art." "Every other doorway has a wonderfully ornate niche, which must have displayed various statues. As for the frieze itself, it is a set of disparate sections where bizarre figures of idols jump out unexpectedly from within the stones. [...] They are framed by zigzagging patterns of finely worked stones and suggest hieroglyphic characters. Then there is a series of very large Greek frets, which alternate at the corners with squares and little rosettes that are admirably finished. In a sign of whimsy, the architect threw up statues in the most extraordinary positions, placed here and there, as if to refute the perfect regularity of the design. Most of these have disappeared and those that remain are headless."

darkroom was set up in the large central chamber, which was 80 meters from the exposure site. Consequently, I had to place a wet cloth over all of my equipment. I wrapped the camera so that during the prolonged period of exposure and during my comings and goings the coat of collodion wouldn't dry.

I had to run in order to save as much time as possible. Since the façade of the palace is quite long, I decided to shoot it in two parts so that I could capture as many details as possible. I felt this would provide the most striking over-all effect. I had set aside a small bottle of collodion for this photo. I had allowed it to rest for quite a while and was depending on it to work. I also had two glass plates—the last two I could find. At this point, I no longer had any other chemicals or plates. Success was the only option. On top of that, I had to succeed twice and in quick

FIG. 31   Nuns' Palace in Uxmal (Yucatán). This is sometimes referred to by Charnay as the Egyptian façade.

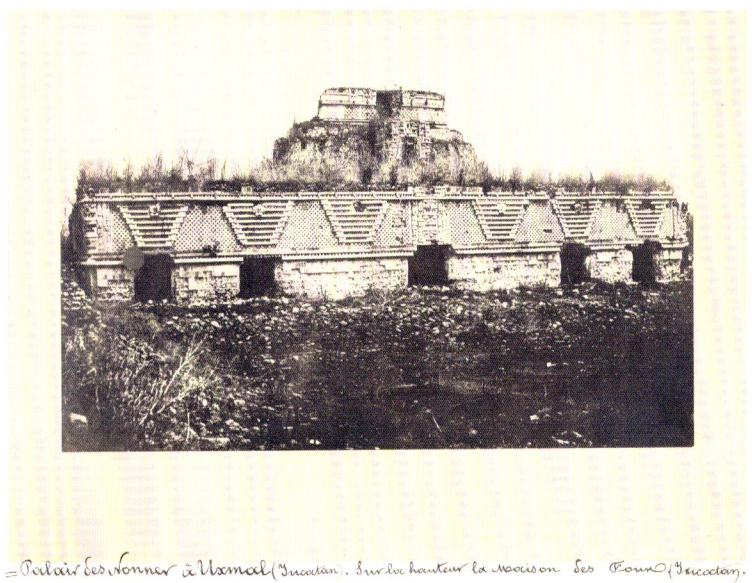

FIG. 32   Detail of eastern façade of the Nuns' Palace, Uxmal (Yucatán). "The corners all have this strange ornamentation, composed of large heads of idols stacked one on top of the other and each with a disproportionally large, crooked nose that is twisted upward in the Chinese style."

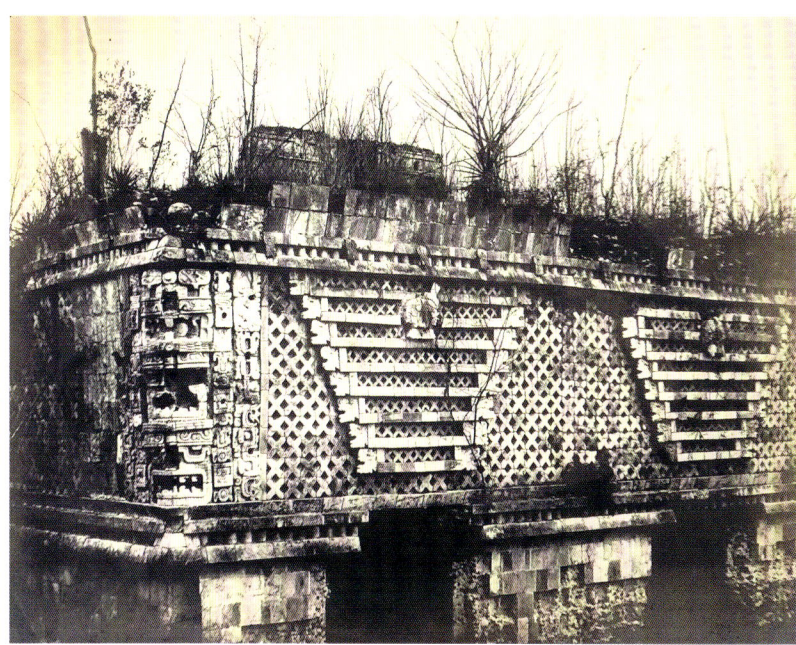

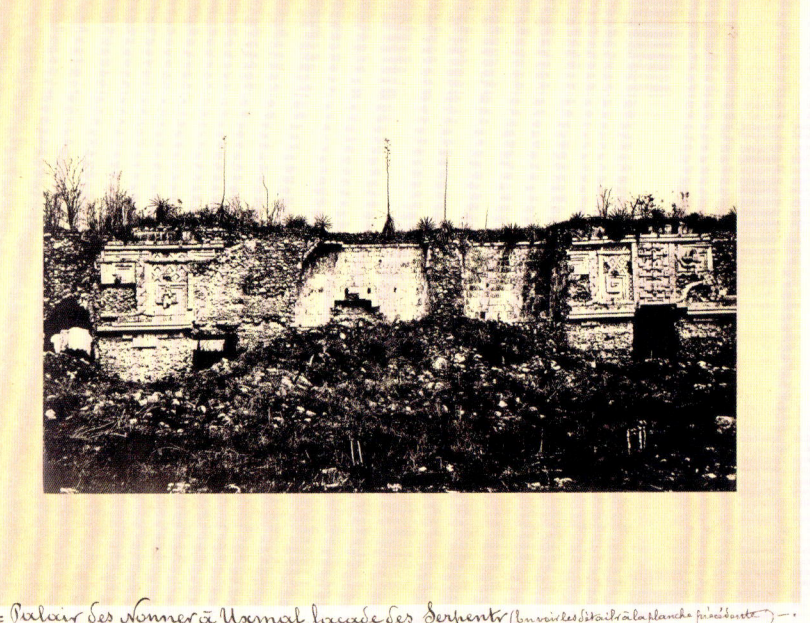

FIG. 33 Nuns' Palace in Uxmal, Serpent Façade.

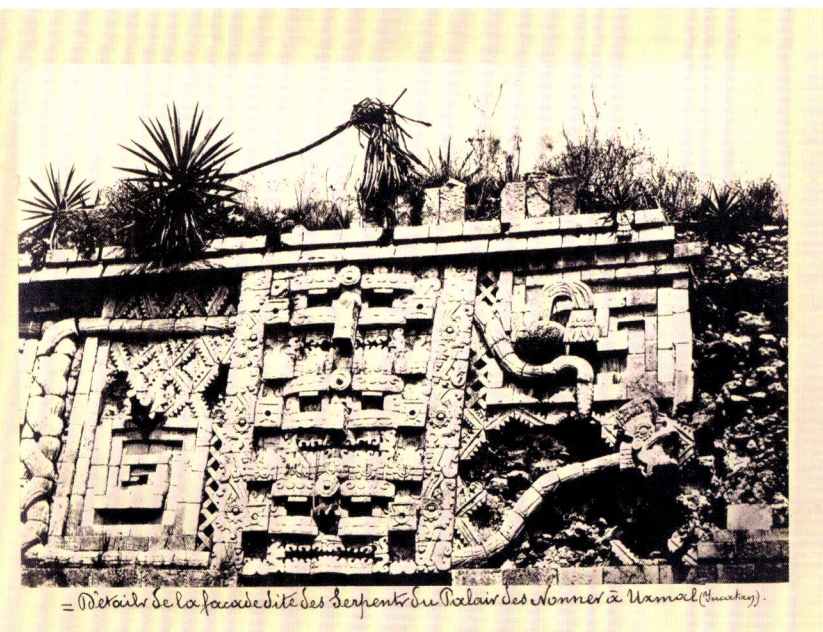

FIG. 34 Detail of the so-called Serpent Façade of the Nuns' Palace in Uxmal (Yucatán): "The left wing (*casa de la Culebra*), called the Serpent Façade, is almost entirely in ruins, but must have been the most beautiful. Its name derives from the immense rattlesnake that runs across the entire façade, whose body twists and turns to create the interlacing frames of the panels along this side of the structure."

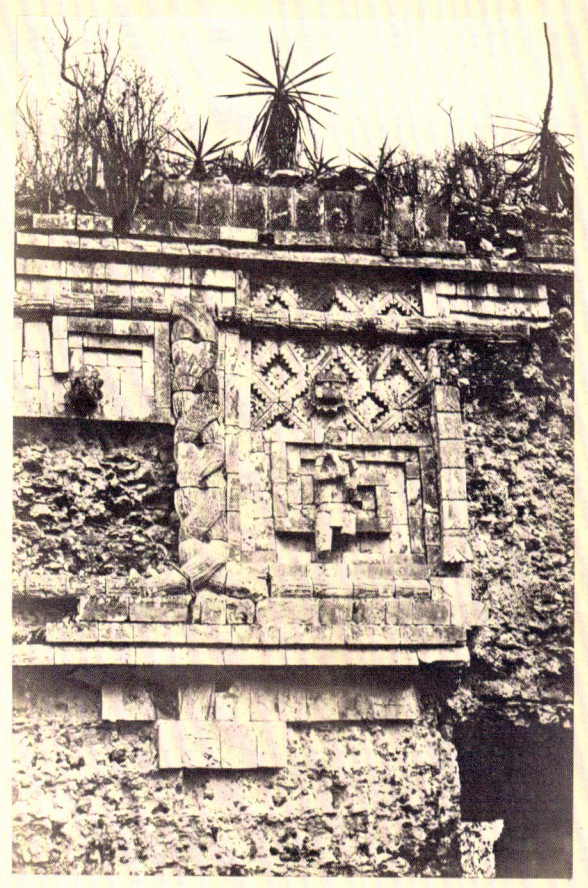

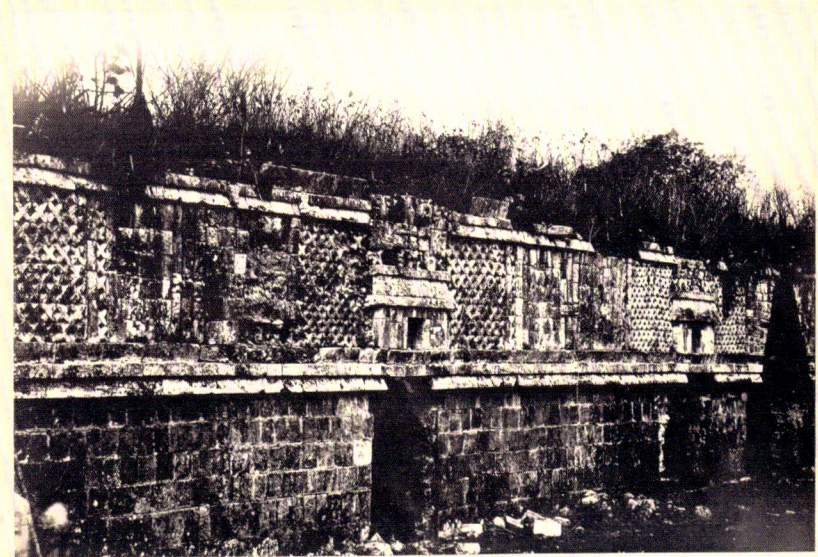

FIG. 35 Detail of the Serpent Façade of the Nuns' Palace in Uxmal. "Only one of these panels still exists. […] A statue of an Indian juts out of the façade, holding a scepter. Above his head there is ornamentation that looks like a crown. The head and the tail of the serpent meet at the other end and the caudal appendage makes it obvious that it represents a rattlesnake."

FIG. 36 Detail of part of the ruins of Uxmal (Yucatán).

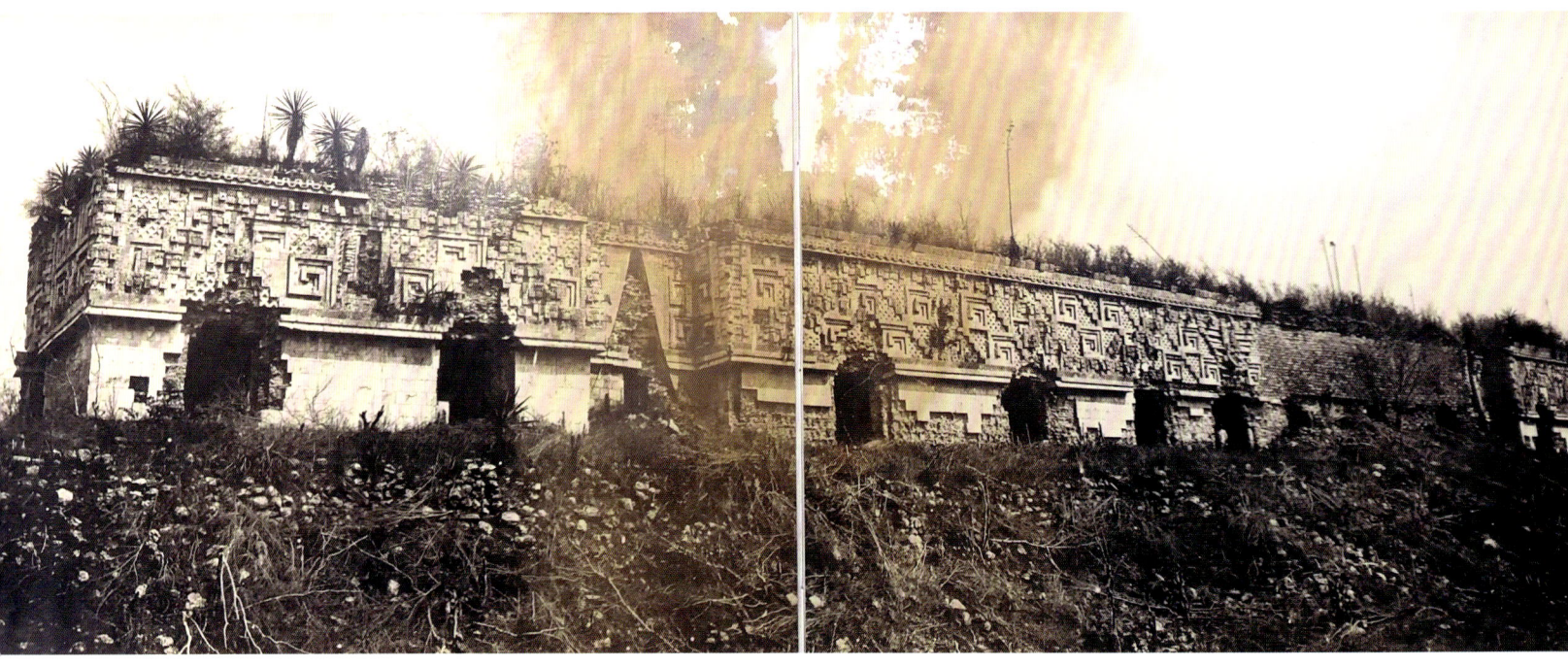

succession, otherwise I ran the risk of the light changing and seeing the two parts of the structure in a completely different light.

I began my work and my first shot came out perfectly. There were no spots. It was transparent, and each detail was highlighted. In other words, it was flawless.

For the second a ray of sunlight had infiltrated the camera frame. This meant that the plate had a black line cutting across it, that ruined the image. I quickly tried to clean the plate. My collodion was getting low and there was none left to spare. I therefore coated my plate as carefully as possible, and since I had seen what had gone wrong with the previous shot it was easy enough to avoid the same problem the second time. Everything had gone well. The shot was good. It had the same tonality. It had the same vigor and I congratulated myself on my triumph in this delicate operation.

FIG. 37 The Governor's Palace in Uxmal (Yucatán) 100 meters by 12 (Assemblage) left side, right side: "The Governor's Palace is the most substantial monument of the ruins of Uxmal. [...] The large decorative elements that used to be above the openings are gone, removed by visitors. Consequently, four niches, placed at equidistance, and which previously contained statues, are now empty. Since the façade of the palace is quite long, I decided to shoot it in two parts so that I could capture as many details as possible. I felt this would provide the most striking over-all effect."

Désiré Charnay (1828–1915)

FIG. 38 Detail of the main doorway to the Governor's Palace in Uxmal (Yucatán): "Above the main doorway is the Palace's inscription. The characters are perfectly visible, and if we had the key to these hieroglyphs they would provide us with the name of the prince or god in whose honor this monument was built. Above the inscription, there is a bust, whose head and arms have been destroyed. It looks like the bust of a woman. The pedestal is decorated with three heads facing in the opposite direction. They are finely chiseled and almost look Greek. Consequently, the Uxmal ruins seem to me to be the ultimate expression of American civilization." Note the red handprints captured in the image.

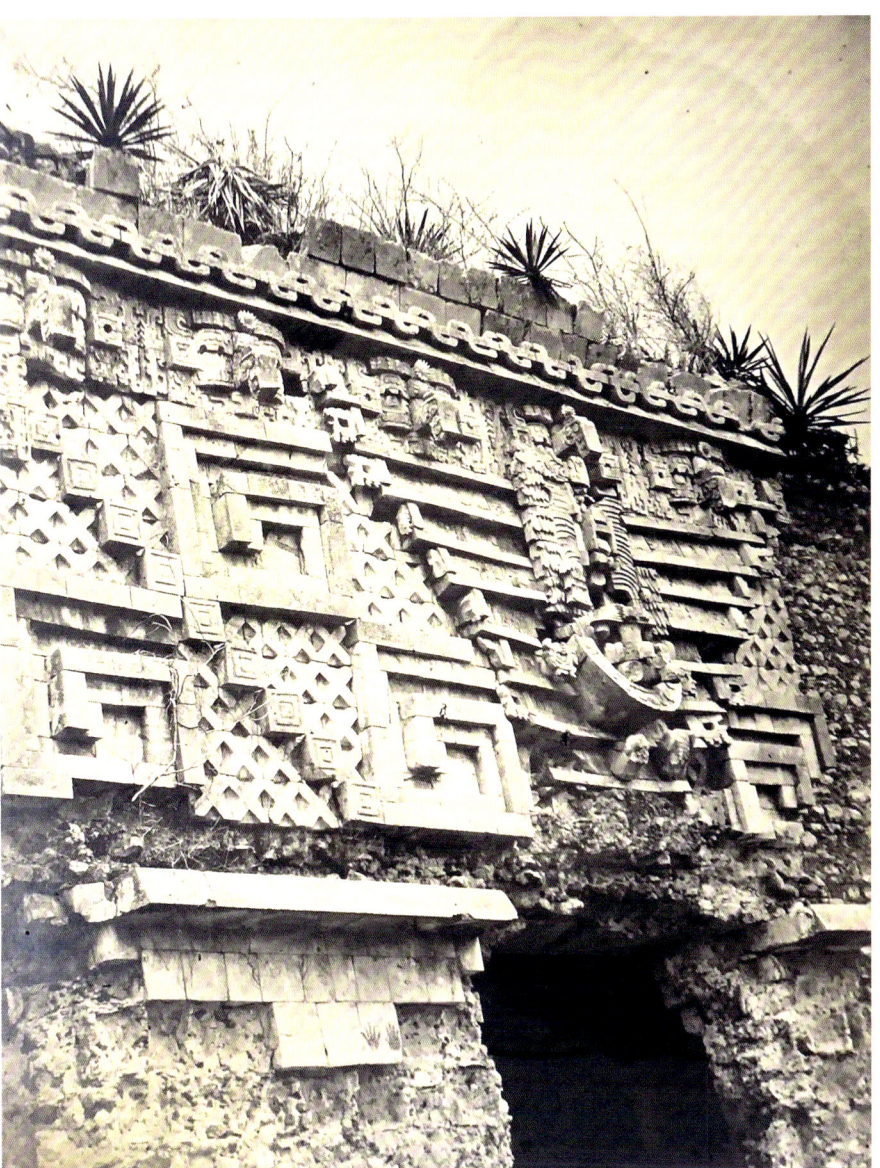

> I set down this second plate to examine the first one and fully appreciate the perfection of my work. I had it in my hand and while I was viewing it as a transparency, I wanted to remove a few foggy areas on the back of the glass plate that had been caused by the chemicals. To my despair someone had flipped the plate over, and my entire handprint was etched onto the impression. Immediately I realized that the whole thing was destroyed. What to do? I remembered that I had left several flasks with remnants of sensitized collodion in the Nuns' Palace and I promised that I would give a piaster to the first person who brought them to me.
>
> The poor men were off in a flash. Watching them run through the cleared brush as if it were the most frenzied of steeplechases, my photographer's rage dissipated. I started cleaning my glass plate once again, and before I could finish, they had returned. It was not too late and although the last shot was not quite as good as the first—it would have to do.
>
> It was time for me to leave this place of damnation. My body was nothing but a giant sore, I had grown impossibly thin, and was as tanned as an old Indian. Moreover, a fever had added to my discomfort.

PALENQUE

Palenque was first explored in the eighteenth century, and the first images of the site seen in Europe—Alexander von Humboldt's *Vues des Cordillères* (Views of the Cordilleras) and Kingsborough's *Mexican Antiquities*—date from that time. Jean Frédéric de Waldeck arrived in Palenque in 1832 and did the first extensive drawings of the site. Seeing influences from South Asian Indian art and highlighting what he thought were elephants in glyphs and decorative elements, Waldeck's fantastical interpretations have since been discredited. Later, Frederick Catherwood would provide engravings that were published in John Stephens's *Incidents of Travel in Central America, Chiapas and Yucatán*. Before reaching the ruins of Palenque, Charnay arrived in the town of Santo Domingo del Palenque, where he was the guest of a government employee, Agustin Gonzales.[8]

> Palenque is still a place where the government of Chiapas sends its troublemaking residents into exile. They tell me that a six-month stay will calm the most mischievous

troublemakers, and a four-year sentence is the equivalent of a death sentence. Boredom, isolation, and fevers will bring down even the strongest of them.

It had been two days since Don Agustin sent twelve Indians into the ruins to clear the forest and the palace for me. I assumed that they had made progress, so I left town to join them. I was accompanied by my servant and the official escort that the state of Chiapas imposes on any traveler at the rate of five francs per day. This escort had two main roles. He was a guide to the ruins while I was exploring the monuments, but he also kept an eye on me. He was under orders to make sure that I didn't damage any of the palaces. There were also four Indian porters who, who carried my kit, as well as a table, kitchen implements, and food supplies.

The ruins were at least twelve kilometers from the village, but it seemed like a particularly long journey. Finally, the sounds of the axes against the tree trunks told me that we were approaching. However, there was no trace whatsoever of the monuments. The virgin forest enveloped us in its thick darkness, and we progressed slowly through it. I soon arrived in a clearing that the workers had created, and despite all that they had chopped down with their axes I still saw no sign of the palace.

"Oh dear, my friend!" I said to the guide, "where is this palace hiding?"

"There it is, señor," he replied, pointing to a black mass, covered in vegetation that was as vigorous as anything I had ever seen growing out of the ground. The façade was partially hidden under a jumble of vines.

In fact, you could easily pass ten meters from the palace and not even notice it. I immediately understood how hard it was going to be for me to reproduce these monuments. Everything here was impenetrable and vermiculated. It had been destroyed and was lost to us. Moreover, I could not get right to work because the Indians had made less progress than I had hoped. They needed two more days before I would be able to get a good view of the façade. At the very least, we had to chop down the most obtrusive trees that covered the roofs and remove the vegetation obstructing the façade.

This temple once contained the stone with the cross that I have reproduced in part [...]. I had no alternative. Torn from its original location by a fanatical hand that interpreted it as a reproduction of the Christian symbol that had been miraculously used by the ancient inhabitants of this palace, it had been removed at the request of a rich widow in the village of Palenque, who wanted it to decorate her home.

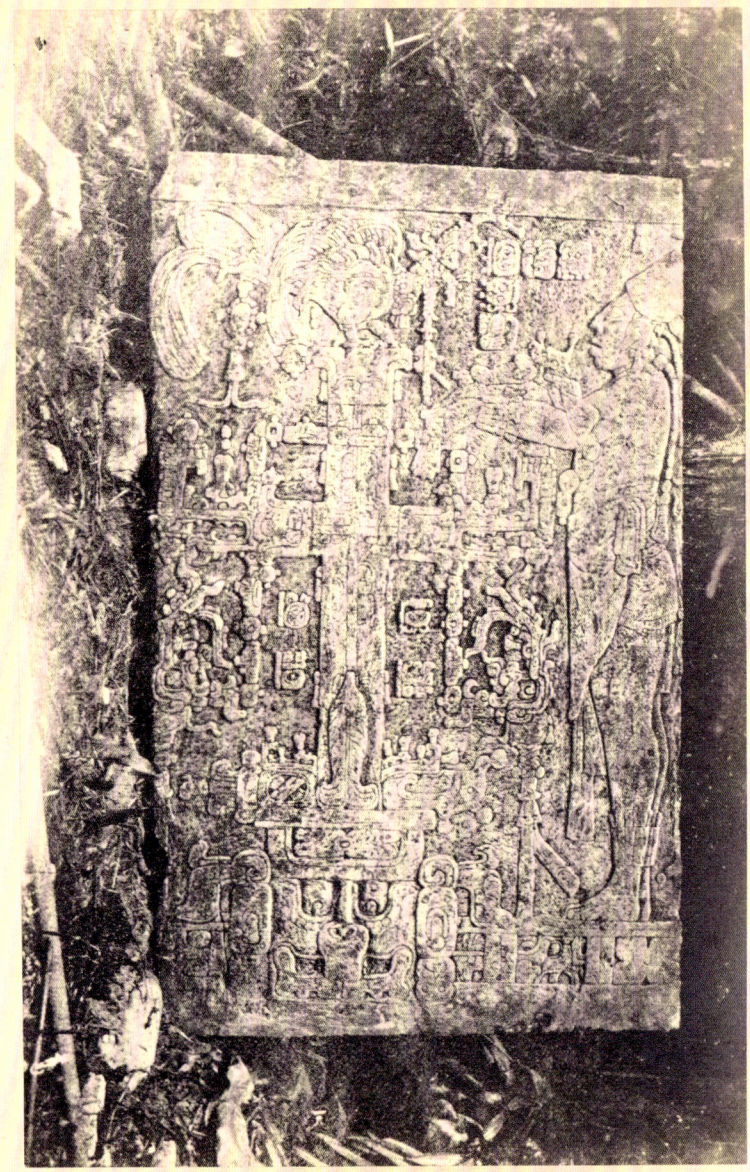

FIG. 39 The Stone of the Cross from a temple in Palenque. Photographed outside the temple from which it had been removed.

Désiré Charnay (1828–1915)

But the authorities were persuaded to stop this plunder and prevented the stone from being moved. It was therefore abandoned in the forest where I trampled it without recognizing it or giving it much thought, until my guide pointed out the priceless vestige to me. The stone was covered in moss concealing the sculptures on it. Later, for my reproduction I had to scrub it clean with a brush and then stand it up against a tree.

The part that is reproduced in my album was the center and represents a cross with a fantastical bird above it to whom a perfectly and purely drawn standing figure is offering a child—who is recumbent in his outstretched arms. There is an inscription consisting of five characters near the figure's head. Four other hieroglyphs of the same type can be found by the section in the lower half of the cross. A hideous idol figure forms the base of the cross.

The façade and the gallery of the palace are dark and covered in moss. I attempted to clean and scrub the pillars so that their color would be more photogenic. But to no avail. In fact, I did this for all the subjects that I wanted to reproduce. Originally, the building was completely painted and there are still traces of color visible.

I had set up my darkroom in an underground chamber. In the morning I prepared my paper there. Although the water there appeared pure and crystal clear when I used it in my baths it caused many spots that I could not prevent. During the day I made my exposures and that was yet another source of trouble. It was so humid in the woods that my camera, which had been subjected to all sorts of difficult conditions over these last two years, was compressing to the point that its joints were breaking. Thus, it was impossible to loosen the frame. Later in the day, towards noon, the heat was so intense that the wood contracted with the same intensity so that everything was exposed to the light. As a result, I had to wrap my camera from top to bottom using bedding and clothing that I shredded for this purpose.

At night, exhausted by the constant back and forth, I began developing the photographs. This task lasted until midnight or one in the morning.[9]

In the end, I must admit that my expedition to Palenque was a complete fiasco. I would have needed ten times the resources, when in fact, I had even fewer at my disposal there than elsewhere. I needed plates and collodion but all I had was iodized paper. This meant that I needed extremely long exposure times that yielded unreliable results. It also required distilled water for developing, which I did not

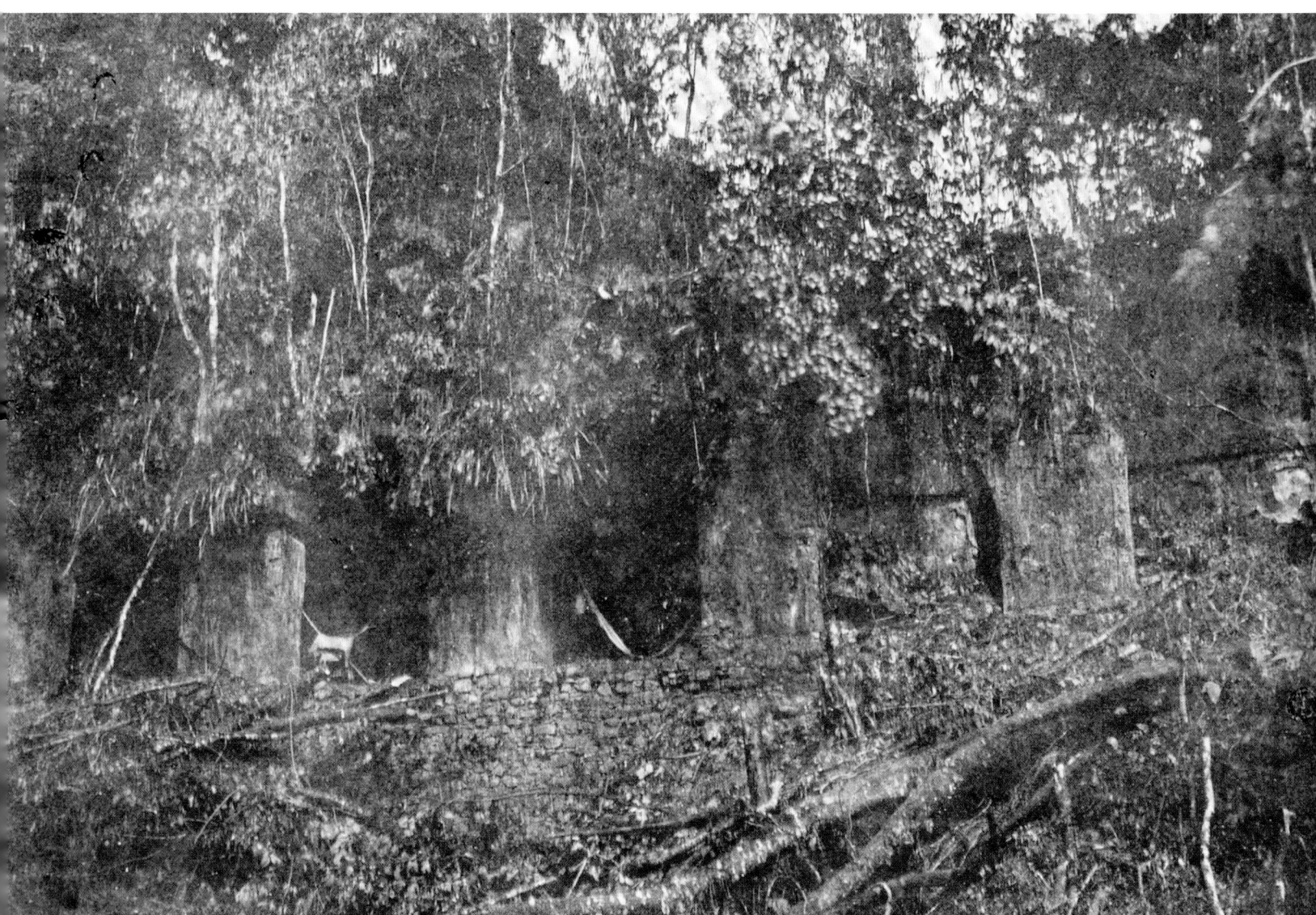

Désiré Charnay (1828–1915)

FIG. 40   The Palace in Palenque (Chiapas).

FIG. 41   Bas-relief in the courtyard of the Palace in Palenque (Chiapas): "The [Palace] courtyard is reached by a perfectly preserved staircase. On either side of the stairway are five sculpted stones representing various figures. They are set on the ground level and reach as high as the gallery, against which they lean at an angle. Some of the figures are particularly well executed but are completely different in nature than the bas-reliefs in stone and stucco that we know of."

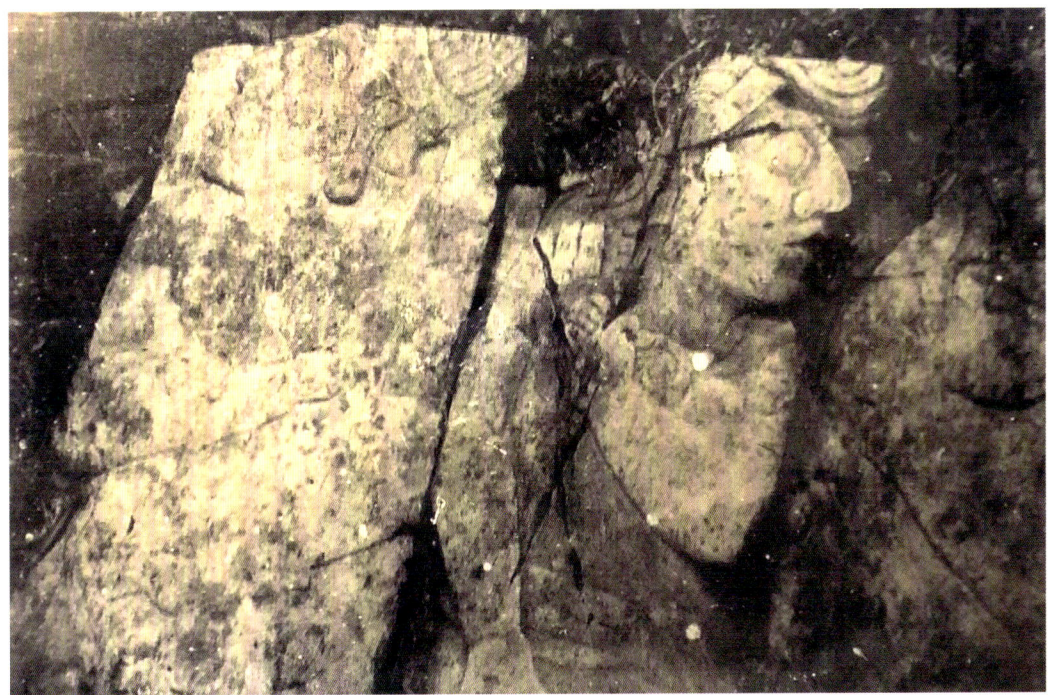

have, and a level of fastidiousness that was impossible in the wilderness. I knew beforehand that it would be difficult but every day new obstacles arose.

My return to the village was a sad one. I walked, like a vanquished man, with a bowed head. Nevertheless, I promised myself that if God gave me life, I would return there one day, to extract more faithful images from these ruins and plaster casts of these precious monuments.

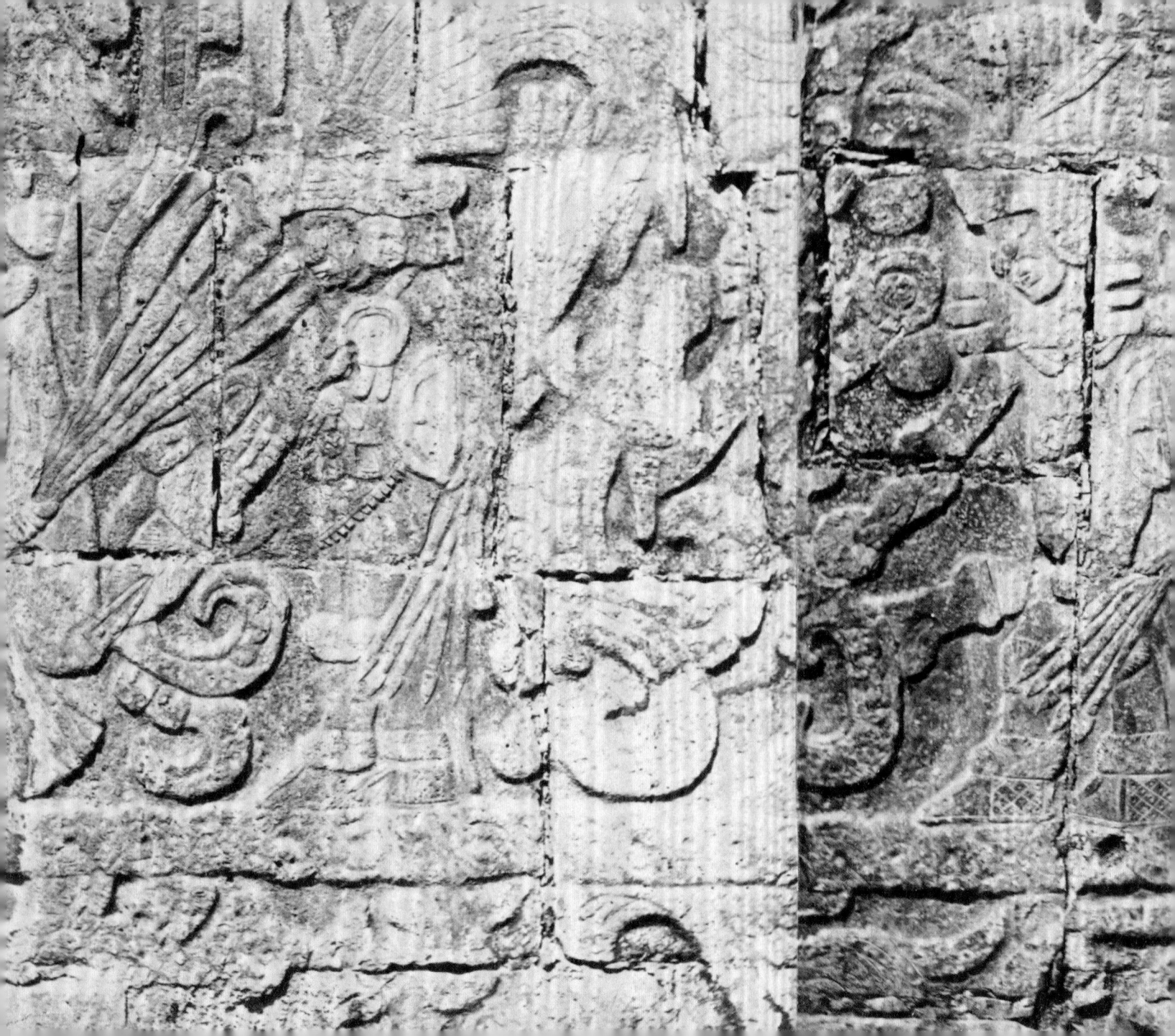

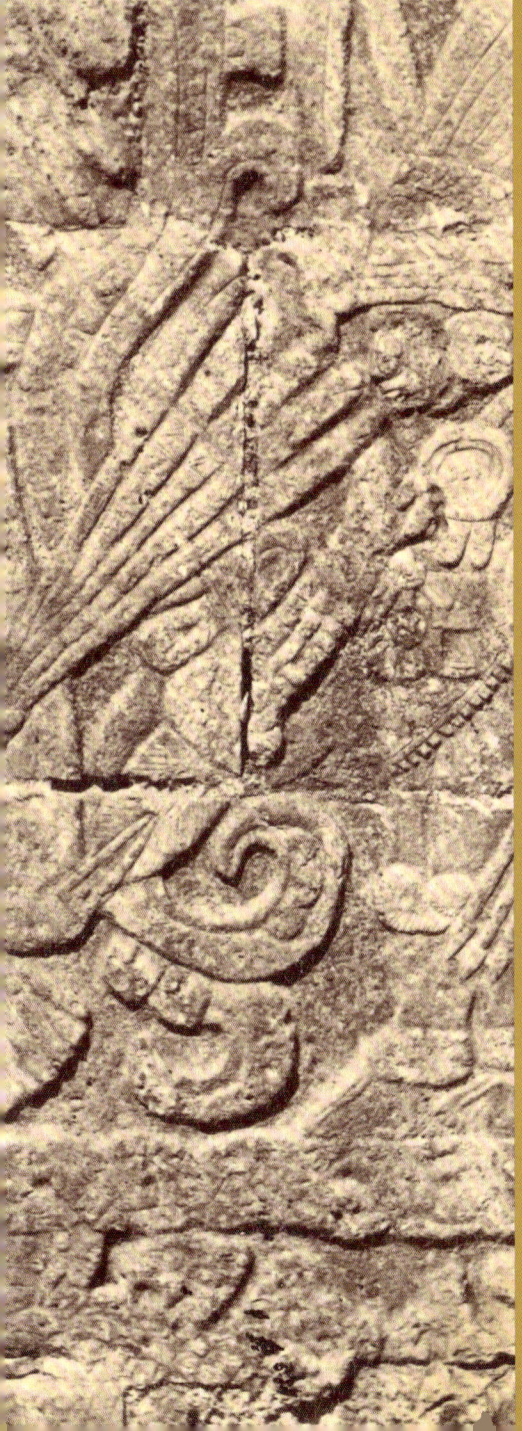

Augustus Le Plongeon (1826–1908) and Alice Le Plongeon (1851–1910)

Exposing the Maya

Augustus and Alice Dixon Le Plongeon are without a doubt the most idiosyncratic of the expeditionary photographers in this collection. Augustus was a French-born, naturalized American, who along with his young wife Alice excavated and photographed major sites in Yucatán in the 1880s and '90s. Today the Le Plongeons are mostly associated with theories that were already characterized as dubious in their day, and, at a time when the field of archaeology was determined to prove its scientific bona fides, they were marginalized. The pair were convinced that they had cracked the code of the stone chronicles found in the vestiges of ancient American sites, where they read evidence that—as Alice wrote—"civilization on this American continent antedated that of the oldest Eastern countries." They argued that, long before the Spanish invasion, "Maya colonists went forth to various parts of the globe" and that archaeological and written records brought to light by nineteenth-century scholars studying the ancient civilizations of Egypt, Assyria, and India provided proof of the presence of the Maya language, tradition, and religion in those distant lands. Augustus's freewheeling interpretations of Maya glyphs led him to believe that the Maya had invented the telegraph and venerated the mastodon among other things. He also created an elaborate epic tale, based on artifacts unearthed during his expeditions, featuring ancient monarchs whom he named Prince Chacmool and his sister-lover Queen Moó—who had fled to Egypt by way of Atlantis to escape her jealous lover, and who would later be venerated in her new land as the goddess Isis.

Born on the island of Jersey to French parents, Augustus travelled to Chile in 1849, made his fortune in the California gold rush as a surveyor and land speculator, dabbled as a lawyer, and later trained as a medical doctor. He began studying photography and subsequently set up a photographic studio in Lima, Peru. There he met the American archaeologist E. G. Squier, who hired Le Plongeon to help him take photographs of Andean ruins in a partnership that quickly ended in a bitter feud.

In 1872, during a trip to England, Augustus met Alice Dixon, who, at nineteen, was twenty-seven years his junior. She became much more than his travel companion. Although Augustus published books, most notably *Queen Moo and the Egyptian Sphinx* (1896), it is Alice's texts that are truly relevant today. Alice's journals and published articles, written over the eleven years the couple spent in Yucatán, describe their daily work in the field. Moreover, Alice—one of the few women who can be counted among the early expeditionary photographers—was an equal partner with her husband, charged with developing and printing images.

Augustus Le Plongeon (1826–1908) and Alice Le Plongeon (1851–1910)

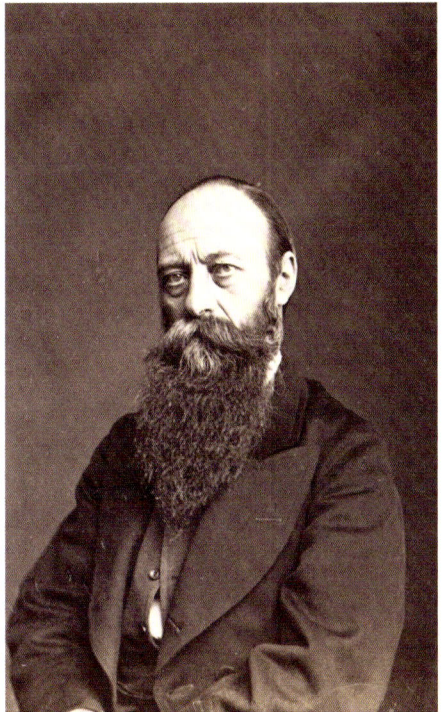

FIG. 42 Augustus Le Plongeon, aged forty-five, photographed by Alice Dixon Le Plongeon.

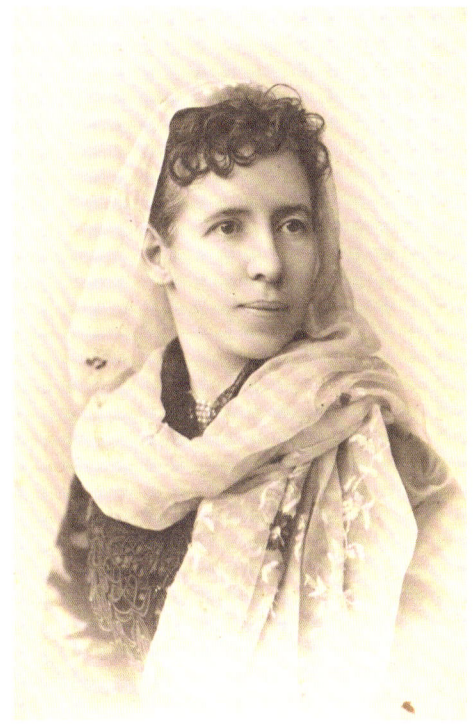

FIG. 43 Cabinet card portrait of Alice Dixon Le Plongeon.

The unfortunate result of the Le Plongeons' association with discredited theories of the Maya past is that the couple's greatest contribution—the extraordinary photographic record they produced of the sites of Chichén Itzá and Uxmal—has been largely overlooked. Theirs was a radical departure from their contemporaries' in the field. Charnay, working in the Yucatán a decade before they arrived, required much heavy equipment which yielded few images. In place of his large glass-plate technique, the Le Plongeons systematically photographed monumental Maya structures using hundreds of small glass plates (10 x 20 cm, or 4 x 8 inches) and stereography—a method that created a three-dimensional visual experience. Of their more than 2,400 prints, negatives, and lantern slides, only a very few were ever published.

Alice and Augustus Le Plongeon arrived in the Yucatán on August 6, 1873 in the midst of an outbreak of yellow fever and political turmoil that pitted Mexican federal troops against Maya insurgents. They stayed in the city of Mérida until the fall of 1875, with only a short visit to Uxmal, as they studied the indigenous Maya language of the region and familiarized themselves with the history of the area.

> I began my work in Yucatan, I will not say without preconceived ideas, but with the fixed intention of finding either the proof or the denial of an opinion [...] that the cradle of the world's civilization is this continent on which we live. I cared too little for the theories that others have advanced, to allow my mind to be influenced by them. But I prefer to listen to the mute yet eloquent voices of the painters, sculptors and architects, who have written the history of their nation on the stones of the monuments reared to perpetuate and make known to succeeding generations the events recorded by them.[1]
>
> Augustus Le Plongeon

> Who can look at the work of these lost races and not feel a thrill of admiration and curiosity? The boasted grandeur of our present civilization fades from the mind when we contemplate these vestiges of a vanished people. That they were mathematicians, astronomers, architects, artists, is proved by the ruins of their cities; but to what further extent their knowledge went no one can at present undertake to say. Future investigations may result in revelations of which we are already catching some glimpses.
>
>   The Peninsula of Yucatan is strewn with fragments of departed grandeur: silent, deserted, fallen cities. Some are not approachable without danger, lying as they do within the territories of hostile tribes. Others—and these are the worst treated—are in the power of the whites.[2]
>
> Alice Le Plongeon

Augustus Le Plongeon (1826–1908) and Alice Le Plongeon (1851–1910)

CHICHÉN ITZÁ

> I took stereopticon pictures of Yucatan in preference to single ones because they are more realistic when looked at with the proper instrument and they enable me to study the monuments as well and sometimes better, than if I stood before them.[3]
>
> Letter from Augustus Le Plongeon to Charles P. Bowditch, December 13, 1902

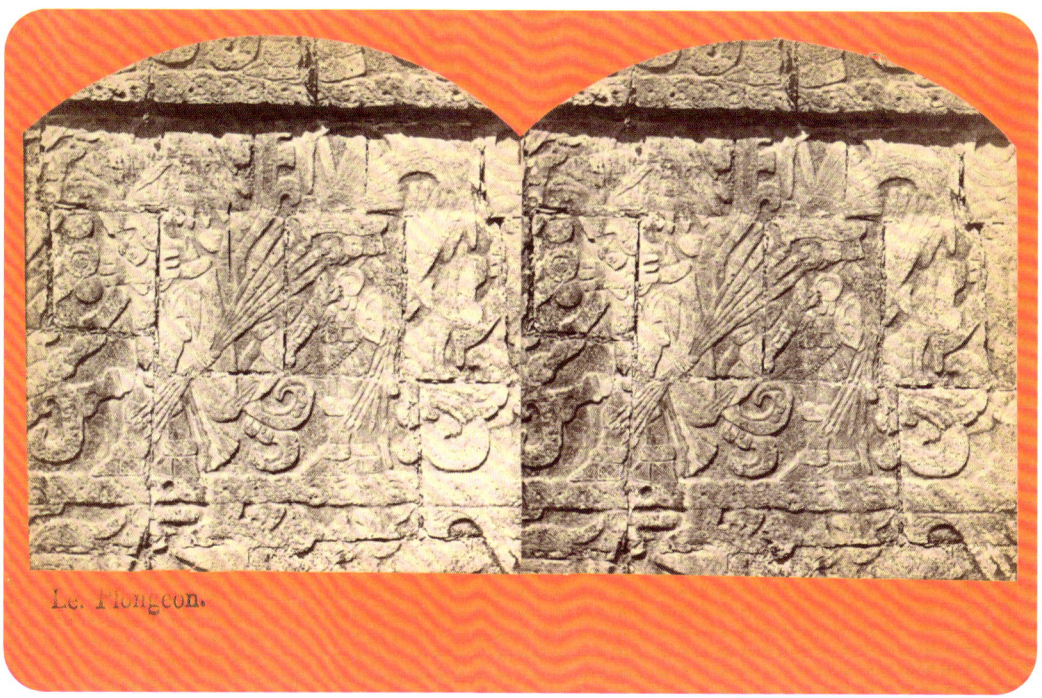

FIG. 44 Bas-relief, Lower Temple of the Jaguars, Chichén Itzá: "The figures all have on elaborate headdresses, or crowns, of various forms, and very long feathers from the top fall over the back of the head. They have large ornaments in the ears and nose. In the right hand they carry [a] battle axe—in the left a bunch of arrows, nearly as long as the men are tall—Some have short skirts with fringe reaching the knees the upper part a tightfitting short coat with a wide belt round the waist from which hang various things behind, apparently ornaments—They have finely embroidered garters. Sandels [sic] that are brought up so as to cover the heel, leaving only the toes and instep exposed. The sandels are highly decorated. Some have serpents for garters[.] In all this procession not two faces are alike[.] All may be portraits. Some are much worn—others are perfect. The face of the queen has been purposely destroyed. There are very handsome faces among them" (Alice Le Plongeon, diary entry for September 29, 1875).

67

Exposing the Maya

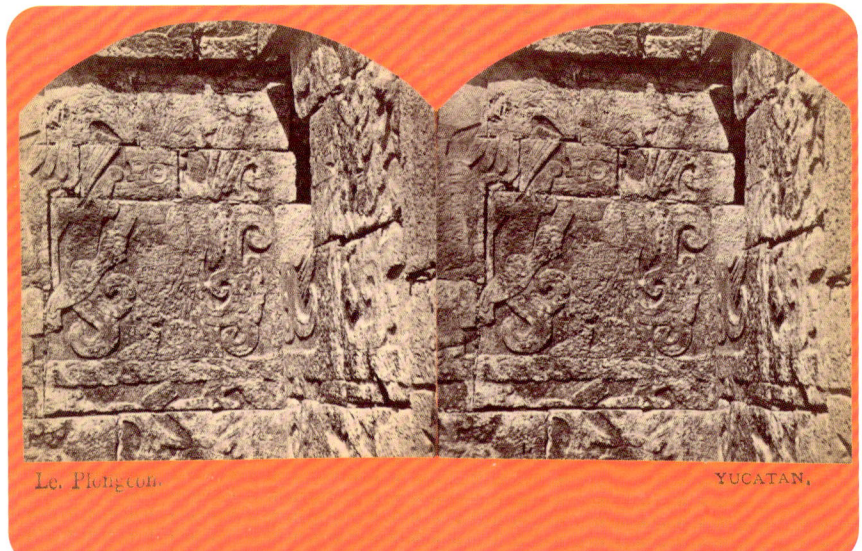

FIG. 45 Bas-relief, Temple of the Jaguars, Chichén Itzá.

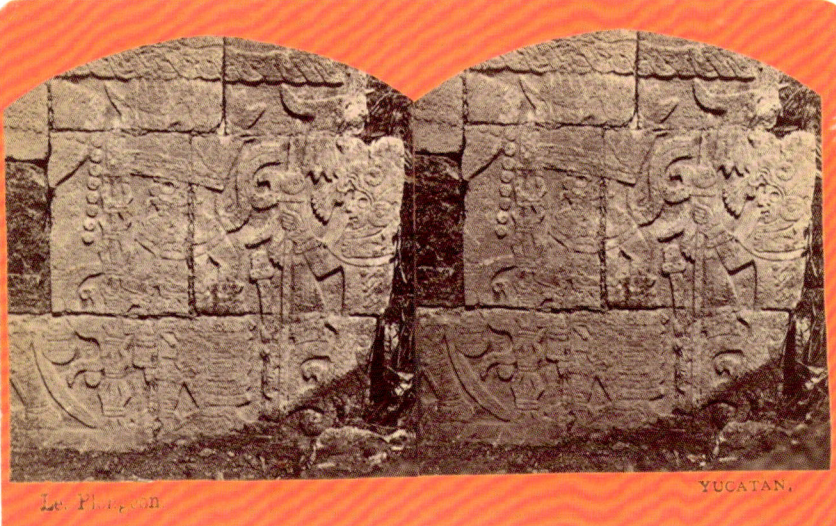

FIG. 46 Corner of the bas-relief room, Lower Temple of the Jaguars, Chichén Itzá.

Augustus Le Plongeon (1826–1908) and Alice Le Plongeon (1851–1910)

Took three views of the Palace. Went home to breakfast at 10 a.m. Found Mrs Diaz almost insensible with a rush of blood to the head. Attended her until restored. then [sic] breakfasted & returned to the ruins. To our intense disgust someone had entered our dark box with a desire to see the negatives, and not knowing how to handle them, had spoiled our mornings [sic] work which had cost the Doctor many tiresome ascents up the Palace stairway of forty steps. [...] On the second floor of the Palace on the wall of a room to the left of the second staircase there are tracings of mural painting.[4]

Alice Le Plongeon

FIG. 47 Doorway of the east façade, Las Monjas (Nuns' Palace), annex, Chichén Itzá. Maude A. Blackwell, who inherited the Le Plongeons' photographic archives, notes Madame Le Plongeon's handwritten inscription: "Portal showing mammoth faces with portrait of deified kings between brows."

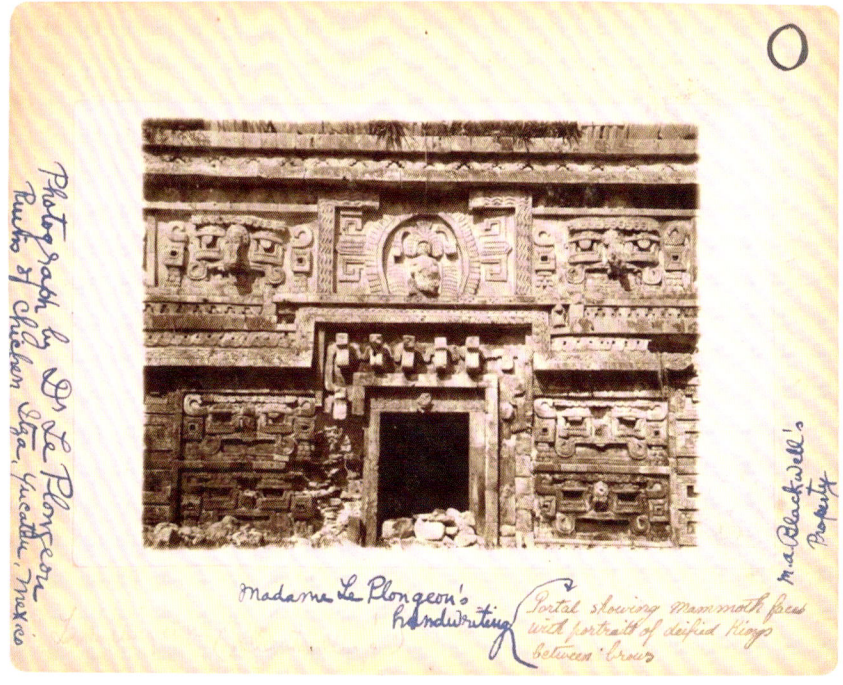

Exposing the Maya

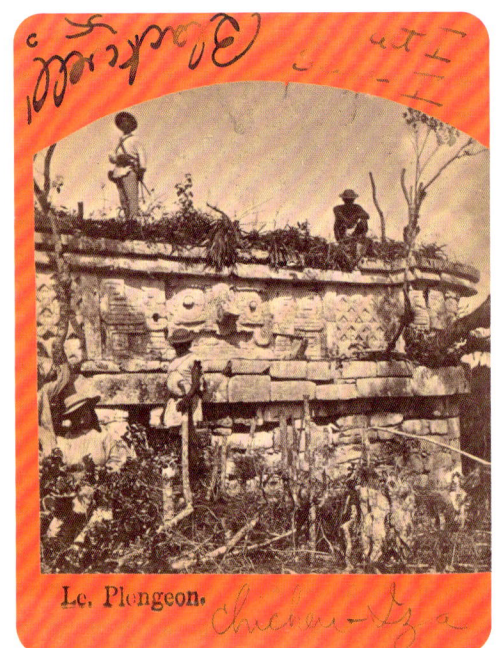
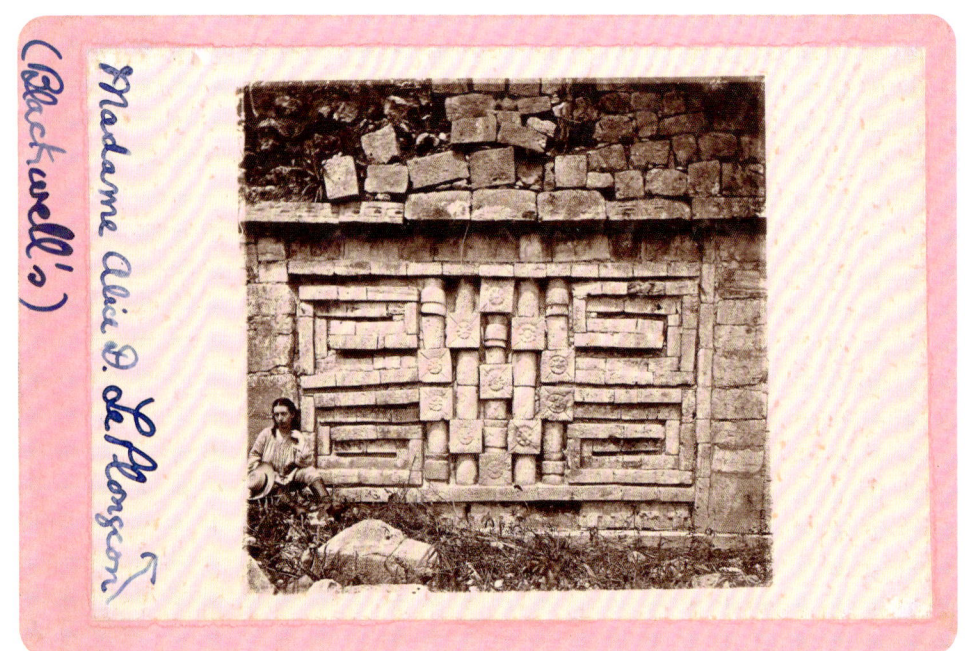
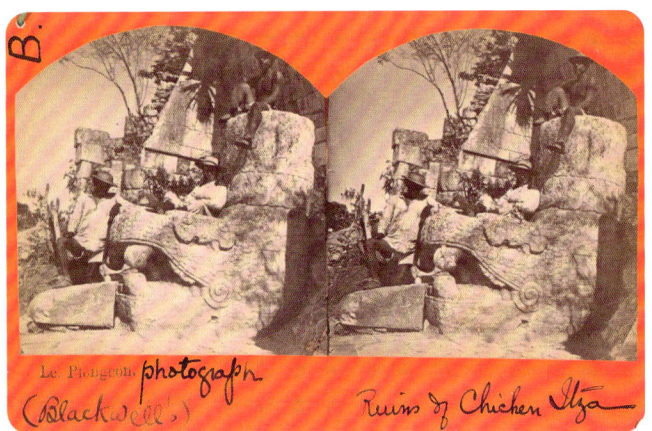
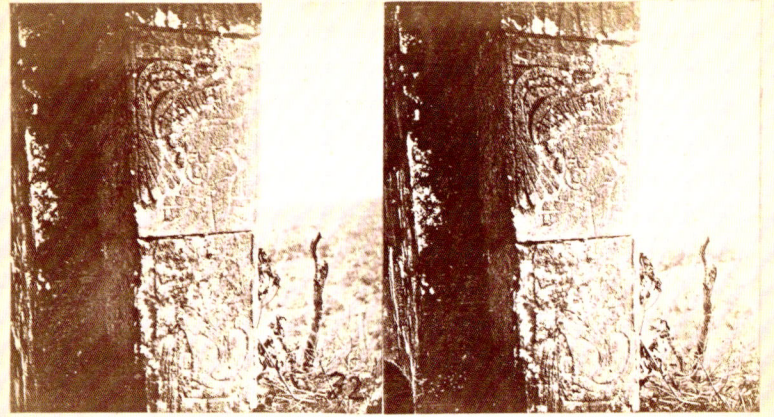

Augustus Le Plongeon (1826–1908) and Alice Le Plongeon (1851–1910)

FIG. 48 East façade of Las Monjas, Chichén Itzá, with Alice and assistants.

FIG. 49 Alice in front of the east façade of Las Monjas, Chichén Itzá, on the second level.

FIG. 50 West side of the Upper Temple of the Jaguars, Chichén Itzá: "We discovered a fallen mound and two large serpent heads. At the entrance of nearly all the buildings in Chichén, these heads are seen" (Alice Le Plongeon, diary entry for October 11, 1875).

FIG. 51 Bas-relief of bearded man, south portico, El Castillo, Chichén Itzá.

FIG. 52 Upper Temple of the Jaguars, Chichén Itzá, which the Le Plongeons referred to as "Chacmool's Funeral Monument."

[October] 16th [1875]: Working in the castle. Our food for the day was a can of lobster & two thick tortillas. At midday I felt quite sick with sleep, but the swarms of flies prevented me from taking a nap. […] We made an intensely interesting and important discovery. On one of the carved pillars of the principal entrance, we found a long-bearded figure dressed in elaborate costume. If I were a disciple of Allen [sic] Kardec, I might swear that it was Dr[5] in his last incarnation, so much do the features resemble his.[6] Having found one bearded man we looked for more and found 12 in different parts of the room in the Castle. As far as we made out, some are suffering torture, others in the act of worship. We had to wash these figures before taking plates of them. […]

Some of the figures were very difficult to take owing to various causes. The stones were discolored. To remedy this, we took some of the fine mortar, and covered the superior parts of the figure with it, leaving the lines black. We also had to make a framework to raise the camera on a level with the stone.

We left work when the sun refused his light, with the conviction that a week would barely suffice to conclude all the work we had to do there.[7]

Alice Le Plongeon

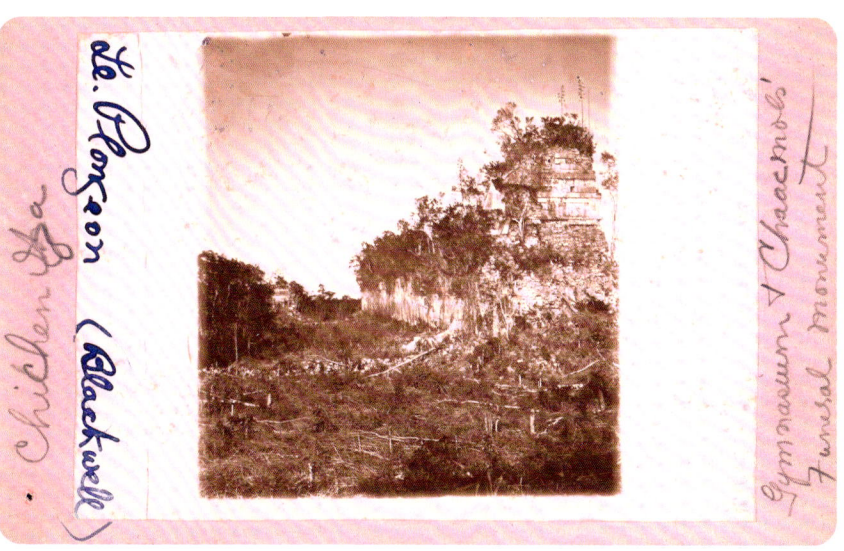

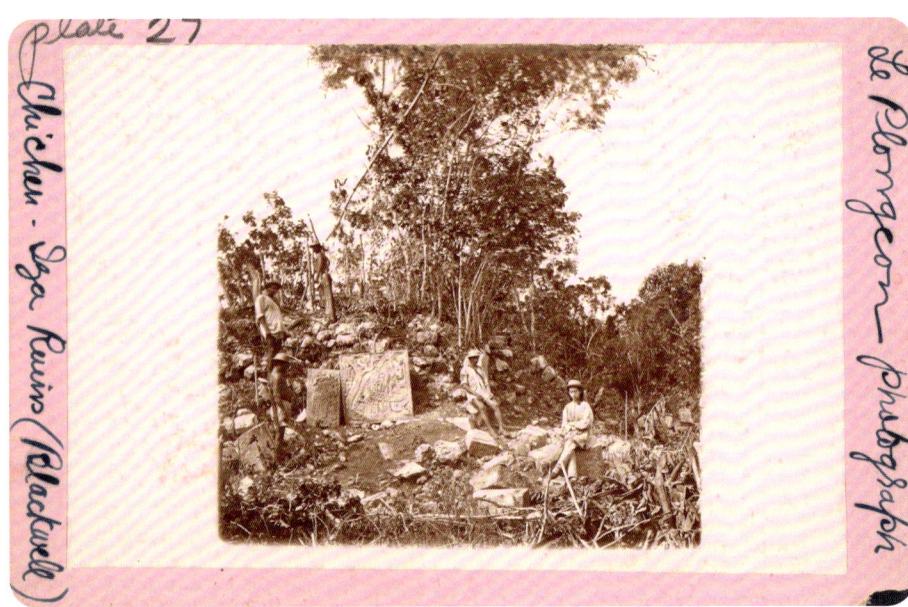

FIG. 53 Platform of the Temple of Eagles and Jaguars, Chichén Itzá, with Alice.

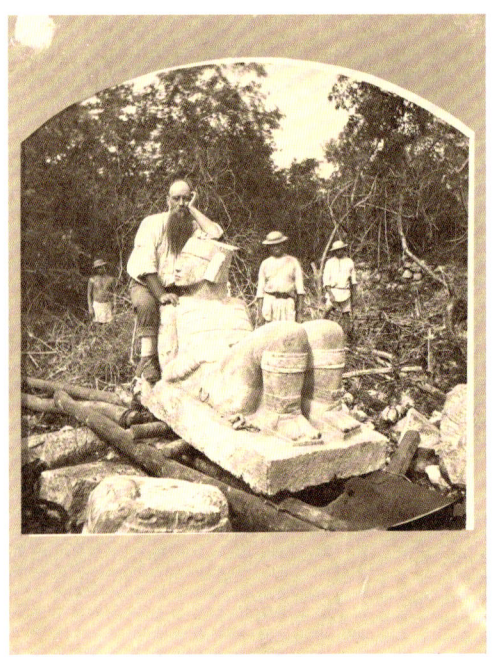

FIG. 54 Augustus Le Plongeon with Chacmool, Chichén Itzá. After the discovery of this statue, the Le Plongeons created an elaborate story involving Chacmool and his lover Queen Moó.

Augustus Le Plongeon (1826–1908) and Alice Le Plongeon (1851–1910)

We worked all day at the painted wall in the <u>Casa del Tigre</u>.[8] With great care we washed it first, then took one or two tracings. Our interest increased as the work proceeded, and the sun was setting before we thought of returning to Piste. We had no tracing paper but made a good substitute by soaking common paper in kerosene oil. We passed the evening preparing this paper, for we saw plenty of work to do in the painted room.[9] [...] We took four plates of the bas-relief wall. Went in search of a building said to exist at the back of the Castle. [...] On leaving work Doctor expressed himself tired of the photographic part. It was not strange, for to get one good plate he often made ten, and for each one walk a long distance and generally make some tiresome ascent and descent. To have a plate procured with such labor, spoiled by one spot of dust just in the middle, was very provoking[.] Yet each day he had to endure it over and over again[.][10]

Alice Le Plongeon

Dr discovered a mound with sculptured slabs, and a statue of a reclining tiger without head half buried in the ground. The slabs represented tigers, and Macaws eating human heart. This mound is not far from the tiger monument. We took it to be a mausoleum...Went to bed without supper[.][11]

Alice Le Plongeon

Went to work for the first time after my fall from my horse. We worked all day in vain. The collodion was bad. At 2 P.M. a heavy rain fell, and were prisoners in the painted room until 5 P.M. We busied ourselves in restoring some of the figures. We started for Piste the rain yet falling.[12]

Alice Le Plongeon

While excavating the Platform of the Eagles and Jaguars, the Le Plongeons found the sculpture that would become known as the Chacmool.[13]

Sunday Dec 26th 1875
Piste, Yucatan, Mexico

My very dear father & mother,

Yesterday was Christmas day, and perhaps before I am able to send this we shall have entered the year—76. I am sure that today you are shivering with cold; while we bask in the sun. Every place and every people with their joys and sorrow. How intensely I should now enjoy a visit to a theater, a little music; apiece [sic] of roast mutton; a cup of tea, etc., etc. Don't laugh—I am very much in earnest. If you were here you would feel the same thing, but you would know the pleasure of life in the wilds. No one to please except yourself and companion [sic], nothing to do except your work. Nothing to bother you except your workmen; complete silence for miles around, save the noise of the insects, the singing of the birds, and the wind rustling among the trees, an almost cloudless sky, for the rainy season is drawing to a close. Brilliant birds, butterflies, and wildflowers in any direction you please to stroll. Large trees here are not common. The forest is close low brush and it is unwise to penetrate far. Tigers and snakes are plentiful and unless you mark your path it is very easy to be lost. Even within the space of a few yards you may find yourself in a complete maze as that of Rosherville Gardens.

January 4th 1876.

[…] In as few words as possible I must tell you of a discovery we have made here. Dr. discovered in the bush a small artificial hill. By the ornamentation surrounding it he judged it to be a burial place. The men were set to dig from the top; and we found it to consist of loose stones. A hole was made, under Dr's direction 7 meters deep: the loose stones, of course, had to be propped up on every side, with sticks cut from the bush, we had no planks. The work was very tiresome, for the workmen did not understand our language nor we theirs. A little below the level of the earth we found a large statue, I send you a picture of it with the Dr. Amid a thousand difficulties this natus[14] had been taken out by the Dr, and 8 men. I leave you to imagine how brain and body have been put to the stretch. With sticks and stones various machines have been made and used to lift this enormous weight, and Dr came out with his statue victorious. There was no road through which to take it, and we wanted to carry it away, and send it to the exhibition of Philadelphia. So Dr put himself to open a road 5 miles long and 6 yards wide.

January 11, 1876. [Vallodid, Yucatán]

In the midst of our work, the workmen were called away from us. We have left the statue hidden in the bush; and we pass on to Merida tomorrow; perhaps to return here very shortly.

As soon as possible I shall have the satisfaction of sending you 80 very pretty views: for the present I send a few that you may see the statue, and the hole from where it was taken.

We have a great deal to do now; drawings, plans, and photos which we wish to send to the exhibition of Philadelphia. We shall return to fetch the statue as soon as we can; meanwhile it remains hidden in the bush; we hope, in safety.

January 27, 1876. [Motul, Yucatán]

And here we are in the house of a very good friend, where we have been just 14 days, I very much occupied in printing the views: We had an order for a copy of the entire collection of 80 plates—they are finished—delivered—and paid for—stereoscopic views at 4 each. We shall send you a like collection as soon as possible. There exists in Mexico an absurd law which forbids the removal of any of the ruins or part of the ruins; and we are baulked in our plan of sending the statue to Philadelphia. Dr had been working hard, writing a petition to the supreme government of Mexico for permission to take from Chichen Itza whatever we please. The governor of the state, Yucatan, put at our disposal men to continue opening the road which we had begun from Piste to Dzitas from where the statue can be carried.

Alice Dixon Le Plongeon[15]

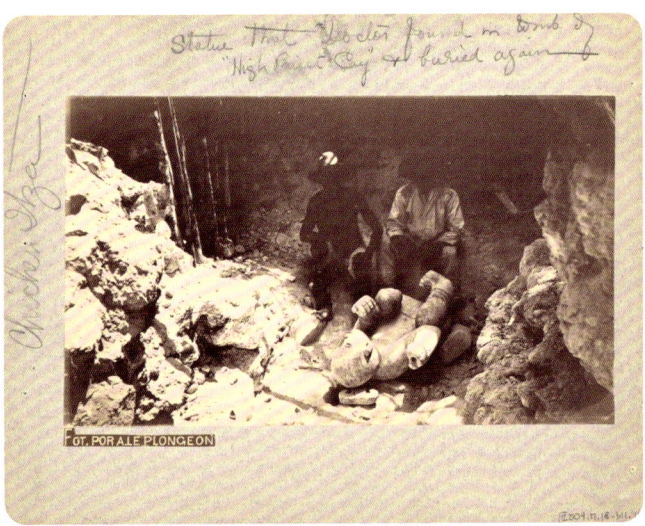

FIG. 55 Statue found within the tomb of "High Priest Cay."

In 1880 the Le Plongeons returned to Chichén Itzá. During this trip they uncovered the sculpture they would call the High Priest Cay, as well as the caryatids—sculptures that Adela Breton and Teobert Maler would later photograph and that Breton would paint.

> On the north side of [a] mound, in a part where there was neither sculpture, stones, nor stairs, we set our men to open a trench one and a half meters wide, to reach the center of the mound, the interior of which consisted of unhewn stones, piled one over another, and mortar that seemed to have been poured among them. As the work proceeded, the sides had to be propped with a strong palisade made of tree trunks cut from the surrounding bush, to prevent the loose stones from falling on the laborers.
>
> On the eighth day of the work, while Dr. Le Plongeon was making moulds in a grand castle, [...] he suddenly heard much shouting, and soon a man arrived, breathless with excitement, to tell him that they had "found a queen"! Arriving at the spot we saw a figure on its back, about one and a half meters north from the center of the monument, and exactly on a level with the surface of the earth. The figure was thickly coated with loose mortar. One leg was broken off below the knee but we found it under the figure, and afterward adjusted it in place to make a picture. The

head of the statue rested on a stone painted bright red, that represents the tongue of a serpent, the peculiar shape of which Dr. Le Plongeon long ago discovered to be the letter *chí* or *ch* of the Maya alphabet.

When the figure was placed upright, we hardly knew what to call it, it appears so human, yet so apish. In the position it occupies it is ninety-seven centimeters (about three feet) high; so if standing would represent a very tall person. It is made of white limestone and painted dark brown. The head is flat at the top and back, and apparently hairless, but painted blue, and over that are red streaks from the forehead down to the shoulders. The eyes are open and painted blue around the lids. The nose is not pierced, but the clumsily made ears have each a large hole. The mouth is closed, and the lips painted red. On the back part of the top of the head a hole is pierced so that a string can be passed through, perhaps to secure a bunch of plumes, perhaps to keep a banner in place, for in the palm of the right hand there is a groove, as if for a round stick to fit in. The hands are not altogether human; where the fingers begin there seem to be mittens, the other ends of which are nowhere visible. The fingers, like the toes, were furnished with nails made of shell, and fitted in place with mortar, so as to look very natural even in color. Unhappily, nearly all were fallen, but we found some of them. A necklace is indicated by a line of red paint around the throat. Garters, below the knee, are painted blue and red. The loins are covered with an ornamental *uiil*, a scanty garment yet in use among the aborigines, and anciently worn by Egyptian laborers. The right foot is turned in, as if the individual had been club-footed. The sandals are painted blue and close up round the heel, but the very elaborate and fanciful fastenings are red. On one heel is the name Cay Canchi, written with red paint. This image may possibly represent the sacred monkey of the Mayas, as the Cynocephalus was emblematic of the god Thoth among the Egyptians.[16]

Alice Le Plongeon

UXMAL

The Le Plongeons arrived at the Uxmal site in May 1876 and lived on site for three months. The couple were able to photograph entire stretches of the façade of the House of the Governor. The task of composing and photographing the architectural details of

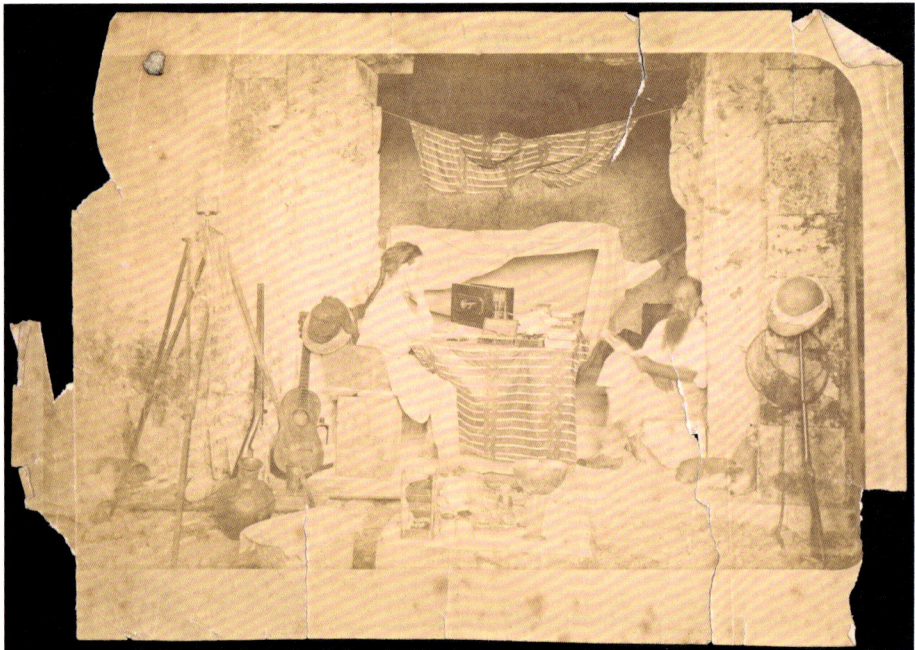

FIG. 56   Alice and Augustus in their quarters within the Governor's Palace, Uxmal. Visible in the photograph are their hammocks, rifles, a guitar, a butterfly net, and their dog Trinity sleeping in the corner.

the façade were particularly difficult because the camera had to be raised far above the ground in order to get good images of the carvings. As the camera the Le Plongeons were using did not have a shutter the exposure was started by simply removing the lens cap, requiring the photographer to also be far above the ground.[17]

> We are settled for the present in what is called the 'Governor's House.' It is the most central building, and from its broad terraces we look upon all the surrounding monuments, which cover an immense extent of ground. Far beyond are the hills, the same that were gazed upon by the people who dwelt here so long ago. We are in a valley, and every edifice is constructed on elevations, in some cases partly natural, but mostly artificial.
>
> There is no solitude here, though far from the abodes of living men. The place swarms with life and perfect silence never reigns, for every tiny insect has something to say for itself. The quietest hour is mid-day, when all seek rest and shelter from

Augustus Le Plongeon (1826–1908) and Alice Le Plongeon (1851–1910)

FIG. 57 Photograph by Alice of Augustus taking images of the east façade of the Governor's Palace in Uxmal.

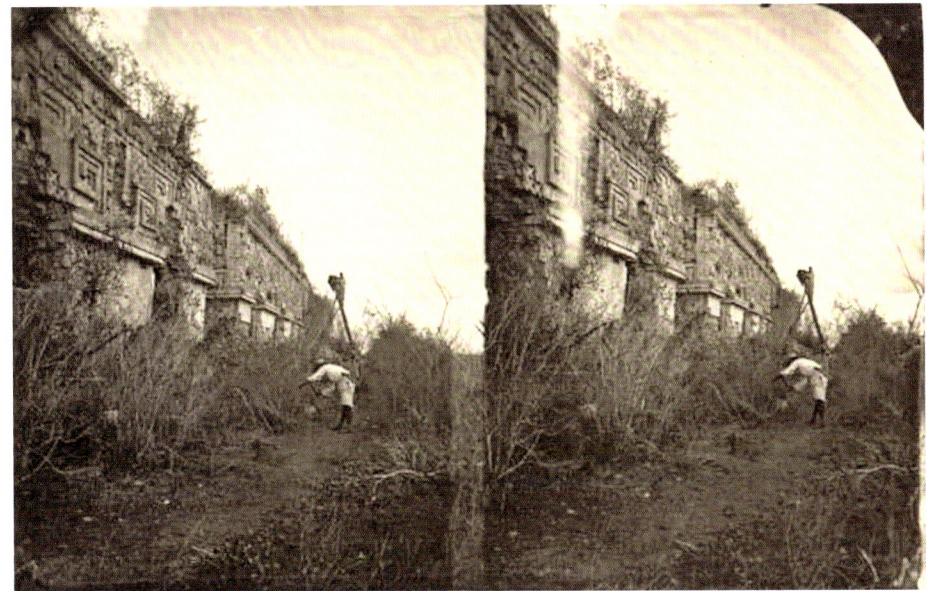

the burning rays of the tropical sun. Not a sound is then heard save the sighing of the wind among the trees of the forests spread out at our feet, and standing above this sea of verdure when the breeze runs through it, it seems to us that we listen to the roar of the ocean. Is it that we hear the waves of time dashing against these old walls? Every creature seems mad with thirst. Suicide is committed every few minutes by foolish bees which throw themselves into any liquid they can find and part with life for a drop of it. […] The iguanas enter our room at night in search of water, and play the mischief generally, besides waking us with their noise. But worse than all are the flies, or 'flying bed-bugs,' as they are sweetly called in Spanish. These are brown beetles about an inch long, which support life by sucking blood from any animal they get hold of, not excepting man. When they begin to feed on one it is like a needle running in the flesh. A dozen of them will give you bad dreams and draw an ounce of blood. Man does not require bleeding every night in a place where food is scarce and work plentiful.

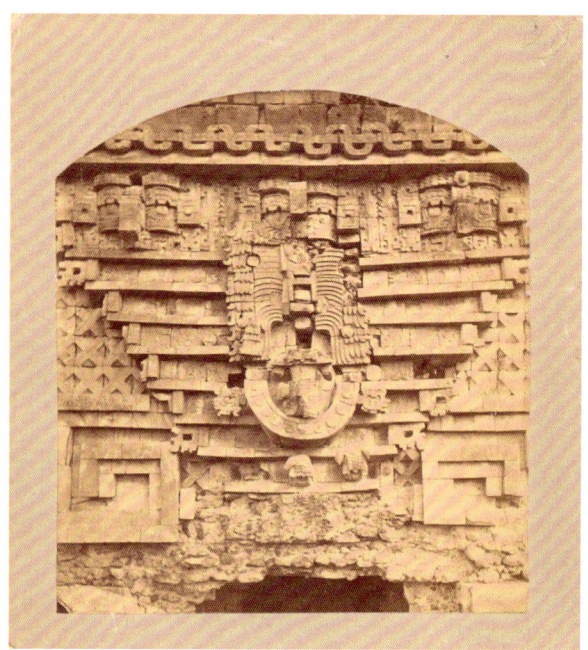

FIG. 58 Detail of east façade of the Governor's Palace, Uxmal.

Sculptured stones are scattered on the platform at the foot of the walls. They are in various stages of decay: some worn by time, some ruthlessly broken, and others worm-eaten, with long winding ruts on their surface. Each of these stones cost many a day's work, particularly if the tools used were of flint and obsidian, and up to the present time no metal has been found by us.[18]

Alice Le Plongeon

Amateurs of the photographic art may find it very pleasant to spill chemicals and spoil plates in studios that have every convenience for the work located in cities where there are unlimited supplies of requisites, but it is quite another affair to operate in the tropical forests, far from any city. Before going to explore the ruins in Yucatan, Dr. Le Plongeon invented a box in which everything could be packed in small compartments, and which could afterward be set up to serve as a dark room, a sink and dark curtain also found a place in the box; and the apparatus could be put into working order by two people in less than five minutes. We carried all that was necessary for the collodion process, as, in the hot climate and with the lime

FIG. 59   Detail of east façade of the West Building, Nunnery Quadrangle, Uxmal.

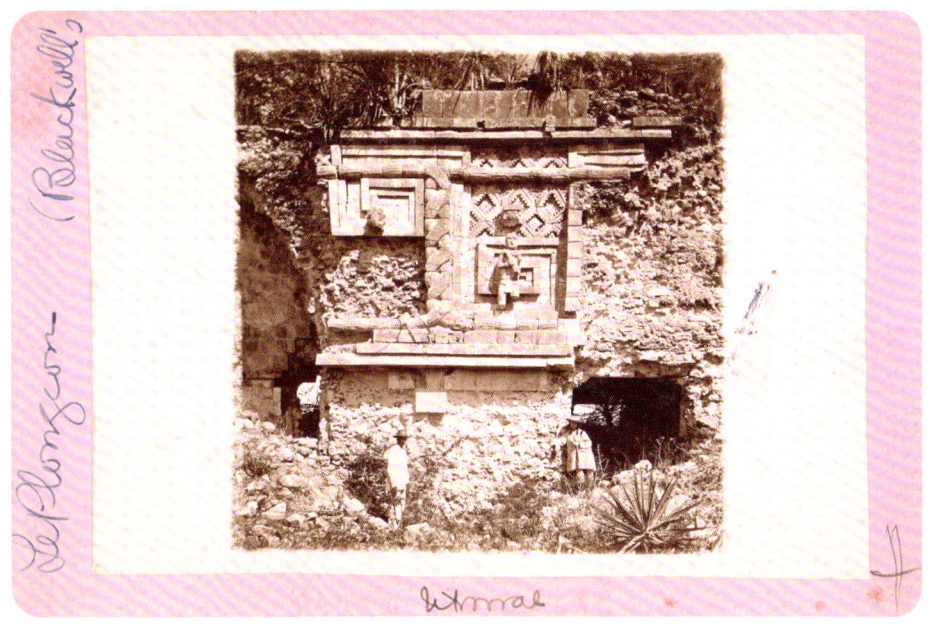

water of that country, dry plates cannot be developed without ice. Of course, there is none to be found in its tropical forests—and we were unwilling to wait until our return to know the results obtained.

The roads of Yucatan are like a stormy sea petrified, so, in spite of our careful packing, we were not quite free from mishaps.

We set up our dark box in an ancient apartment, the abode, thousands of years ago, of some haughty nobleman or feather-robed priest, when such apartment was handy. When not, we had a spot cleared in the bush, and stood the box out in the open air, putting lead in the bottom of the curtain to prevent the wind from blowing it about.

Dust and heat were our great enemies. The first we were never able to conquer, but the heat was made harmless to the plate by using honey in the silver bath. We have kept plates half an hour after silvering, and had no spots on them. But for the honey, we could not have obtained such perfect plates as we brought home, for frequently they had to be carried quite a distance, and even if not very far, it took time to move carefully step by step over *débris* and fallen tree trunks. It is easy to be tripped on such ground, at the risk of cutting one's face or hands on the sharp edge of a stone, of running a few thorns into them, or of coming in contact with

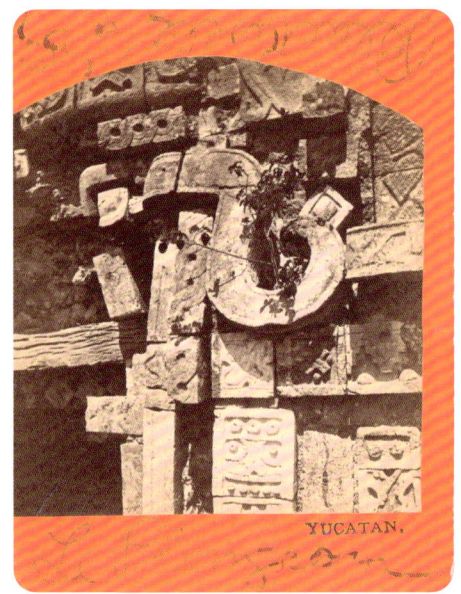

FIG. 60   Chac nose, Chenes Temple, Pyramid of the Magician (El Adivino), Uxmal.

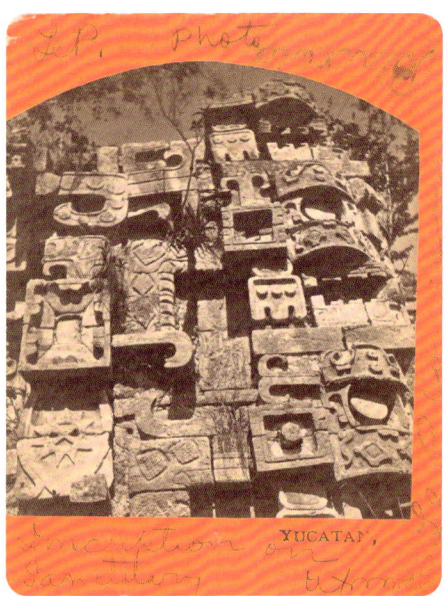

FIG. 61   Detail of façade, Chenes Temple, Pyramid of the Magician, Uxmal.

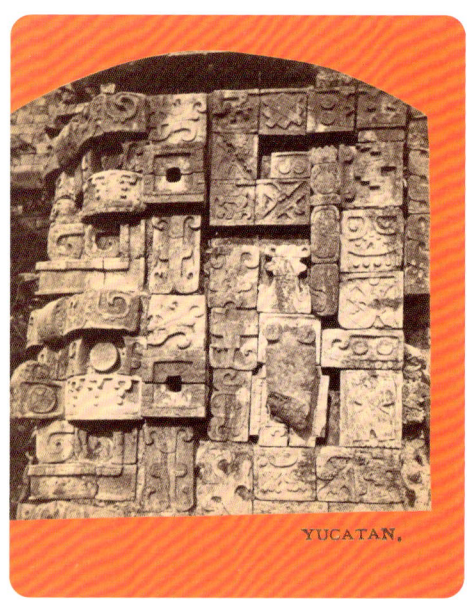

FIG. 62   Detail of façade, Chenes Temple, Pyramid of the Magician, Uxmal.

ants crawling in every direction and never losing a chance to bite. You may even rouse some deadly reptile, that will at once thrust its ugly head from under the stone you disturbed in falling; and you may consider yourself lucky if your dark slide has escaped unhurt by the angular stones over which you tripped.

The work of photographing the ancient buildings can hardly be realized unless experienced. Their sculptures cannot be moved, so the camera has to be brought near them and placed now on the ground, now on giddy heights. One grand edifice stands on the top of a wall forty feet high. All means of ascent were long ago destroyed, so we had to clamber up the wall as best we could, catching at bushes and stones to balance ourselves. The dark box could not be taken up, hence, to expose each plate there was a journey up and down. Above, on a stone platform, were beautiful pillars, with portraits of ancient warriors carved on them. Dr. Le Plongeon had to put the camera on the platform and lie flat while focusing. Dust, changeable light, etc., made it necessary to repeat an exposure several times, and for each there was the dangerous ascent and descent. When we thought to get a certain number of views, it seemed that everything conspired against us. While we were

FIG 63   Crouching figures above Chac nose, Chenes Temple, Pyramid of the Magician, Uxmal.

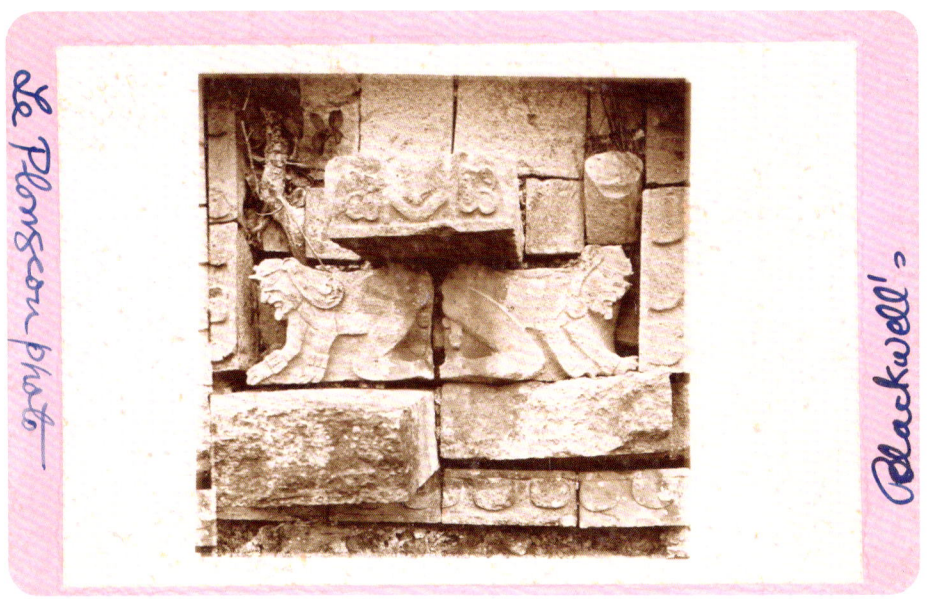

in the dark box the sun would shine, and when on the road shower scorching rays on us, making us long for the shadow of a passing cloud. But the cloud did not come till we were about to expose a plate, and then would stay so long that we had to choose between letting the plate dry or exposing it without sun; then no sooner did we start on the return journey, than the great orb again rained fire upon our defenceless [sic] heads. If the light favored us, the foliage, fanned by the breeze, made unshapely blurs on the plate. When wind and clouds troubled us not, the Indians, carefully posed to embellish the picture, would be sure to move just at the wrong time, though motionless a minute before.

To make photographs of the ornaments on the edifices at Uxmal, it was necessary to work from the top of a ladder, so we directed our Indian servants to make one. We explained that we wanted a double ladder joined at the top. [...] [The] tripod was tied to the top. Thus dangerously perched, the doctor put his head under the dark cloth, and found the camera too near the object. The cumbersome ladder and poles had to be moved farther back. Meanwhile, the iron point fell from a leg of the tripod, and I found it only after moving all the stones and weeds round about, disturbing some ants that speedily revenged themselves on me. The ladder was so unsteady that, standing on it, breathing was enough to move it and spoil the plate.

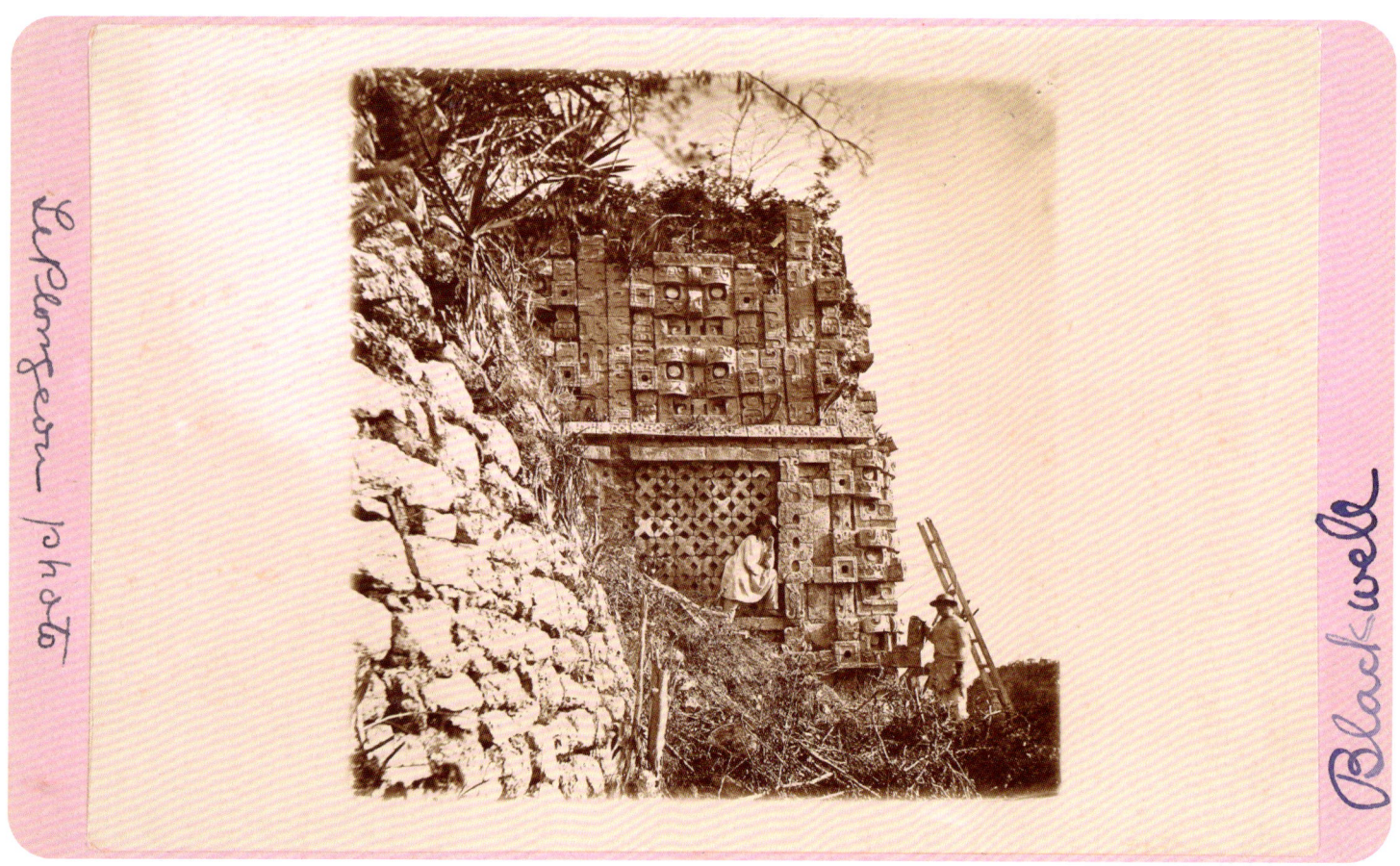

FIG. 64 Chenes Temple on the north façade of the Adivino Pyramid, Uxmal. Alice on the north side of the Chenes Temple near the top of the Pyramid of the Magician, Uxmal, with the ladder used to photograph details of the main façade visible in the background.

Augustus Le Plongeon (1826–1908) and Alice Le Plongeon (1851–1910)

So after drawing the slide the doctor came down, and by means of a long pole, uncovered and re-covered the lens from below. The light changed during exposure, timing was impossible and the plate was over-exposed. Only after several attempts was a satisfactory result obtained. [...] This experience led the doctor to invent and manufacture a legless stand on which he could move the camera back and forth on the top of a ladder. [...] Still, the ladder had to be moved for each picture, and it was tiresome work to run back and forth, ascend and descend, be closed in the dark box and so get scorched and steamed alternately.

The pictures of the Sanctuary at Uxmal [...] were made at the risk of my husband's life. The foot of the ladder, which was about twenty feet high, was attached to two tree trunks just over the edge of an almost perpendicular side of a mound 100 feet high. The ladder was supported by two forked poles, and held by ropes tied up in the room to two stone rings that once served to hang a curtain. The ladder was secure, but the danger to him consisted in any false motion or vertigo. Twice one day was he nearly sun-struck, and only able to continue his work by keeping wet cloths on his head. For one particular picture, even the ladder was not high enough. After it was placed almost perpendicularly, still on the brink of the precipice, its top was not then on a level with the object. A long pole was cut and planted at the base of the ladder. Then the doctor carried up his tripod, and tied the lower extremity of the legs, two to the top of the ladder and one to the pole he had planted. The half hour it took to arrange this was most trying; it was a perilous and exhausting task, depending altogether, as the doctor did, upon standing steadily on a round stick, while his hands were busily employed. Owing to dust and other petty annoyances, he had to make eight plates to obtain one to our satisfaction. He worked bared to the waist in order to have freer movement, and his shoulders were baked brown when he finished.

How little people imagine, when they cast a hasty glance at the photographs that we have to show of ruined edifices, among which the doctor and I have toiled for the last ten years, what they have cost, and how precious for history they are. I think I do not boast when I say that no other will make all the pictures made by him; requiring as it did, to secure them, the knowledge of an archaeologist who understood the importance of each object exhumed or seen, and the fearless daring of a gymnast of indomitable will—one who never hesitated in the face of difficulties which seemed unsurmountable.[19]

Alice Le Plongeon

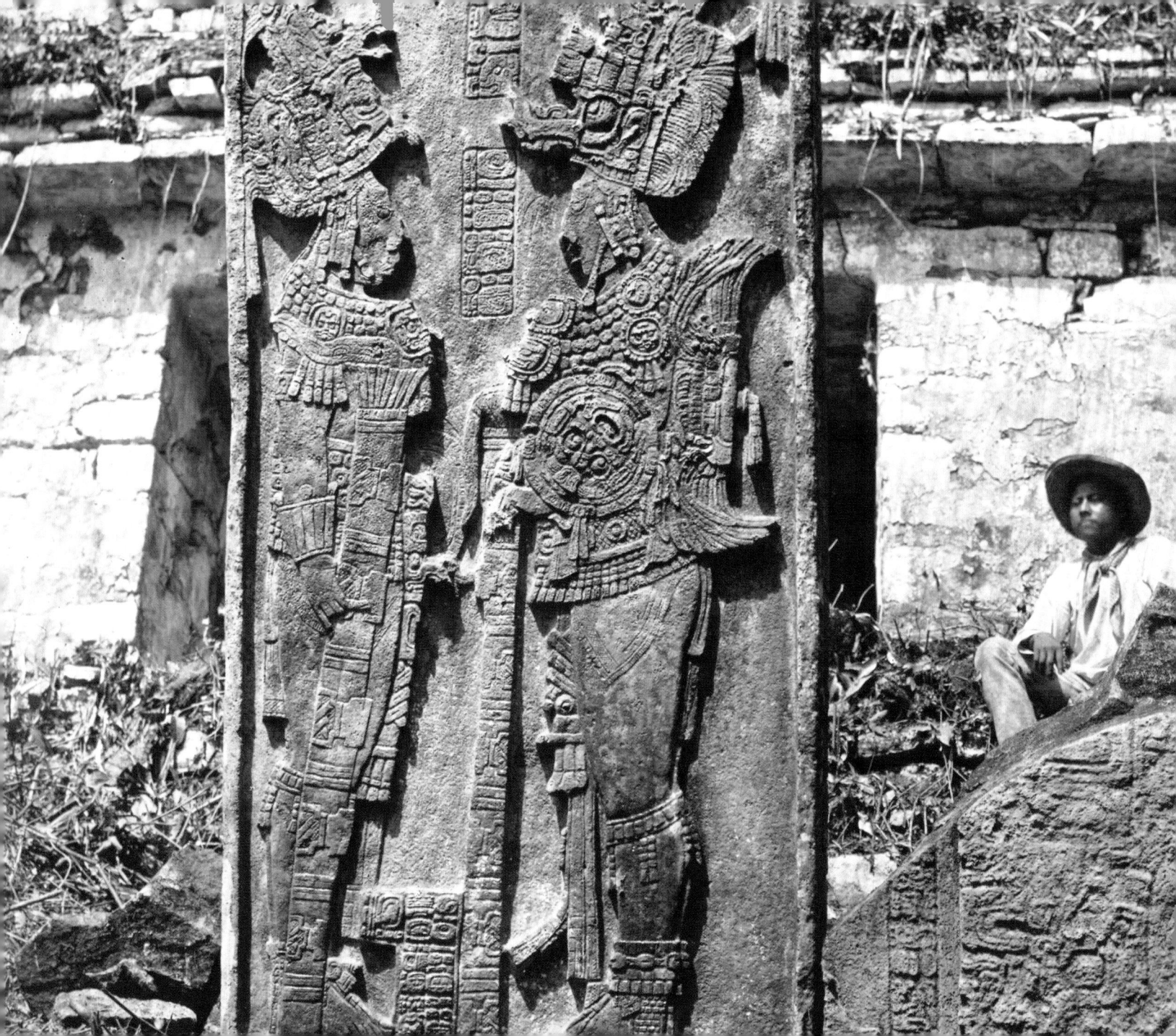

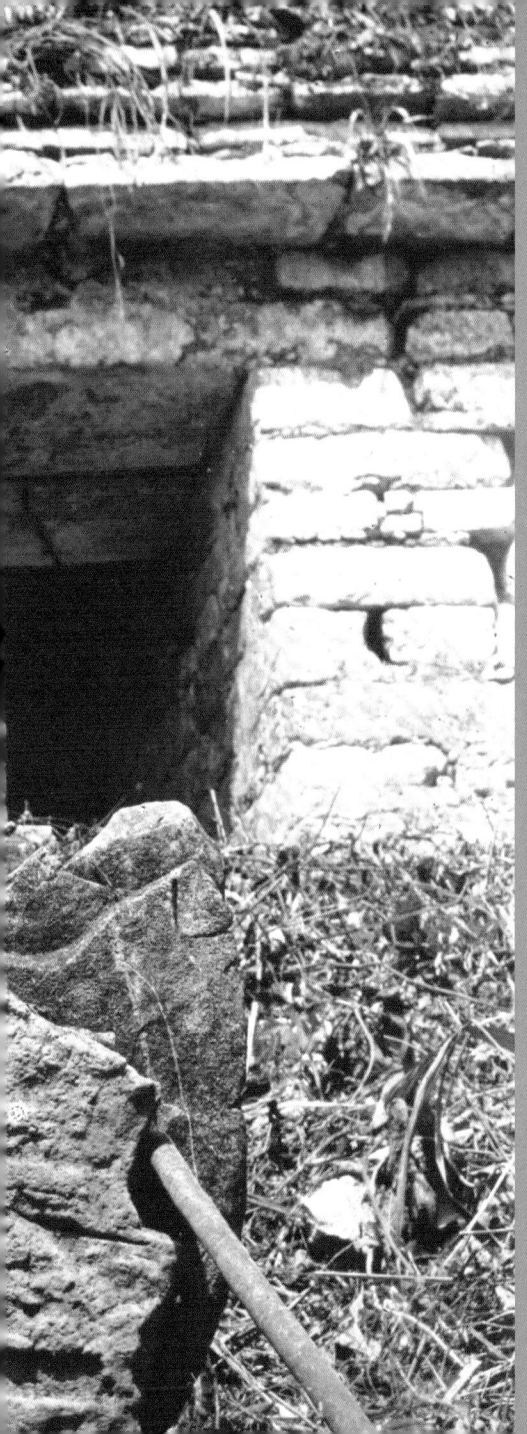

Teobert Maler (1842–1917)

Teobert Maler, who was born in Rome of German parents, first came to Mexico as a soldier to fight with the Imperial Army during the French intervention that briefly put Archduke Maximilian in power. After the fall of Maximilian, Maler remained in Mexico and discovered photography. With the exception of the period between 1878 and 1885, when he returned to Europe to deal with his father's inheritance upon the latter's death, Maler spent the rest of his life traveling around Mexico and other parts of Central America with camera at hand. At first, he worked as an itinerant photographer, making money by taking portraits. But by 1885 he had started to meticulously seek out "old stones" and to document Maya sites. His approach, like Maudslay's, heralded the new age of scientific archaeology "located at a transitional position between the explorer-photographers and the institutional archaeologists."[1]

Maler, who was always scrounging for financial support, secured funding from Harvard's Peabody Museum starting in 1898, and for several years his photographs were published in the scholarly publications of that institution's Memoirs. Under the Peabody's auspices, between 1898 and 1909 he undertook expeditions that systematically documented sites—many of which were unknown to scholars. The portrait that remains of Maler in the historical record is that of a cantankerous soul who ended his life as an embittered drunk, but on the few occasions that he placed himself within the frames of his photographs, long-haired and bearded, and within the pages of his accompanying texts, we glimpse a man consumed, who spent months obsessively combing through sites both big and small. He rants against the woodcutters and natives who vandalize ruins and grouses about his fellow archaeologist-photographers Charnay, Le Plongeon, and Maudslay, whose methods he frowned upon and whom he saw as exploiters rather than explorers.

Maler's photographic work was unsurpassed, and he developed techniques that allowed him to produce exquisite images even in the difficult conditions of these isolated tropical sites. As with the other photographers in this collection, Maler's texts provide insight into the work of the nineteenth-century expeditionary photographer. He tells of waiting for hours or days for the sun to hit an object just right or taking photographs at night using magnesium light (and attracting rare nocturnal butterflies in the process). He used his camera to preserve vestiges that have since degraded and are illegible. He also used it to reconstitute already destroyed monuments by photographing their fragments "piece by piece, taking pains to keep the lens-to-object distance constant" in order to "reassemble" them.[2] His commentary is as crisp and precise as his detail-rich

Teobert Maler (1842–1917)

FIG. 65 Plan of the ruins, Piedras Negras, Coahuila.

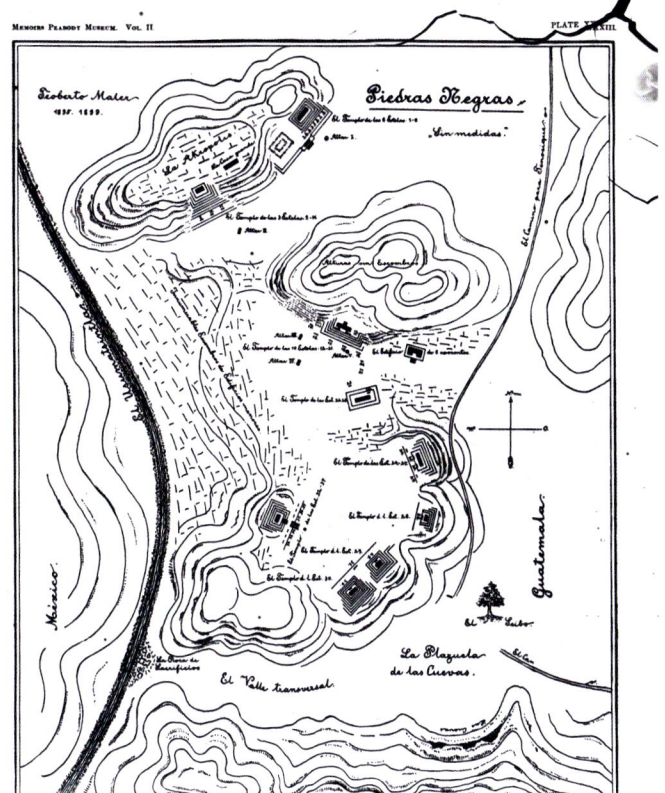

photographs. Having often spent months at the same site and pored over each stone he encountered, he is able to offer close readings that enhance our viewing of the objects captured in his photographs. His texts, which are devoid of the grandiose theories and speculation on the obscure past and origins of the Maya, highlight features that make even his best photographs more readable.

PIEDRAS NEGRAS[3]

Maler visited Piedras Negras in July 1895 and, again, in 1899. At the time of his first visit, the site, which lies along the Usumatsintla (Usumacinta) River, had only recently been established as being on the Guatemalan side of the border with Mexico, and Maler frequently refers to Mexican logging camps whose workers served as his informants. He began photographing the site which had "succumbed to the weight of an overpowering vegetation,"[4] with a particular attention to the stelae.

STELA 1

It took a whole week of hard work to prepare for photographing these stelae, which probably marked the graves of persons of rank and also represented the principal divinities. Each stone was carefully excavated and set up on one of its narrow side faces by means of a windlass we had borrowed from a neighboring montería [hunting ground], and then washed and brushed off in order to secure as good a picture as possible, after felling some trees which excluded the sunlight. Most of the stelae had sculpture on the two broad faces and inscriptions on the narrow side faces. The face which had lain next to the ground was generally well preserved, while the upturned face was mostly destroyed.

The sculpture on the front is wholly destroyed; that on the back representing Ketsalkoatl [Quetzacoatl], is very well preserved. Each narrow side face has a double row of glyphs, which have become quite indistinct.

The preserved relief represents the front view of a male figure, with an oval beardless face carved in very high relief. Upon the brow is placed the serpent's head, the upper row of teeth forming a diadem. Above the serpent's head is the turban, from the centre of which rises the ornamented feather-holder, and the plumes of feathers proceeding from it fall to the right and left. The god is clothed in a tunic reaching to his feet, ornamented with delicately incised Maltese crosses, and finished at the neck by a cape of scales. In his right hand the god holds feathers, and his left lies on the medallion of the cape.

The upper part of the relief consists of three horizontal rows of glyphs: 3x7=21. Along the edges a row of glyphs reached down to each shoulder: 8+10, one glyph in each row being wholly destroyed, owing to the fracture of the stone, while all the rest are in an excellent state of preservation—thirty-nine glyphs in all, two of which are destroyed. A small glyph also occurs at the base of the feather-holder.

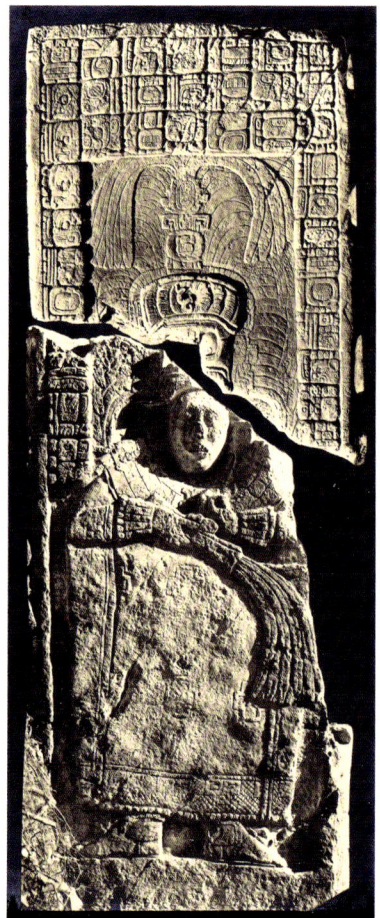

FIG. 66 Stela 1, Piedras Negras.

Teobert Maler (1842–1917)

Remnants of color were still visible, as follows: face, arms and garment, bright red; background, dark red; edge of garment, blue; breast cape, blue; feathers, always green.[5]

STELA 6

One of the narrow side faces has an upright figure in bas-relief; the other has two perpendicular rows of glyphs. On one of its broad faces the stela had a bas-relief, now quite crumbled away, and on the other the figure of a god sitting in a niche in half or almost high relief.

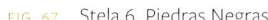

FIG. 67   Stela 6, Piedras Negras.

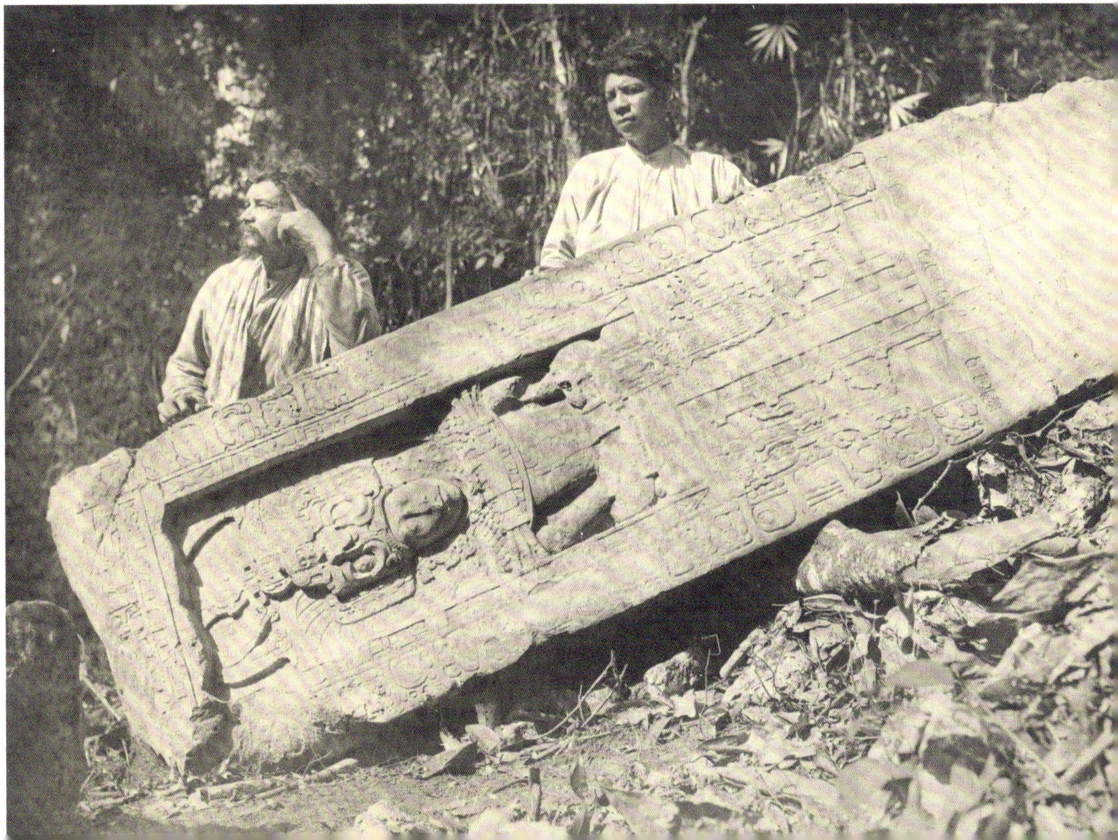

> While the niche with the deity is cut very deep into the stone, the surrounding glyphs and ornamentation are in very low relief. Owing to these contrasts, it is difficult to obtain a satisfactory photograph of the whole.
>
> The god supports his right hand at his girdle, and holds in his left an ornamental pouch, which hangs far down over the edge of the niche. He wears a breast-cape of scales and the familiar horizontal breastplate. His head is surmounted by a serpent's head. Over this is a small human head and over the latter the closed hand out of which proceeds the feather-holder with the feathers.
>
> There is ornamental work on the surfaces above and below the niche, and a perpendicular row of glyphs of about twenty little characters runs along the right and the left edge of the stone. Most of the glyphs are well preserved, but some have become indistinct and others have been broken off. In addition to these there are some very delicately incised miniature inscriptions: 3+4+3 at the very bottom; 3+4 on both sides of the feather-holder, and 3+3 still higher up.
>
> Remnants of color: face, arms, body, and thighs of the deity, bright red; serpent's head, hands, and feather-holder, likewise red; breast-cape, green and all the feathers green.[6]

At the end of August 1899 when Maler returned to the site to undertake further exploration under the auspices of the Harvard's Peabody Museum he wrote: "I was able to leave Tenosique with three men and the necessary pack-animals." Once at the site, "the palm-leaf huts of the montería of Piedras Negras had entirely disappeared and everything was already quite overgrown by the luxuriant tropical vegetation. For this reason, I had to find quarters for myself and my men in one of the caves near the place of the ceiba [tree]. These caves afforded us excellent shelter in the rainy season, which was now in progress. We supplied our animals with fodder by daily cutting branches from the ramon-tree, which fortunately abounds in these forests. We devoted the months of September, October, and November (of 1899) to the further exploration of the ruined city, with such good results this time that Piedras Negras now ranks with Palenque and Yāxchilan in respect of the number and importance of its sculptures."[7]

FIG. 68 Lintel 2, Piedras Negras.

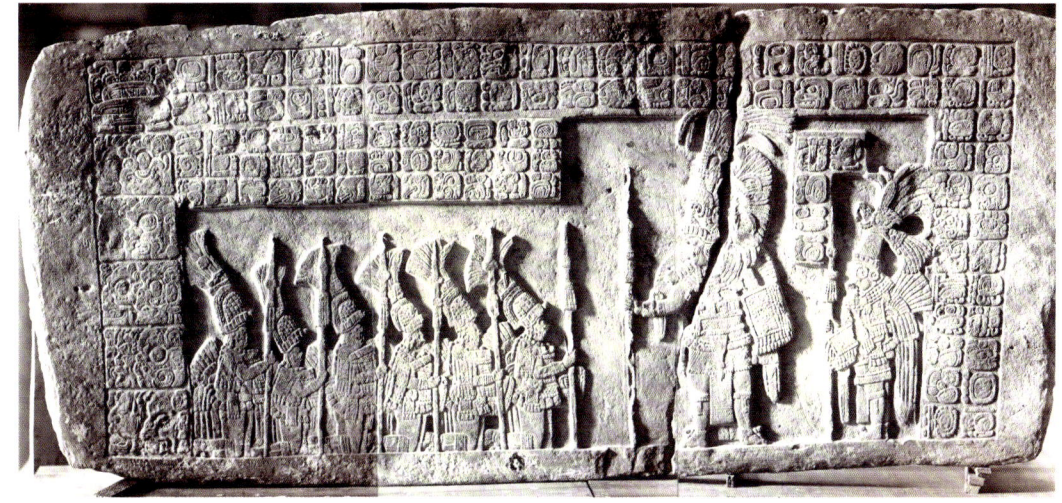

LINTEL 2

I made a slight excavation [...] near the middle of the mass of ruins in front of the temple [known in Spanish as El Templo de la Estela de la Víctimas] and was fortunate [...] to find the sought-for middle lintel, which was adorned on its lower face with a well-executed, very interesting piece of sculpture. The slab was cracked in two, but, excepting the line of fracture, the sculpture is admirably preserved, only the colors have entirely disappeared. I called this lintel No. 2.

Upon the base-line of the picture stands the principal figure, the Halachvinic (halatšvinik), or warrior chieftain, richly dressed and wearing a great helmet with plumes of feathers. In his outstretched right hand he holds a lance, on his left arm a quadrangular shield. Behind him stands the second in command or adjutant, likewise armed with lance and shield. To the point of the lance are attached five little hieroglyphs, probably expressing the command which the Halachvinic is giving the six warriors kneeling before him. These warriors, doubtless subordinate chieftains, are all well dressed, and wear on their heads helmets with plumes of feathers. Each holds a lance in his right hand; the shield on the left arm being concealed, owing to the position of the body. The sculpture is bordered on the left (from the spectator) by six large hieroglyphs,—one large initial glyph and five chronological representations of faces; on the right by two perpendicular rows of small glyphs, 10+10; on top by two horizontal rows of small glyphs, 22+22. In addition there are thirty-six still smaller glyphs, in three rows of twelve each directly over the kneeling warriors. It seems evident that six of these glyphs, in two columns of three each, belong to each of the warriors. In all six large glyphs and one hundred and five smaller ones.[8]

STELA 14

Buried deep under a mass of debris at the foot of the half-pyramid, I found a stela with a niche resembling No. 6, but of better workmanship. This also has doubtless fallen from the top terrace, and in its fall had been broken in two pieces,—a large upper and a small lower one. The back face is perfectly smooth. The narrow side faces have two perpendicular rows of glyphs, very well preserved on one side and entirely worn away on the other. The relief on the sculptured side is injured only in a few places; otherwise it is preserved in all its nicer details, but only partially as to its original colors.

On the lower base line stands a man of rank, in profile, looking expectantly up to the god in the niche. He is dressed in a long tunic, which reaches to his feet. His head covering seems to terminate in a tiger's head in front, and a plume of feathers falls down at the back. In his right hand he holds a little leather bag tied up with a fine cord, and in his left a flabellum of green feathers with a red handle.

At the feet of this exalted personage is a round altar. Here [...] also is seen a victim, flung across what is doubtless a tiger-skin and pieces of wood laid crosswise. In this case the face, hanging down over the edge of the stone, is represented in full-front view. Three beads of the necklace are still plainly recognizable. Rising flames seem to meet over the breast, and above them is the bulbous vessel, [...] with a plume of feathers proceeding from its thick neck. The scroll-work and the structure of beams also recall the decoration on the lower part of Stela 11. Bright-red scroll-work runs up the right and left edges of the niche as far as the curtain, which is divided into four parts (that is, tied up with cords in three places), and has a horizontal band of six simplified glyphs (second manner of writing) above it. Above this band is a fantastic green mask with red eyes and mouth. It is crowned by a diadem of large discs with scroll-work on either side and feathers on top.

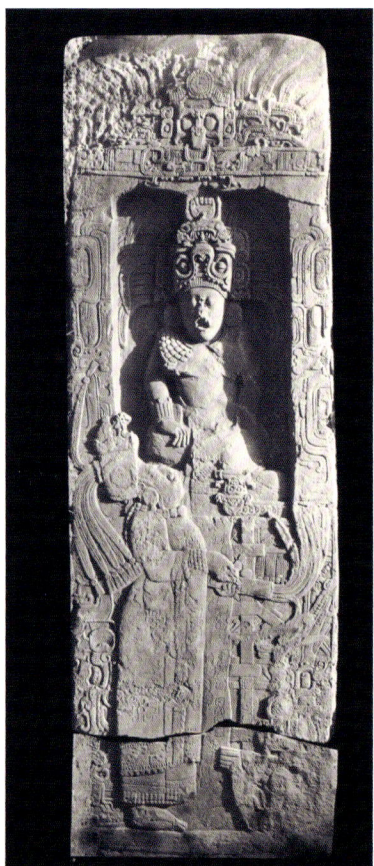

FIG. 69   Stela 14, Piedras Negras.

Teobert Maler (1842–1917)

All the sculpture described above is in very low relief, but the bright-red god, who sits enthroned cross-legged in the niche, in Asiatic fashion, is in very high relief and is represented in front view. His right hand rests upon his right knee; his left hand, now broken off, held an ornamental pouch with the appendage of conventionalized rattles, which in this case does not hang down over the edge of the niche, but lies upon its floor. The breast is covered by a green cape of scales and a horizontal breastplate, but the latter is very much injured. The bright-red face of the god is smooth and beardless. The lips are wide apart, as if the god were speaking to the people. Large round ornaments are in the ears. The head is crowned with an elaborately executed serpent's head, surmounted by a fantastic little human head. Both are for the most part green, the eyes and mouths only being red. The teeth in the serpent's mouth are saw-shaped. The little head is in its turn surmounted by an oval with the closed hand, which, being contiguous to the curtain, leaves no room for a crowing plume of feathers. Green feathers, however, fall from each side of the headdress.

Here and there delicately incised glyphs are applied.

After having thoroughly examined the terraces and temple described above, my men and I felt convinced that it would be quite impossible to find more stelae in Piedras Negras, because we had so carefully explored the entire forest in which the ruins lie, unless of course, another suburb should be discovered higher up the stream from the sacrificial rock. We had discovered and examined no less than thirty-seven stelae, of which twenty-three were photographed and fourteen were rejected as no longer fit for that purpose.

Our life in the wet forests by day and under shelter of the caves by night was full of hardships, and we had repeatedly to contend with dangerous fevers. But our daily bath in the refreshing water of the Usumatsintla, which often rose high above the sacrificial rock, together with ample provisions and now and then a dose of quinine, helped us through. In the beginning of December 1899,—at the beginning of the rainy season,—we were able to begin our journey to Yāxchilan, where we were quite as successful as we had been at Piedras Negras.[9]

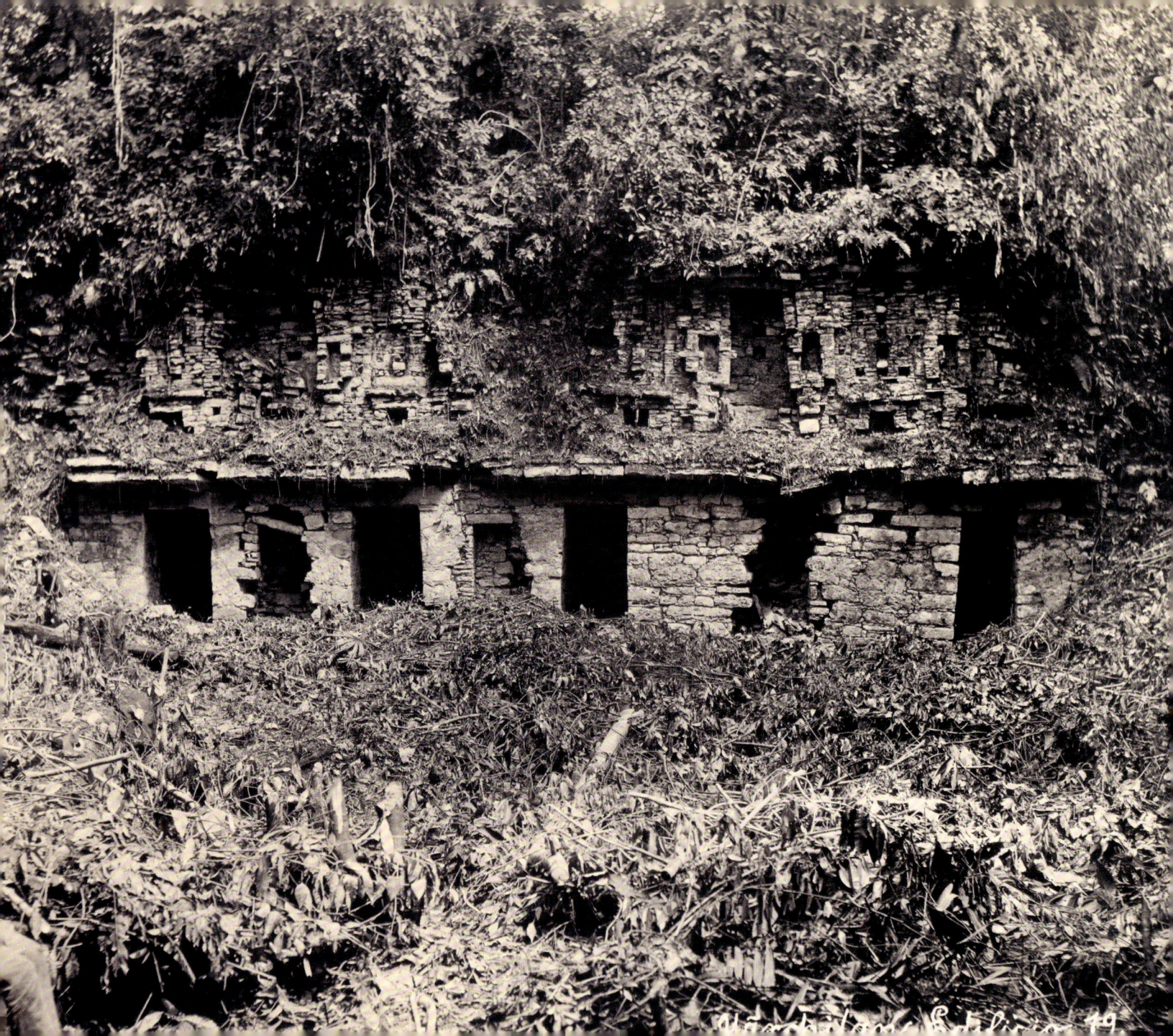

FIG. 70   Structure 19, "The Labyrinth": "My men constructed for themselves a palm-leaf hut, *una champa*, while I, after discovering the 'Labyrinth' (Edifice 19), settled myself within its walls with my most important baggage, for the ceilings were dry, and the great stone benches were very convenient for sleeping purposes or for spreading my things out upon them."

YAXCHILAN[10]

Maler made three trips to Yaxchilan—in 1895, 1897, and December 1899. As he explains, Yaxchilan, which Alfred Maudslay called Menché, and Charnay called Lorillard City, translates as Piedras Verdes or Green Stones, "an allusion to the greenish color caused by the moss or algae on the stones in the bed of the river which flows into the Usumatsintla above the ruined city."

Commenting on his predecessors' work at the site, Maler reports that Désiré Charnay, "amply provided with funds by the French Government and the American millionaire Lorillard," undertook an expedition to Yaxchilan in 1882. Finding on his arrival that Alfred Maudslay had got there before him, Charnay "limited himself to making an examination of the principal buildings, and to taking photographs and moulds of some of the finest carved lintels." Maler notes that the results of Charnay's explorations are "included in his interesting volume *Les Anciennes villes du Nouveau Monde*" before going on to discuss Maudslay's endeavors: "Mr. Maudslay's work at the ruins was continued for some time, and to my great disappointment I found that he had removed many of the carved lintels, taking them with him to England. However, I do not doubt that in the splendid work now being published (*Biologia Centrali-Americana, Archaeology*), Mr. Maudslay will give an interesting account of the condition of the ruins as he found them, and that all the sculptures at the time available will be reproduced by phototype process for the benefit of students."[11]

Structure 19: It was rather dangerous to spend the night quite alone in that solitary ruin on account of the tigers. But fortunately, we escaped all collision with these felines, which are always to be greatly feared. We were so fortunate as to have a month of glorious weather, which greatly lessened the difficulties of my work among the ruins. It generally rained at night and hardly ever by day. Even the Usumatsintla soon sank again to a less dangerous level. But we had another trouble to contend against. Our stock of provisions had run very low, because the men when living at someone else's expense eat enormously and know no moderation. I therefore hastened all my preparations for photographing the façades and the sculptures.

I succeeded in discovering three magnificent temples, never yet visited by Europeans, at the southern end of the mountain range of the great Acropolis. I photographed with magnesium light at night under great difficulties the lintel sculptures still in position over the entrances to the temples. Others, already fallen to the ground, and some wholly buried and excavated by me, I placed in such positions that they could be photographed in sunlight. I also prepared a dozen mortuary or deity stelae for photographing. Of these stelae I found only one still in an upright position; all the others had fallen to the ground; many were broken in pieces and sunk in the earth. Notwithstanding the lack of provisions which greatly hampered us, the result of my explorations (July and August, 1897) may be said to have been on the whole very satisfactory. Leaving the excavation of additional pieces of sculpture for a future occasion, I returned for the time being to Yucatan [...].[12]

While we actually suffered from famine [in 1897] during the first expedition, we fared very well [in 1900], for we had a superfluity of provisions. I had brought along a little machine for grinding maize, *el Azteca*, so that my men could daily make fresh maize bread, *tortillas*. José María Jiménez, who had settled a little way above the ruins, opposite the embouchure of the Yāxchilan, from time to time brought us maize, beans, bananas, and even a little pig. Besides, we frequently succeeded in shooting birds and little mammals, which afforded us savory roasts. Passing Cayucos occasionally sold us spirits, which largely contributed toward keeping the men contented."[13]

"The stelae of Seibal and Piedras Negras are on as grand a scale as those of Yāxchilan, but in regard to the sculpture on the underside of the lintel[s], Yāxchilan stands alone. It is necessary to see these sculptures to convince one's self [sic] of the truth of this assertion. It is no exaggeration to say that in fineness of execution and general artistic value they can be compared with the best that Assyria and Egypt have produced.[14]

Maler explains that in 1897 he photographed some of these at night with magnesium light: "In order to attain my end, I was obliged to invent an illumination especially suited to the case, and to make many experiments. At last, the three undersculptures were beautifully reproduced, and the nicest details came out perfectly."[15]

FIG. 71   Lintel 9, Yaxchilán, Chiapas.

Teobert Maler (1842–1917)

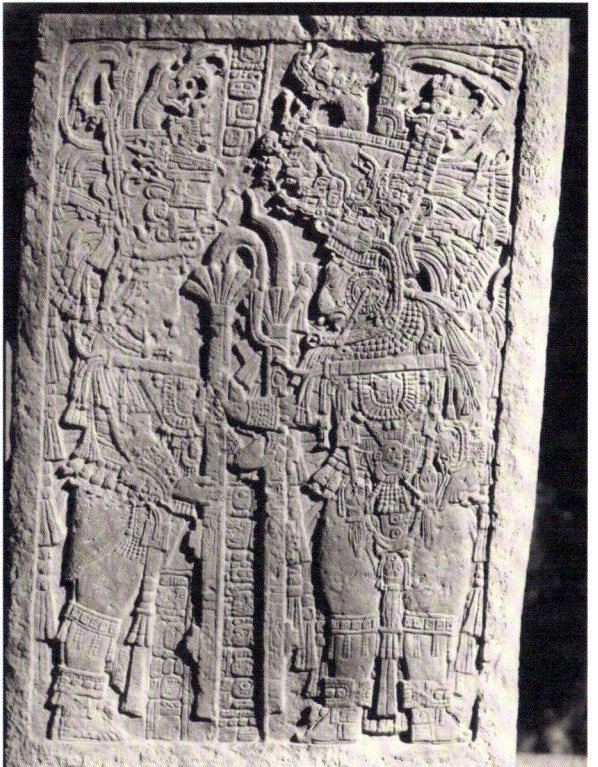

LINTEL 9

This piece of sculpture taken from the most insignificant pile of rubbish imaginable, I consider the finest of all I found in Yāxchilan. It was executed in the finest of fine-grained limestone of an agreeable light-yellow color, and looked as new as if it had just left the hands of the sculptor. Only the face of the second personage of rank was somewhat oxidized or affected by moisture. The work is of extraordinary delicacy, and the general projection of the relief is not more than 1 cm. As this low relief was completely concealed and protected,—hence could not have been subjected to rubbing off, to having moulds taken, and to calcination by ignorant explorers,—and still had no visible trace of color, I am inclined to think that the artist preferred to retain the natural yellow color of the stone.

Exposing the Maya

The *Halachvinic* (halatšwinik) or generalissimo, who, with the exception of his face, is represented in front view, holds with his right hand what I am inclined to consider as a quiver with bow and arrows toward a second chief represented quite in profile, who on his part extends with his left hand a similar object or quiver with bow and arrows toward the generalissimo. The Halachvinic, very richly adorned, wears below the breast-cape of beadwork a large horizontal breastplate, below which appears a large medallion with a little mammal represented upon it. From the shoulders of the Halachvinic hangs down to his thigh a pendent ornament of cords, to which are attached five human heads, and a sixth head attached to an intervening pendant fills out the background below the mammal medallion. All these heads of slain enemies hang with the crowns downward. The gigantic helmet of the Halachvinic has two conventionalized faces on the lower part, and to the front is attached the little figure of a man holding out a small human head with both hands. A serpent's head rises up from the top of the helmet, and an elaboration of feathers falls down at the back.

The second chief, adorned almost as richly as the first, but not hung with human heads, also wears a towering helmet, out of which rises a serpent corresponding to that of the generalissimo, while close under the jaws of the serpent (that is, on the front of the helmet), is a delicately executed human head, likewise corresponding to the little figure on the other helmet. The background is filled out with 4+8+4 glyphs.[16]

FIG. 72   Structure 6: The Red Temple on the Shore, or El Tiemplo de la Ribera, Yaxchilán, whose façade is richly ornamented with serpent-head decoration. "All the exterior parts, principal wall surfaces, friezes, and superstructures had once been colored bright red [...]. One can easily imagine what a fantastic spectacle this bright red temple with its airy superstructure must have afforded during the most flourishing period of the city, in the blaze of the tropical sun, while at nocturnal feasts numerous firebrands and incense vessels shed abroad their light from the windows above."

STELA 1

In connection with the description of Stela 1, it will be well to remark once for all that the stelae of Yāxchilan which may be regarded as mortuary monuments have one wide side devoted to the memory of a person of rank, generally some great warrior with his prisoner, while the other is reserved for the representation of a divinity (Ketsaltkoatl?), generally a beneficent god distributing the good things of life to supplicants. I, therefore, for brevity call one side *the human side*, and the other *the deity side*.

The deity side of the Yāxchilan stelae *without exception* faced the temple to which it pertained, while the human side was turned toward the city or the people. In other words, whoever leant his back against the temple façade saw the deity side of the

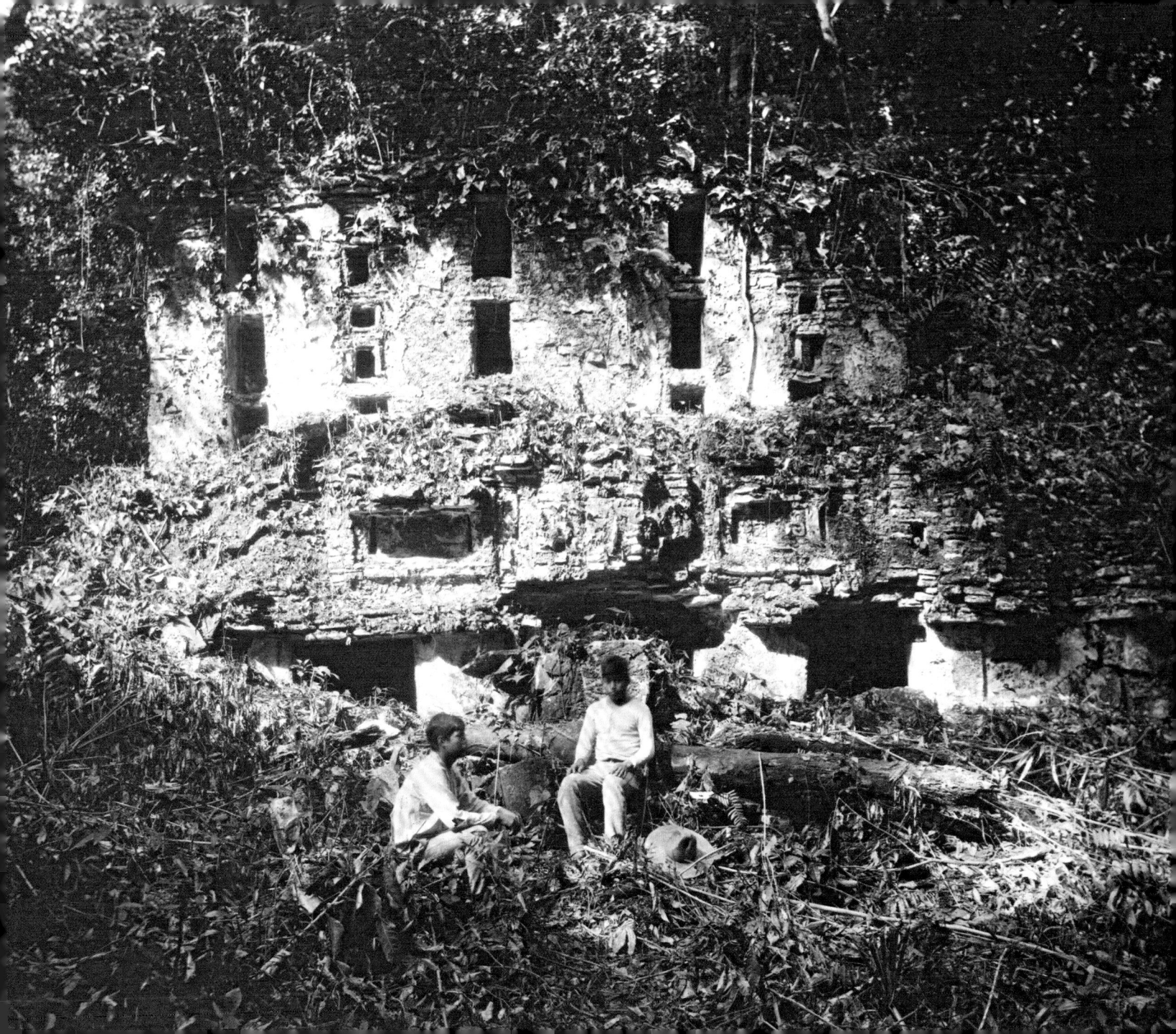

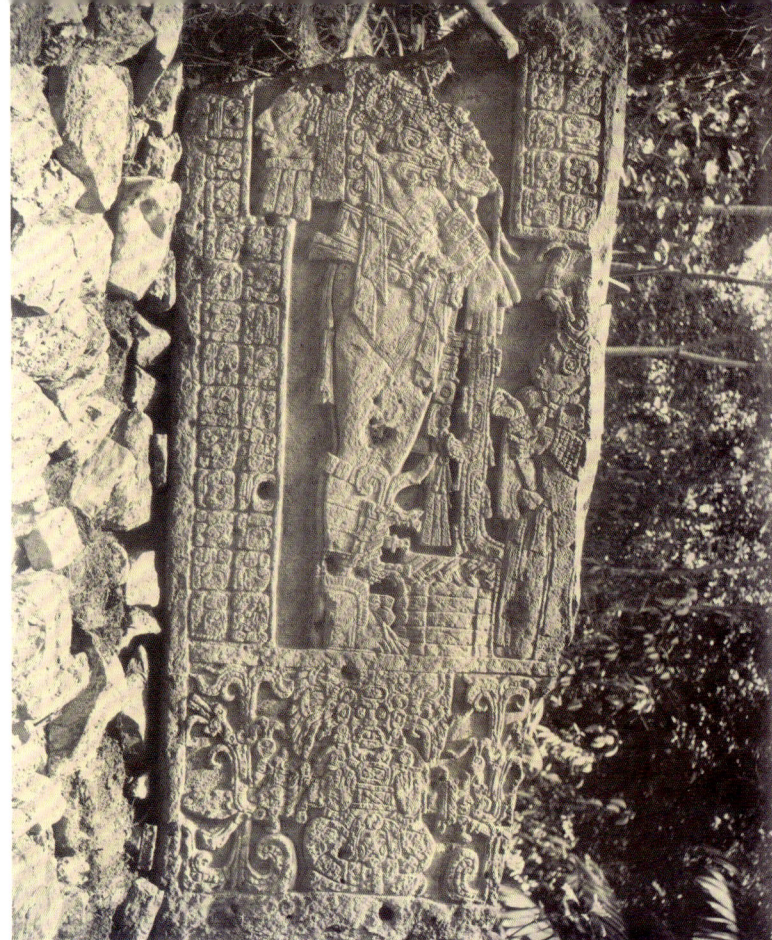

FIG. 73 Stela 1, Yaxchilán.

stelae, but whoever looked at the façade from a distance saw the human side of the stelae.

I would further remark that the low relief of the human side, though very nicely executed, shows as a rule less projection than that of the deity side, the work of the latter side being invariably much bolder.

The huge stela [Stela 1] in falling to the ground broke into a large lower and a smaller upper piece, and between the two a very acute-angled triangular piece was broken into splinters, causing a hiatus which is very much to be regretted.

The deity side fell face downward and is admirably preserved, with the exception, of course, of the triangular piece, and also some injuries on one of the narrow side faces. The human side having fallen face upward is almost entirely worn away by the action of the elements.

With great exertions and reinforced by José María Jiménez's men, we succeeded in setting up the large lower piece on one of its narrow side faces, and the photograph taken of the deity side in a favorable light turned out very satisfactorily. The missing upper part was nowhere to be found in spite of a careful search. Not until we explored the terrace of Structure 9 at a distance of more than fifty paces, did the missing top of the stela make its appearance, much to my surprise. There is not the slightest doubt in my mind that some persons, inspired for the moment by the sight of the beautiful decoration which finishes the top of the stela, determined to drag the fragment to the river and there put it on board of a boat. As long as they could drag the stone over the level surface of the curved embankment, all went well. But when they came to the high barricade formed by the debris of Structure 9, they were evidently unable to drag the stone over it. Before, however, they abandoned the stone to its fate, they luckily turned it over, whereby the sculpture nearly completing the deity side was preserved. This removal of the piece must have been many years ago,—perhaps when the wood-cutters of Encarnación Carrillo, before alluded to, made such havoc among these ruins,—for I found the stone completely sunk in the earth.

Both the narrow side faces had rows of glyphs which are now partly worn away and partly broken off.

The worn-off flat relief on the human side displays a symbolical design serving as a base, upon the upper edge of which stands a personage of rank in an upright position with a staff of office (perhaps a lance) in his right hand. Below, in front of him, also standing upright, is a kind of monkey or animal with protruding snout. The upper finish of the human side of the stela is formed by horizontal rows of glyphs, which are more plainly recognizable than all the rest of the relief on this face of the stela.

As for the deity side, it has for its base a figure with an evil distorted countenance, holding in both arms a great "ornamental beam," the ends of which develop into elaborate scroll-work. An expressive face-mask is attached to the girdle, and an oval with a St. Andrew's cross to the necklace.

The fierce expression of the monster, which recalls certain east Asiatic figures, is in remarkable contrast to the quiet majesty of the beneficent deity standing above him. The god has taken from the chest of plaited work the string (serpent?) of joys

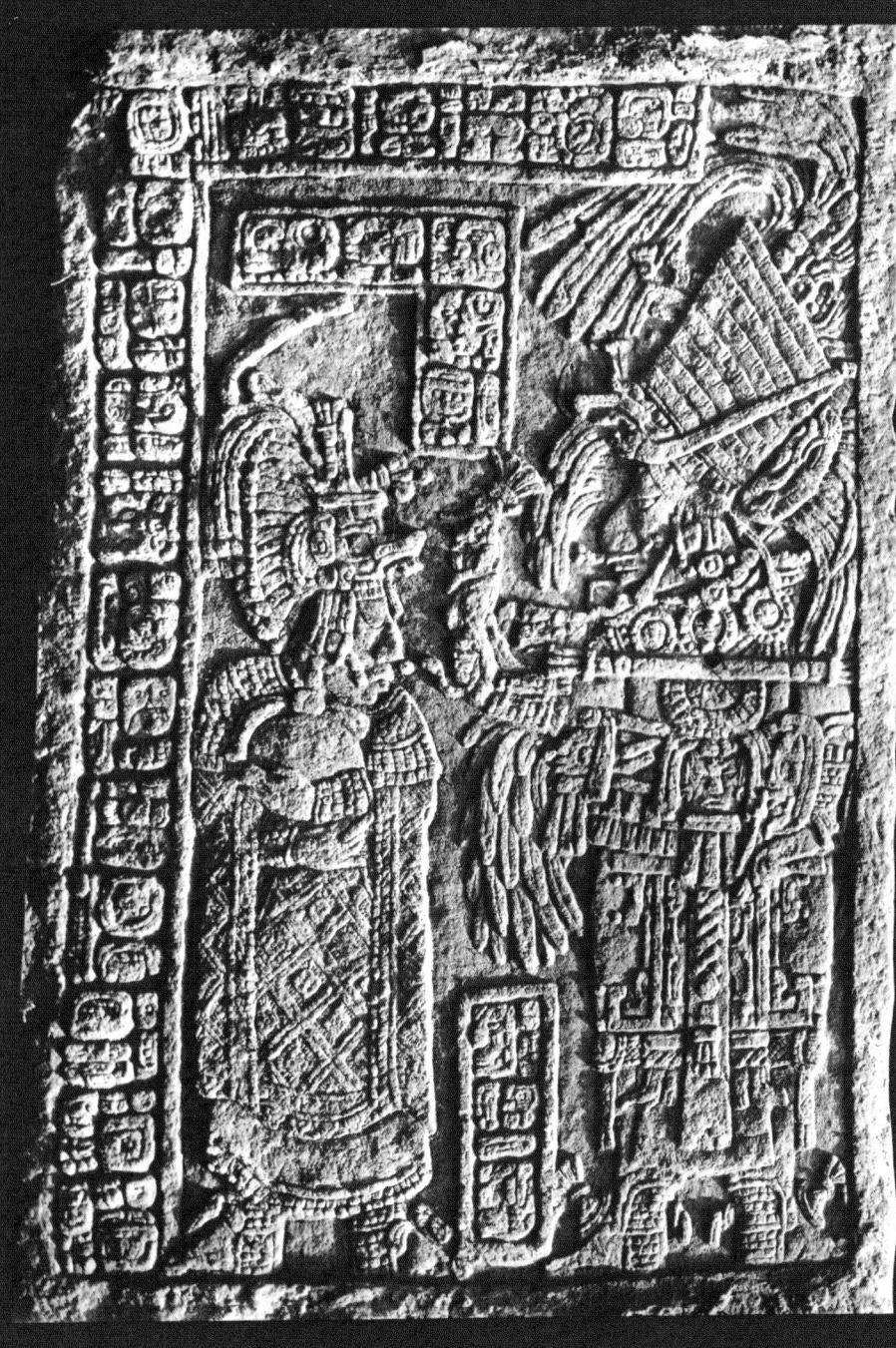

FIG. 74 Lintel 32, Yaxchilán.

adorned with little heads of bees and bordered with beads, and is holding it out with both hands to a personage of rank who kneels before him and holds up his hands to receive the gifts. The god, represented entirely in profile, wears high buskins, so carefully executed that the little straps passing from the sole up between the toes are plainly discernible. The girdle is ornamented with St. Andrews's crosses and the shoulder-cape with medallions. The fracture runs obliquely through the face, and the helmet belongs to the shattered portion. The great human head which this deity always wears fastened to his back has come out especially well on my photograph.

Above the head of the suppliant rise two vertical rows of glyphs, each row containing probably eight characters. The great initial glyph occupying the space of four of the ordinary glyphs, joins this double row above on one side. Behind the god, extending the whole length of his form, there is another double row of glyphs, which becomes single when it reaches the head attached to the back; its topmost glyphs belong to the missing portion. Of these rows behind the god 13+10 glyphs are preserved. There are three small glyphs incised on the back-ground in front of the face of the suppliant. These are not visible in the plate […].[17]

LINTEL 32

This magnificent sculptured lintel belonged to one of the entrances of the wing built at right angles to the main structure. I dug it out of the debris of the façade. After it had been carefully brushed and washed off and placed in favorable light, a fine photograph was obtained, notwithstanding the very slight projection of the relief.

A richly clad woman of rank brings a pouch with sacrificial gifs to the Ahaucan, or high priest, who holds a little image toward her. The woman wears the petticoat (*enaguas*), over which is thrown a cloak-like garment ornamented with a handsome reticulated border. Her headdress consists of a grotesque face, with a crest of feathers falling backward.

The priest is richly adorned from head to foot. Especially noticeable is the girdle with the great face-masks, while a great mask also adorns the cuff on the left wrist. Three small medallions containing little faces adorn the breast-cape, which might also be regarded as a broad necklace. Below the latter is another larger medallion crossed by the long narrow breast-plate. Out of the calpac-shaped priest's hat, which has eight stripes, rise several erect plumes of feathers sloping toward the back. The little image or idol has a snouted face, and wears a little helmet with feathers. The leg by which the priest holds it ends, as always, in a serpent stretching forward. On the border and on the background I find 18+3+5 glyphs,—a total of 26. The colors on this exceptionally fine piece of sculpture have totally disappeared.[18]

LINTEL 33

Notwithstanding the fact that this stone was broken in two, it was otherwise in a perfect state of preservation. [...] The sculpture represents a warrior of high rank, in front view, with his face in profile, who holds in his right hand what I believe to be a decorated quiver containing bow and arrows. Of the warrior's ornaments the most noticeable are: low buskins, leg-bands with a small medallion attached to each, a girdle with a border of flowers from which depends a large sash ornamented with a remarkable death-mask, a breast cape quite covered by a double row of medallions,—five smaller ones in the upper and five larger ones in the lower row, all with little faces,—long, narrow breast-plate, and a great medallion with a mammal (tiger?) below it; a large cuff on the left wrist, heavily ornamented in front, which may be a bow-string guard; large ear-ornaments; upon his head a large scroll-work helmet from which rise serpent-like designs falling toward the front, and plumes of feathers, which slope backward. The body is surrounded by radiating feathers! I find about twenty-five glyphs along the border.

Everywhere—on the face, on the medallions, feathers, helmet, feet, background, etc.—traces of bright red color are visible; therefore, I am of the opinion that the entire piece of sculpture was painted bright red, without the application of any other color.[19]

STELA 5

This stone is broken in two. The upper half had fallen with the human side turned upward, which was consequently worn away, but it is still discernible that the subject of the very flat relief is the figure of a man standing upright. The lower half of

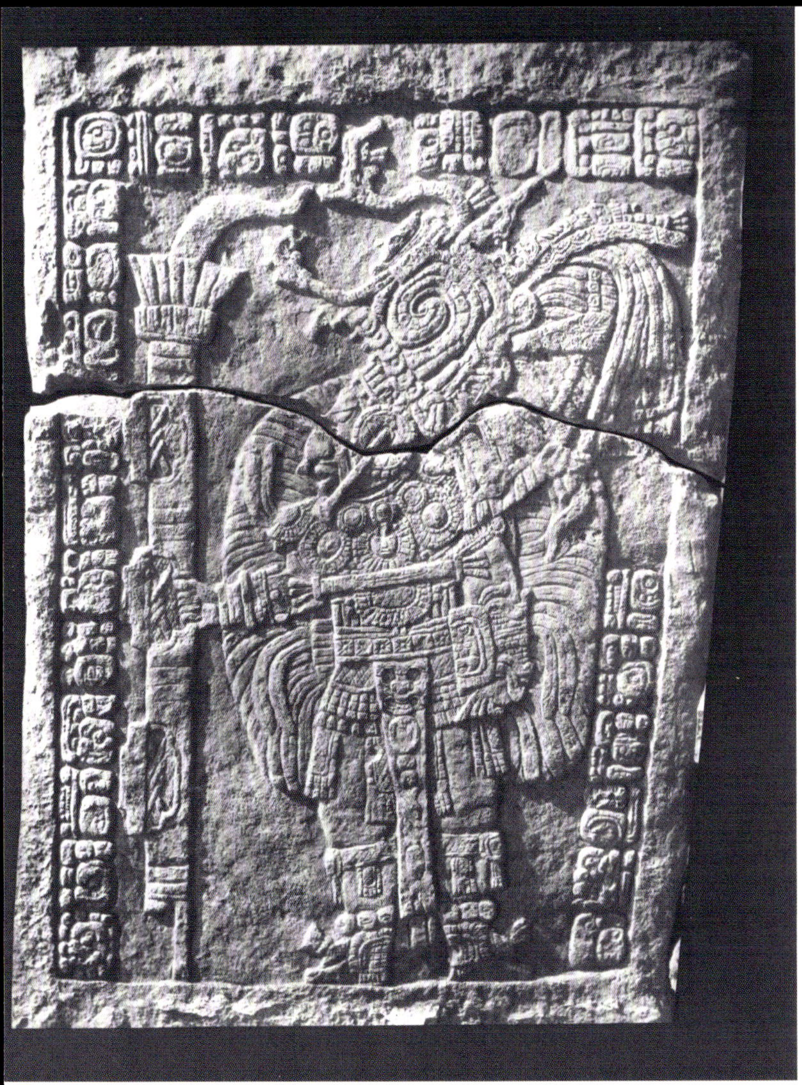

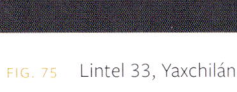

FIG. 75 Lintel 33, Yaxchilán.

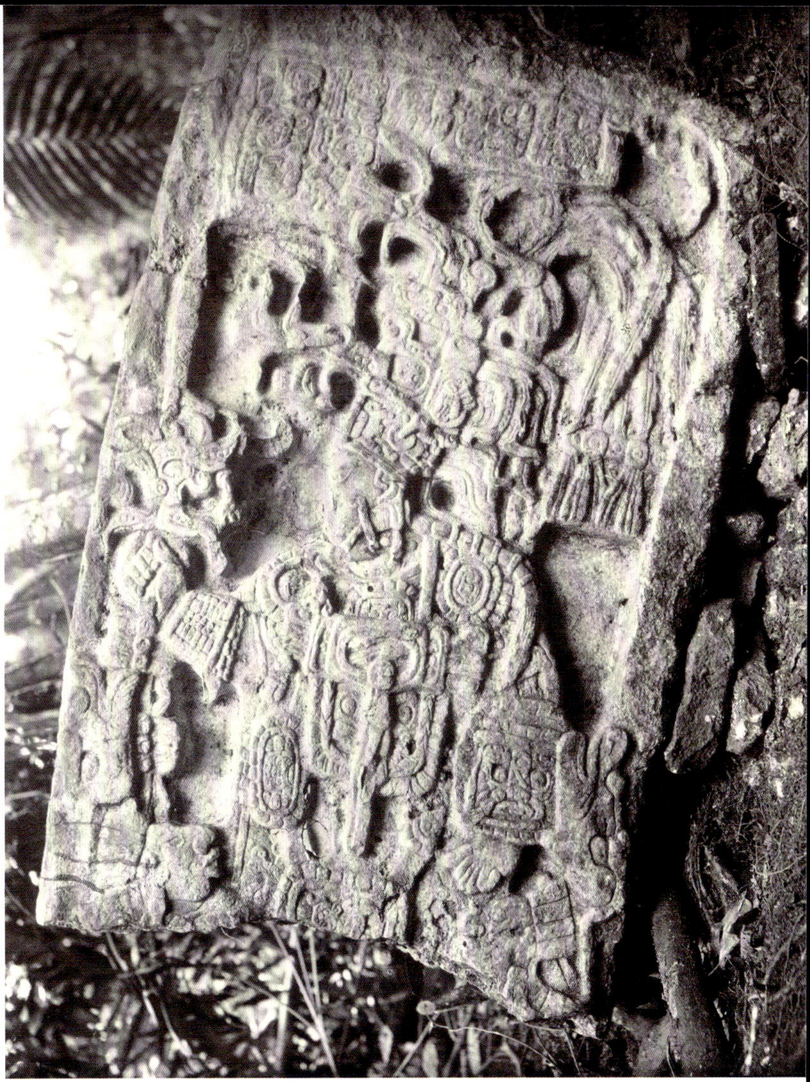

FIG. 76 Stela 5, Yaxchilán.

the stone—on which comes about one-third of the sculpture—had fallen with the human side down, and shows only the uninteresting lower part of the legs and the feet of the figure. The portion of the deity side which belongs to this lower piece is totally destroyed. The upper two thirds of the deity side, following the general rule, exhibits much greater projection than the other side.

The divinity is adorned with a superabundant number of medallions,—round ones and square ones, eight in all,—which almost entirely conceal his tunic, which is covered with a pattern of cross-bones. Three medallions with small round faces are attached to the breast-cape of scales. To a strap reaching down as far as the abdomen are attached, first, the breast-plate with a St. Andrew's cross and pendants, and then below this, a great four-cornered medallion with an elliptical one on either side, and at the very bottom a large square one. There is a cuff on the right wrist and on the left one a large four-cornered medallion, which may be regarded as a little shield for the protection of the artery of the wrist. The head-covering consists of confused scroll-work out of which rises a great plume of feathers falling backwards. These feathers are toothed like a saw, and have rayless stars and feather tassels at their tips. The divinity rests his left hand upon his hip. In his well-modeled right hand he holds a lance, the shaft of which is ornamented with small intertwined serpents. The fantastic head of a monster has been impaled upon the point of the lance.

A male figure kneels on either side of the divinity. The fracture fortunately passes below the heads, diagonally across the stone. Above the head of each of the kneeling figures is an animal's head looking upward. On the upper part of the stela there are nine glyphs. Only on the background were traces of dark-red color visible.[20]

STELA 6

The lower part, which was let into the earth, and on which were the beginnings of the ornamental base, was broken off. The side devoted to the memory of a human being fell face upward, and is entirely worn away by the downpouring rains. The side devoted, again in this case, to the beneficent divinity, having lain face downward, is sufficiently well preserved. There were no inscriptions on the narrow side faces.

A mass of roots at the back of this exceedingly heavy stone proved an obstacle to placing it in a perfectly perpendicular position on one of its sides, and it therefore

FIG. 77   Stela 6, Yaxchilán.

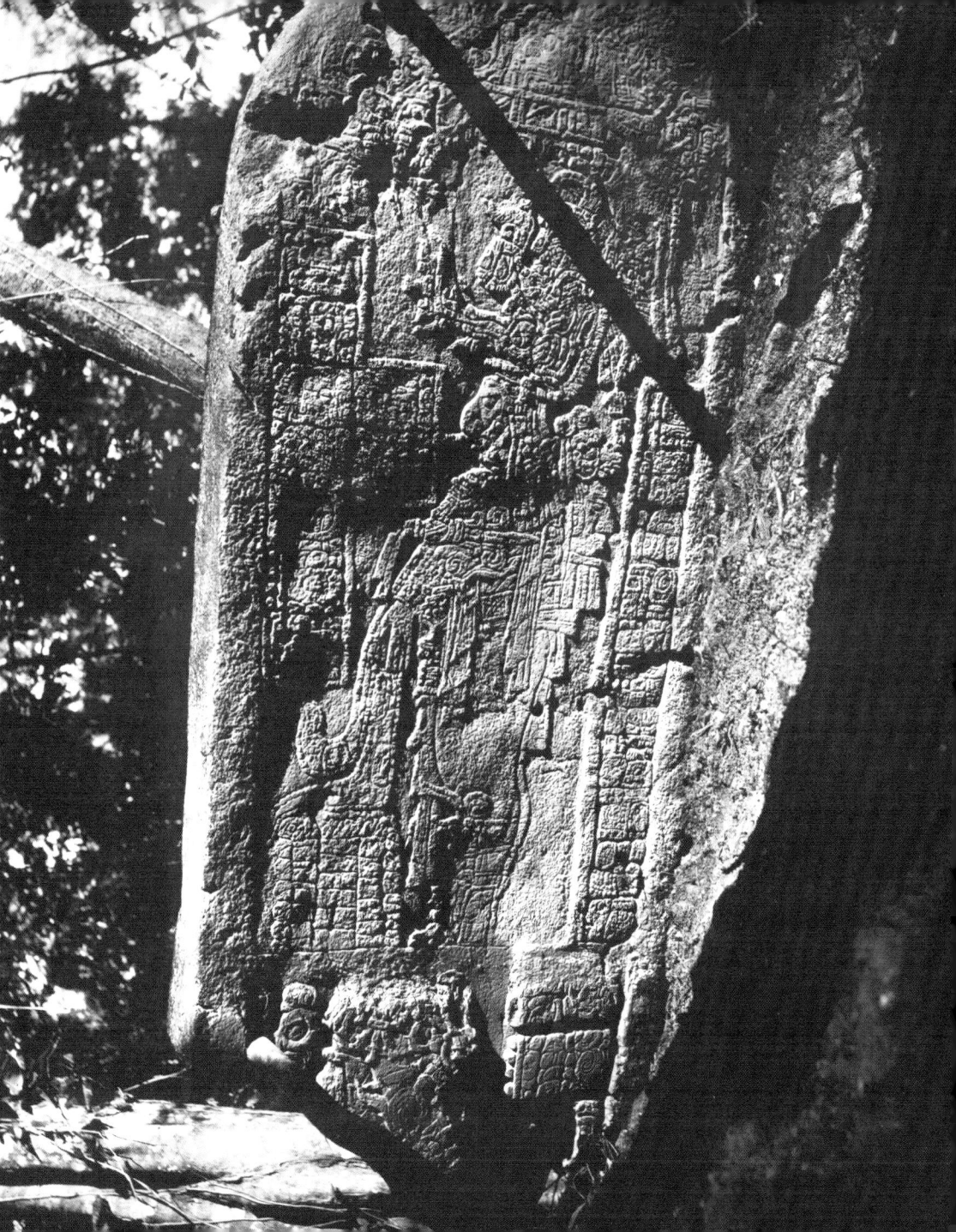

remained leaning forward a little. The sculptured surface could only be lighted up by the rays of the sun as they glanced through the clearing in the front very early in the morning. In order not to lose the favorable moment on the day on which I had arranged to take the photograph, I had my breakfast brought out to the stela, where I had set up my apparatus, deeply sunk in the earth, so that the middle of the lens should correspond as nearly as possible with the middle of the stone. Fortunately, no clouds obstructed the sunlight, and the photograph turned out well.

The ornamental base of the deity side is executed in very high relief and exhibits a richly adorned figure sitting Turkish fashion. The head has been broken off. On the right of the figure are certain symbolic signs, and on the left are the remains of three very much involved glyphs.

Upon the top line of the ornamental base stands the beneficent divinity, executed quite in profile, and in much lower relief than that of the base. Before the god stands the chest of plaited work, from which he has taken the string of sweets ornamented with little bees' heads, which he holds out before himself with both hands. He wears buskins and leg-bands; cuffs on his wrists; on the upper part of the body a garment with a great mask in front at the neck; a scroll-work breast-plate, with a St. Andrew's cross; a loin girdle; a large head attached to the back. The high head-dress consists of peculiar scroll-work.

In front of the divinity I find nine large glyphs; behind him, in a vertical row, ten smaller ones.[21]

STELA 2

[On] the platform of the stone stairway, which I consider a part of the plan of the Temple of the headless Ketsalkoatl (Structure 33) [...] between two heaps of stones, marking the site of two very small structures, I found a moderately large stela lying on the ground.

The stela was broken off just above the piece which had been let into the ground. The narrow side-faces have no glyphs. The broad face turned upward was entirely destroyed, but it was probably once ornamented with sculpture.

The sculpture on the side which lay face downward had lost its most delicate outlines, but the photograph taken in strong sunlight brought out the low relief

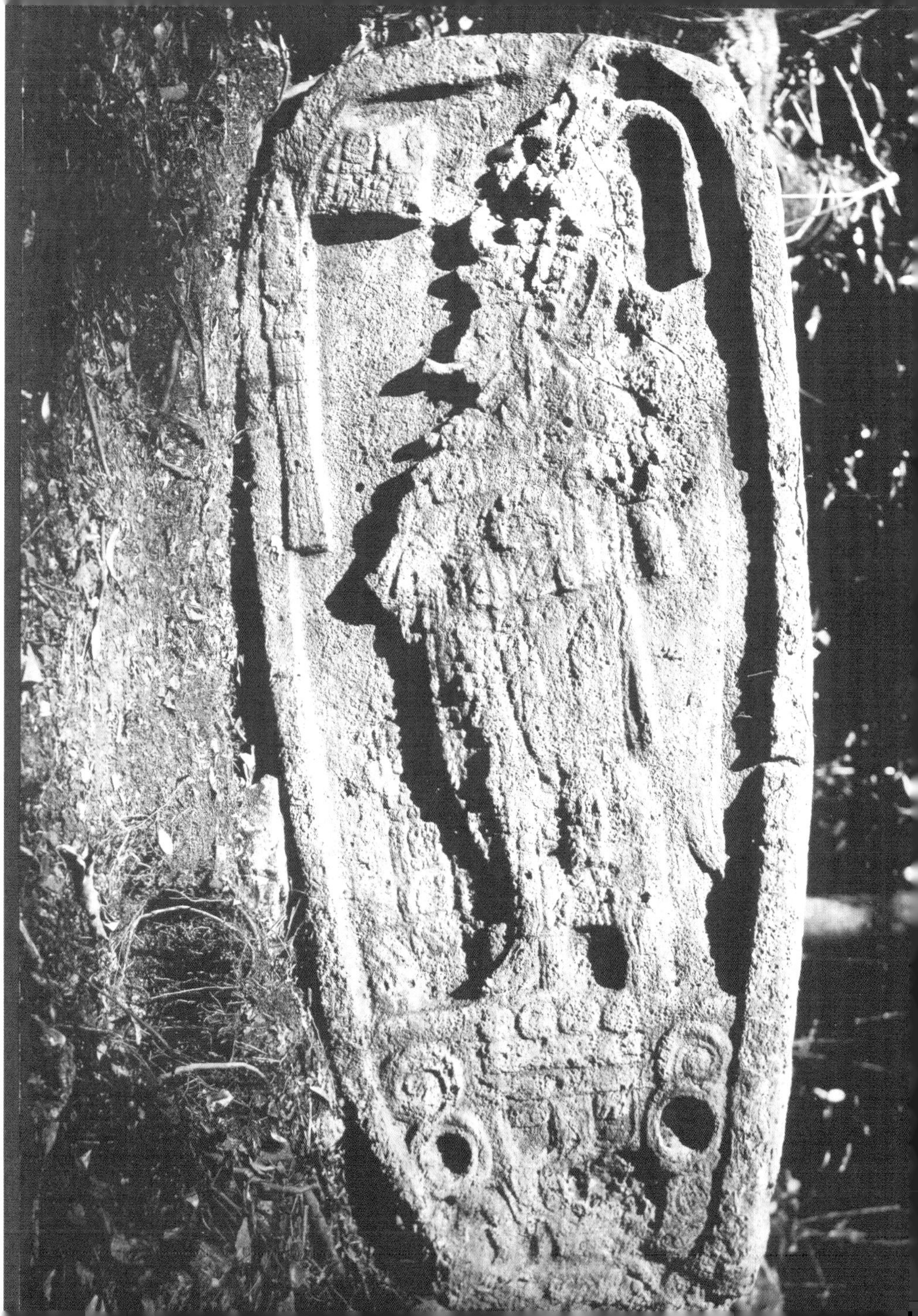

FIG. 78   Stela 2, Yaxchilán.

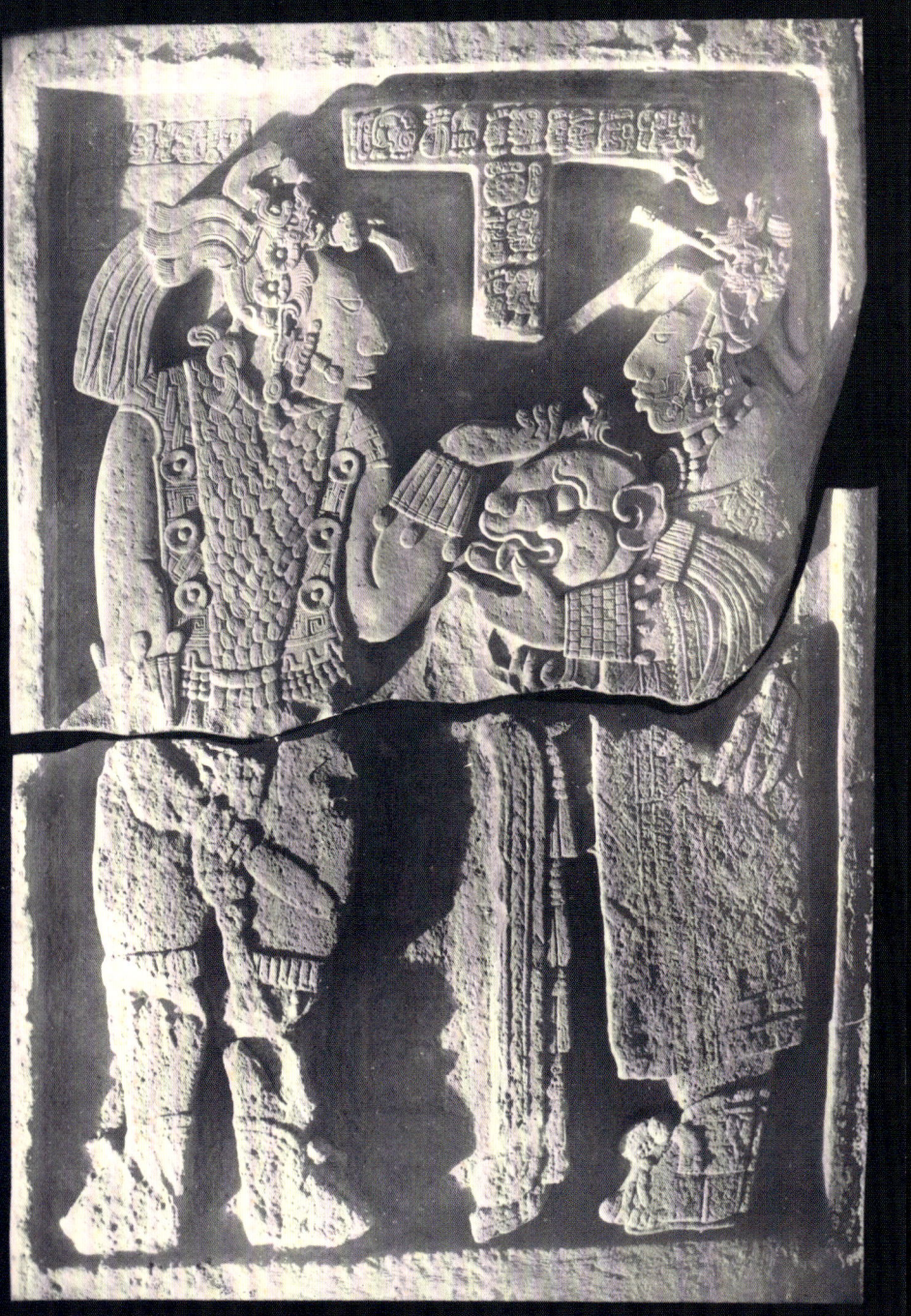

FIG. 79　Lintel 26, Yaxchilán.

splendidly, to the very grain of the stone. The design perpetuates some bloody event, for the better understanding of which I refer to the photograph.

The ornamental base consists of a single chronological glyph, which can be interpreted as the ninth series of years or bolonahau. (The face represents the word *ahau*=king, above which the number 9=*bolon* is distinctly recognizable). Above the chronological glyph stands a warrior with both arms cut off. He is represented in front view, the face only being in profile. Upon his head-dress a gnome (*ppus*) seems to be sitting, from whose occiput a great feather falls backward. A feather projecting forward is drawn through the nose of the warrior.

In front of the warrior, near the border, is a stone lancehead with pendants, but without a shaft in order thus to indicate that the shaft has become useless since the warrior has lost his arms and can no longer hold a lance. On the background there are four glyphs above and four below, not counting those placed transversely below the latter row, with the death's-head (?) lowest of all. There are no traces of color.[22]

STRUCTURE 23, LINTELS 24 AND 25

[T]he lintels of the three principal doorways [of Structure 23] were once ornamented with beautiful sculpture on the under sides, and with a row of glyphs on their exterior faces. [...] The stone lintel 24 had been torn out of the doorway, which had a span of 100 cm., and as no sawed-off stone lay near-by, we were in doubt as to what had become of it. An examination of the heap of ruins at that spot resulted in finding out that the back of the lintel had been hacked off with an axe, which still lay close by, in order to lessen the weight of the sculpture. By this rude process the inscription on the exterior face (probably eight characters) was unfortunately all broken to pieces. The chips were lying all about! [...] It was not very difficult to find out what had become of this stone [lintel 25]. The enormous mass of frieze and masonry which it had been necessary to take down in order to get at the precious stone lintel, formed a mound reaching to the top of the central doorway, which has a span of 121 cm. At the foot of the mound lay the stone sought for, with the inscription and the relief on the exterior and under faces very neatly sawed off.[23]

LINTEL 26

As the wielders of axe and saw had apparently done their work most thoroughly, there was little hope of finding the stone lintel belonging to the third entrance. At this part of the building the vaulted ceiling and the frieze had already fallen down. But as we found no sawed-off stone nor chips, I set to work to fathom the heap of ruins. Our excavation resulted in finding the sought-for stone, which was broken in two. The lower half of the sculpture was considerably weathered, but the upper half was remarkably well preserved.

Undersculpture: A woman of rank presents a tiger's head, prepared as a helmet, to the sacrificial priest. The woman has on shoes, her cuffs are of scale-work, her tunic (*huipilli*) shows a reticulated pattern, her head-dress is of medium size and adorned with conventionalized flowers, her ear-ornaments are very distinct, and a line of small dots borders the lips and ends in a scroll on the cheek turned toward the spectator. Below the face is a necklace of stone beads, with a medallion in front. The woman carries with both hands a tiger's head, with a great plume of feathers, probably meant as a head-covering for the priest. I must also add that a pendant ornamented with tassels hangs from the woman's hands down to the ground.

The priest has buskins, leg-bands, and striped cuffs; his jacket shows a tasteful pattern in lines, and is ornamented with six rayless stars; a broad sash of shell-work reaches from his neck to his knees; the ear-ornaments are peculiar. His head-dress, with handsomely executed flowers, has a grotesque face on top, and out of the knot at the back falls a plume of feathers. In his right hand the priest holds a sacrificial knife, and his left hand lies against the front of the tiger's head.

A T-shaped inscription of nine characters executed in very fine detail is above between the two personages; six miniature glyphs in low relief are seen on the background near the head-dress of the priest, while about six glyphs, which have become almost invisible, lie between the left thigh of the priest and the pendant described above. The projection of the beautifully executed relief is only about 1 cm., but the background is sunk 3 ½ cm. There are traces of blue color plainly visible on the background, the head-dresses, the garments, the tiger's head, etc., for which reason I am inclined to believe that the whole sculptured lintel was once painted sky-blue.

Exterior face sculpture: Eight rounded-off glyphic characters, most of which seem to be composed of four glyphs, ornament the exterior face of the lintel. Some of these have been battered off, but a good deal of the inscription can still be recognized in my photograph. The tiger's head occurs repeatedly among the glyphs.[24]

STELA 11

While the wood-cutters of Encarnación Carrillo were camping among these magnificent ruins, occasionally also taking up their baleful abode in the beautifully colored chamber of the central South Temple—about thirty years ago—they felled a gigantic caobo tree, which must have stood close to the temple. Whether intentionally or not, they let the tree fall right across this grand monument of Maya sculpture, by which means a corner was struck off and the entire stone forced forward into a leaning position. Before very long the huge stone will fall, and, striking the circular altar in front of it, will be shattered into many pieces. In order to comprehend the enormity of the vandalism perpetrated in this case, it should be remembered that the Mexican government at that time received on an average 50 centavos for the cutting down of a tree, and only about 25 centavos for trees of an inferior quality, and that the wood-cutters knew well how to include in their cargoes many a tree which had not been marked, for which the Mexican state treasury received no equivalent. This magnificent monument, then, was sacrificed for the miserable pittance of 50 centavos, or perhaps for nothing at all!

Owing to the inclined position of the stela, it was extremely difficult to photograph it. In order to avoid a distortion of the perspective, I slanted the apparatus upward in photographing the human side, and downward for the deity side. I set up the broken-off piece on one side, but not in the correct vertical position, owing to the unfavorable fracture.

The Human Side: The sculpture on this side has for its base four horizontal rows of nine glyphs each, excepting the top row, where the initial glyph occupies the space of two of the others,—hence, thirty-five glyphs in all. I took a special photograph of this group of glyphs early in the morning and the principal portion of the sculpture was photographed about an hour later.

Exposing the Maya

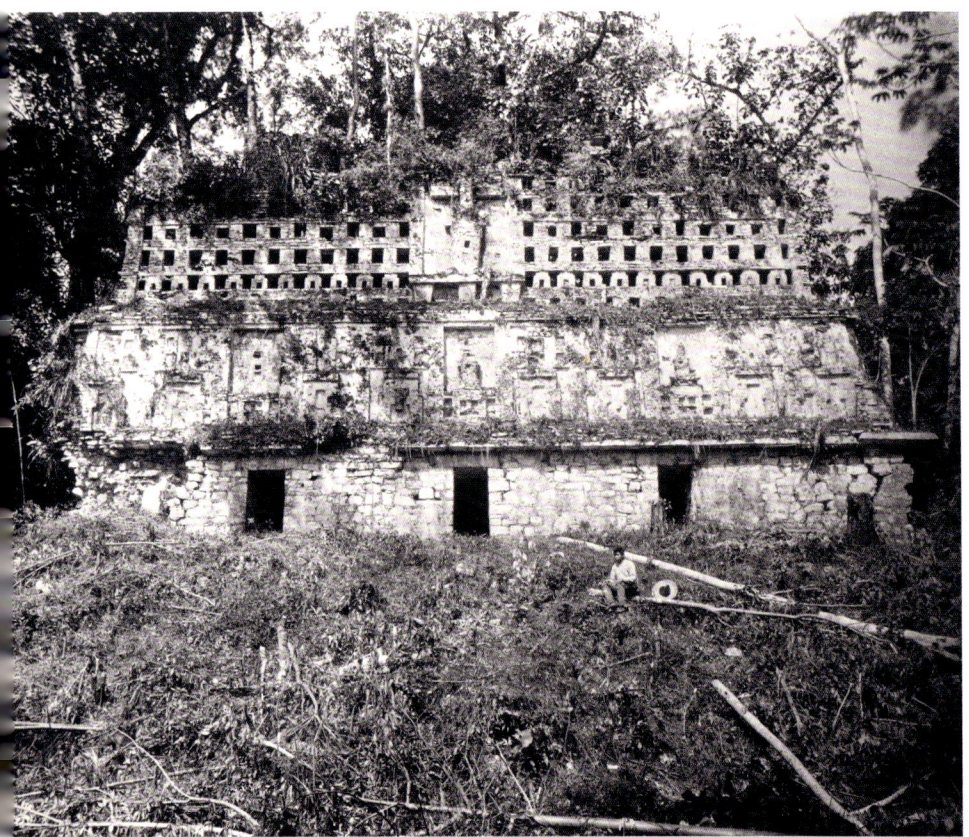

FIG. 80   Structure 33, Yaxchilán.

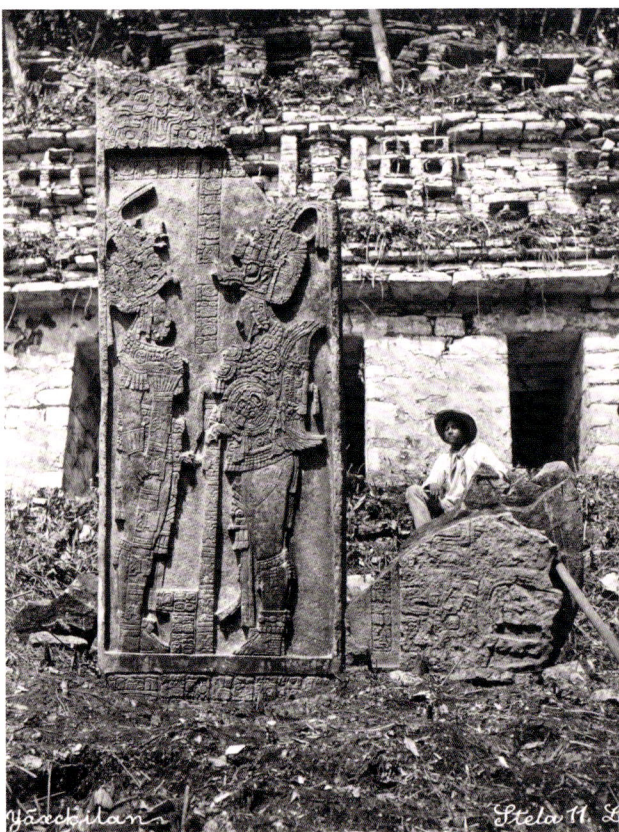

FIG. 81   Structure 40 with Stela 11, Yaxchilán.

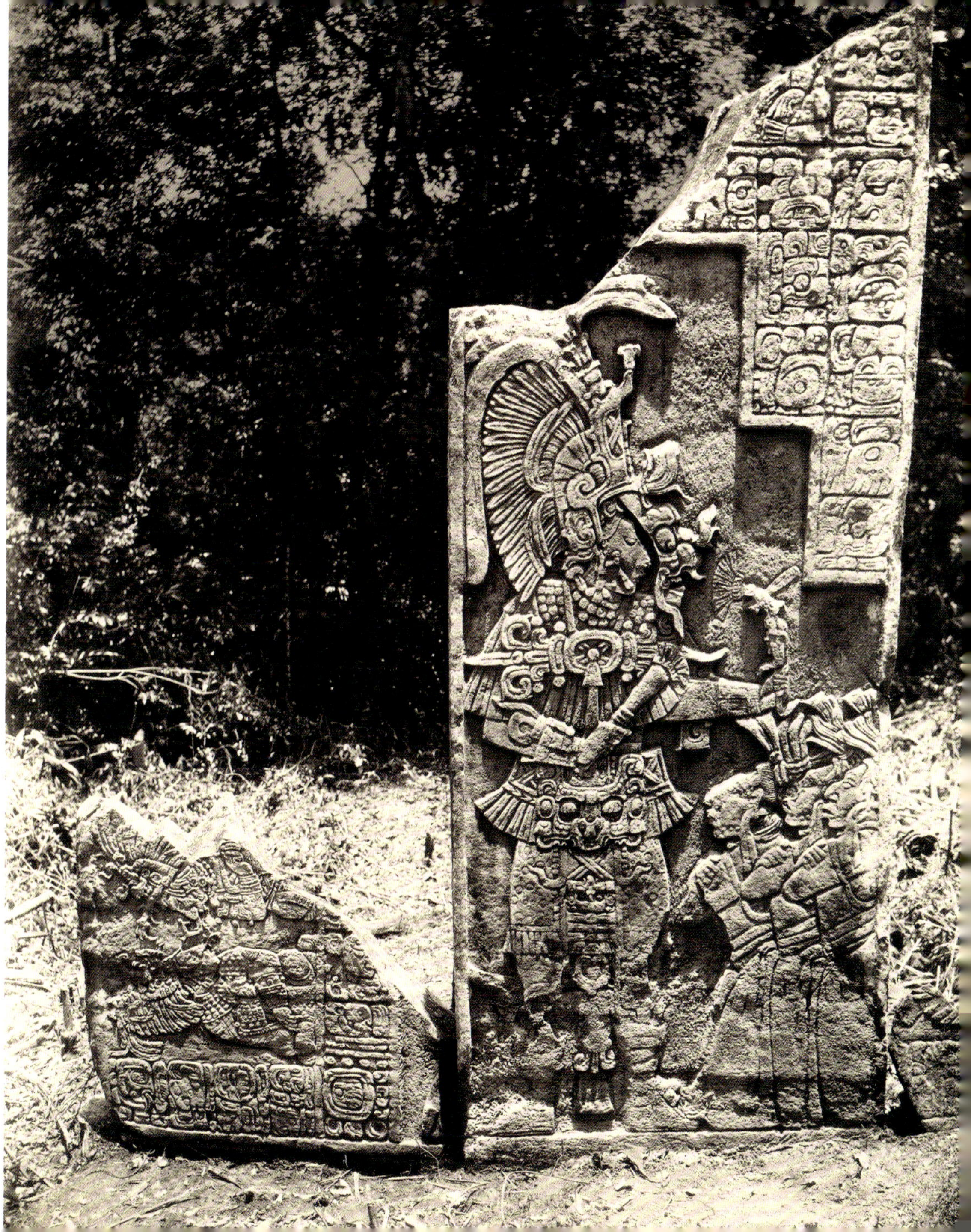

FIG. 82   "Deity side" of Stela 11, Yaxchilán.

Upon the upper edge of a group of glyphs stand two warriors of proud bearing, probably the chieftain first in command, or *Ahau*, with the second in command, the *Sihuacohuatl*, as the Mexicans would say. The two chieftains, drawn in profile, are standing face to face in a strictly military pose, carrying what seem to be quivers with bows and arrows. Both wear buskins and leg-bands, crossed loin-cloths of thin material lying closely to the form and partly concealed by the richly ornamented girdle. The second chieftain holds his quiver with his right hand, on the wrist of which the cuff is visible, while both the cuffs of the first chieftain are invisible. A shield or possibly a large cuff-medallion is on the left lower arm. Both chieftains wear elaborate breast-capes of bead-work, each with three medallions, of which only two can be seen, owing to the position of the wearers. The Ahau has a second row of medallions under the upper one, and he furthermore wears on his back (as a guard?), a large oval disc surrounded by feathers, with a projection in the middle from which a tassel depends. Both warriors wear tall helmets adorned with grotesque faces, scroll and feather work. On the helmet of the Ahau the animal's head with a large eye and projecting snout is especially distinct. Unoccupied spaces of the background are filled in with glyphs: 4+8+9=21.

The finish at the top, now incomplete, owing to the fracture, was probably ornamented as follows: At the bottom four grotesque faces in profile looking downward (two of them very distinct on my photograph), and resting upon these, symbolical scroll-work. Then to the right and left an oval containing a small figure sitting Turkish fashion (one of the ovals can be recognized on the smaller fragment), and a large half-length picture between the ovals.

The Deity Side: This side, which faces the temple, is quite as interesting and as spirited in design as the human side. A circular altar dedicated to the deity side stands above on the edge of the platforms. Upon this altar, where in past ages the heart of many a miserable victim may have been torn out, I set up my harmless photographic apparatus (directly upon the stone, without the tripod), giving it a decided forward incline. I took the photograph a few moments after the sun had passed the zenith when its rays fell almost perpendicularly upon the stone, lighting it at a very acute angle and imparting to its usually colorless surface a truly wonderful animation. The photograph came out beautifully in spite of a slight distortion of the perspective, which was quite unavoidable. The sculpture represented on this side has no glyphic base. A soothsaying priest is here represented in an attitude of zealous ecstasy, his body in front view and his face in profile, the latter concealed by the mysterious mask of a terror-inspiring god. With his right hand he holds out toward the worshipping populace the augur's stone, *sastun,* and with his left the small image of a god with a snouted face and a raylike plume of feathers. The people, kneeling with hands crossed over their breasts, devoutly receive the utterances which proclaim good or ill fortune. The populace is symbolically represented by three simply clad men kneeling close together. The priest wears breeches of tiger skin, a St. Andrew's cross girdle fringed with feathers, and a tiger's head or death mask (?) in the middle, buskins as usual on his feet, and cuffs on his wrists. A feather mantle with a bead cape which covers the upper part of the body is horizontally intersected by a breast-plate of handsome scroll-work with a St. Andrew's cross in the central oval. The helmet is large and of handsome design, and has another St. Andrew's cross in front, above which rises a gigantic plume, the feathers of which curve backward and downward, and wave about a close, comb-like border of feathers.

The upper part of the deity side is occupied by twenty large glyphic squares arranged like steps. At the top, space was found among them for a picture square, within which two personages, probably a man and a woman, sit side by side in Turkish fashion, and are evidently engaged in very animated conversation.

This sculpture in low relief, which enlightens us with regard to the religious procedures of a long-vanished epoch, is absolutely the only one of its kind among my collection of photographs.

The narrow side-faces are also decorated, each with a row of large, fairly well-preserved glyphs. Generally speaking, there were no traces of color remaining, only on the group of glyphs protected by debris I thought I detected some remnants of red.[26]

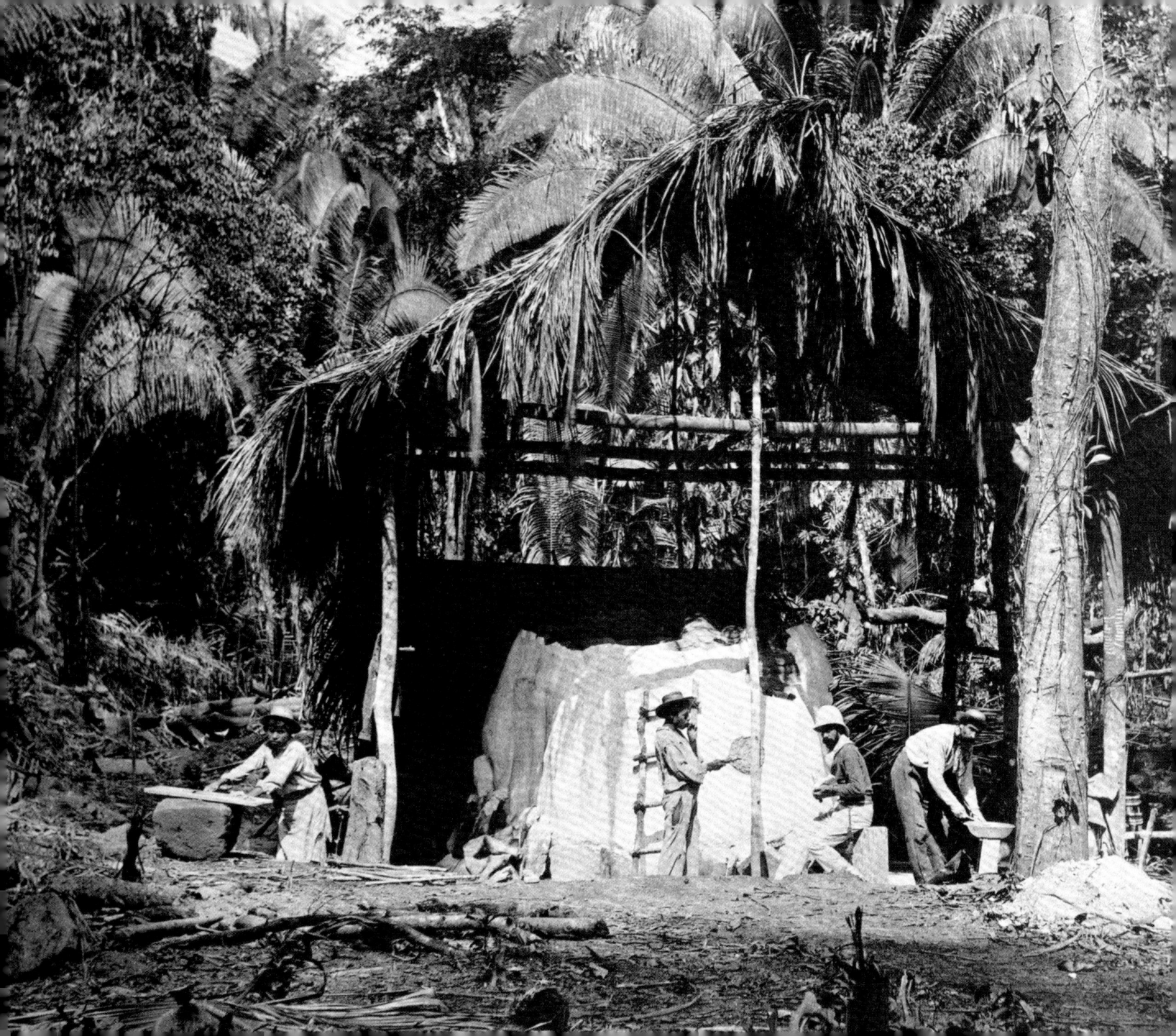

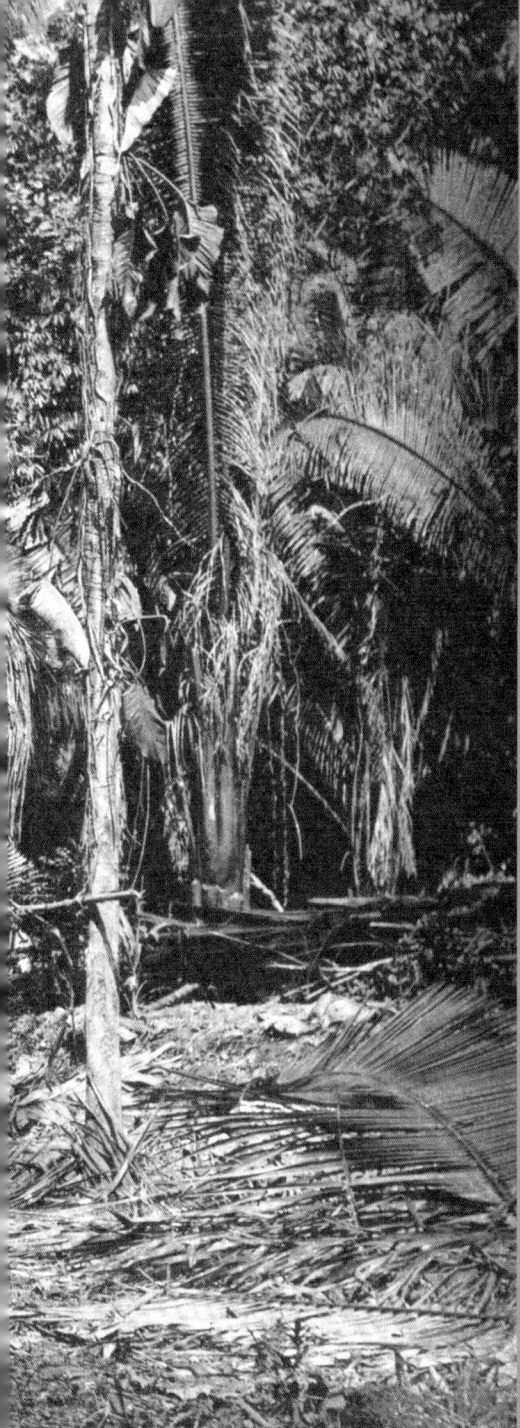

Alfred Maudslay
(1850–1931)

Alfred Maudslay, born at Lower Norwood Lodge, near London, worked for more than twenty years to provide the most precise record of the ancient buildings and monuments of Mesoamerica; he hoped, in particular, that his exact reproductions of the carved hieroglyphic inscriptions of the Maya language would help preserve them from the destructive forces of man and the tropical climate in Mexico and Central America.[1] The result—published as part of the *Biologia Centrali-Americana*—was the most accomplished and systematic documentation of Maya sites to date, widely seen as both an artistic and a scientific milestone. Within the *Biologia*'s volumes are photographs, drawings, and maps from across the Maya world, including the sites of Copan, Quiriguá, Ixkun, Yaxche, Chichén Itzá, Tikal, and Palenque. Maudslay was a photographer in the service of scholars and linguists. He methodically surveyed and photographed the sites he visited, leaving behind a corpus that is devoid of speculation, or flights of fancy. His prime years in the field coincided with the development of ready-to-use photographic dry plates, which made the work of capturing images of sculpted stone easier than it had been for photographers in previous decades.

Maudslay's photographic project found its home in the *Biologia Centrali-Americana*. The publication of his photographs within this corpus was a major undertaking. The *Biologia* was itself a massive project, with fifty-one volumes being published on every aspect of the natural history of the region. The work was composed of beautifully produced fascicules, conceived of and edited by two of the most creative naturalists of the late nineteenth and early twentieth centuries, F. Ducane Godman and Osbert Salvin. At sixty-three volumes in total, mostly dedicated to zoology and botany, it completed its run in 1915, thirty-seven years after the publication of its first volumes.

The *Biologia* was inspired by Salvin and Godman's reading of Darwin's *On the Origin of Species* (1859), two chapters of which—entitled "Geographical Distribution"—outlined the lack of complete species data for any one region in the tropics that might answer the question of why a species is found in one place, and not in another. Salvin and Godman thus set out to compile the data Darwin said was lacking. They found a fascinating and fertile area of study in the lowland jungles of Central America.

Forming part of the *Biologia*'s comprehensive survey of the region's biogeography are the seven meticulously produced and impressive volumes of photographs and drawings of the great ruined Maya cities of Central America by Maudslay. Maudslay would spend years traveling through the jungle to the newly rediscovered archaeological

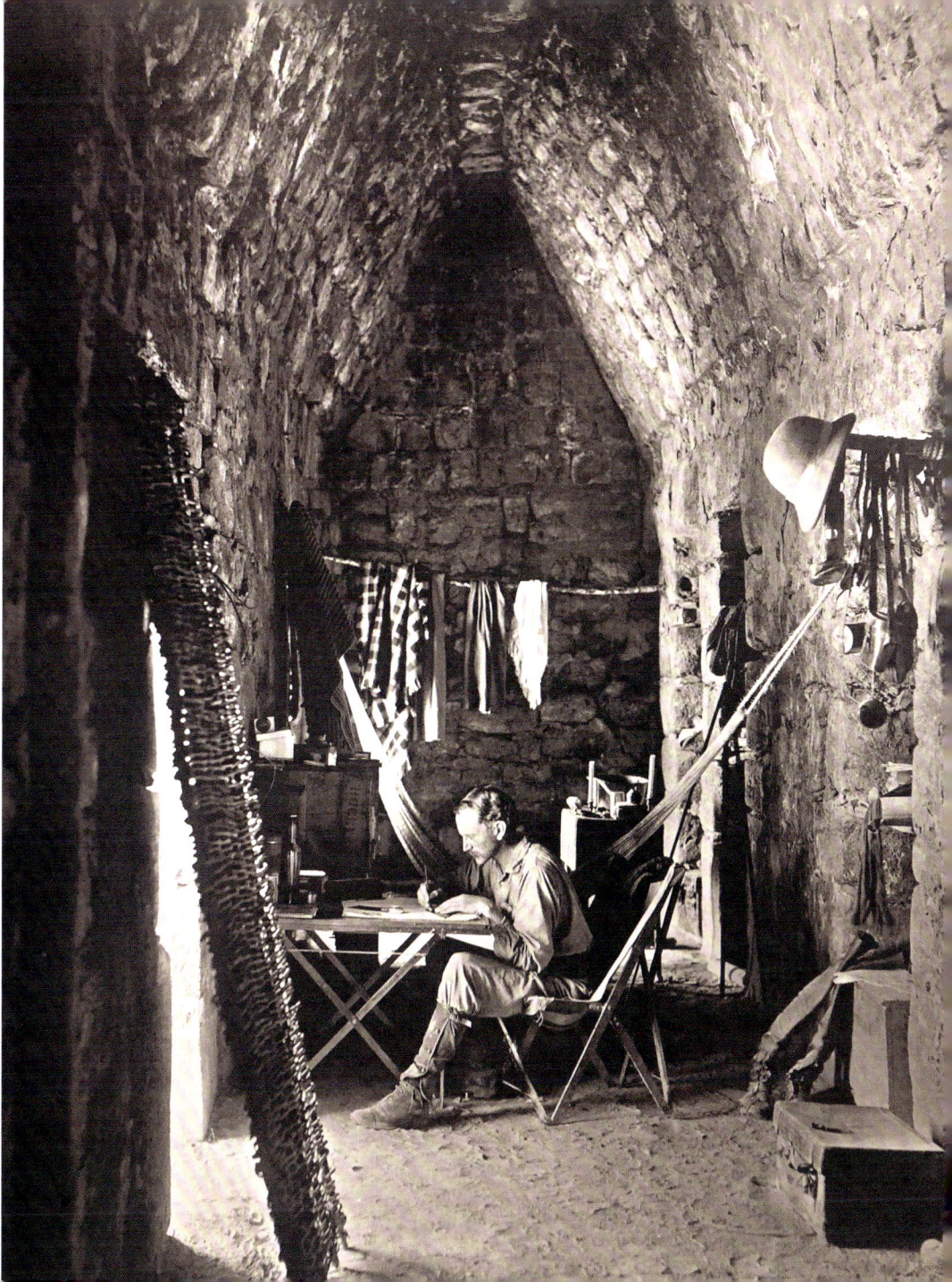

FIG. 83 Self-portrait of Albert Maudslay in his quarters within the southern chamber, Casa de Monjas (Nuns' Palace), Chichén Itzá.

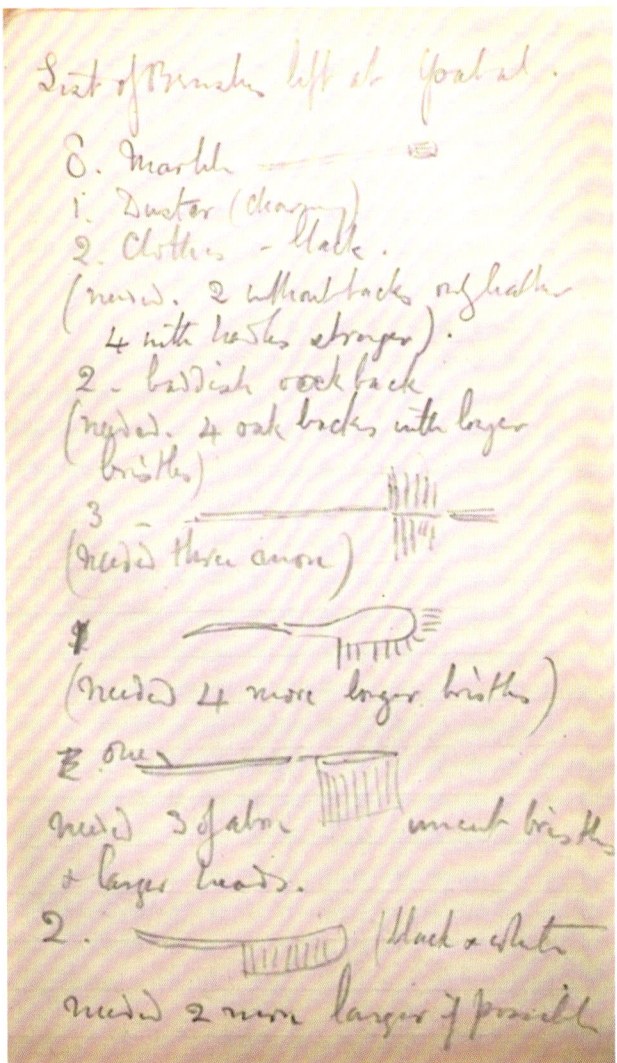

FIG. 84 Field notes from Copán, featuring a description of brushes for cleaning epigraphic inscriptions.

sites of the Maya with camera and notebook in tow. Unlike many of the photographers in this volume, his undertaking was expedition-like—by using his personal fortune, he could hire trained craftsmen, rely upon massive supplies and carry out a logistically challenging enterprise that would soon become possible only with institutional or national support.

For archaeologists and epigraphers, his photographs would be the starting point for most serious attempts at deciphering the long-forgotten writing system of the Maya. For Godman and Salvin, however, these volumes on archaeology fit well into the environmental history of the region as they conceived it, placing man and his modification of the landscape in their proper place within the natural world.

Maudslay's fieldwork, which took place mainly in the years between 1881 and 1894, entailed many of the activities that today might be considered part of modern archaeology. He mapped, photographed, and made molds of monuments and carved hieroglyphs. The photographs themselves were produced using dry-plate photographic techniques that were more forgiving than those employed by Charnay and that, when combined with the new gravure reproduction techniques used in the *Biologia*, yielded what "arguably reign as the best printed pictures of Maya sculpture ever produced."[2]

To make the photographs Maudslay wanted, and that would represent the details of the fine carving with enough clarity to be used by scholars, the play of light on the stela and architectural monuments was a critical factor. To that end, employing many local laborers, he cleared the trees, vines, and centuries' worth of jungle growth from the plazas, façades, and sculptures he photographed, allowing for unprecedented reproductions of ancient Maya epigraphy.

In March 1882, a chance meeting in Yaxchilán with Desiré Charnay would greatly impact one aspect of Maudslay's work and the accuracy of the reproductions found in the *Biologia*. In his journal, Maudslay noted: "Showed Charnay around the ruins and he immediately set his secretary at work to make paper molds of some of the carved lintels. It is a very easy process and I wish I had known of it before." Charnay, for whom papier-maché molds, or "squeezes" of vestiges had long been a practice, introduced Maudslay to a process credited to Victor Lottin de Laval, who had himself used this method for creating lightweight but faithful reproductions of sculpted reliefs in early excavations of Nineveh.

Thanks in part to this meeting, as well as his growing experience as a field photographer, Maudslay concluded that relying on photography alone for recording sculpture

Exposing the Maya

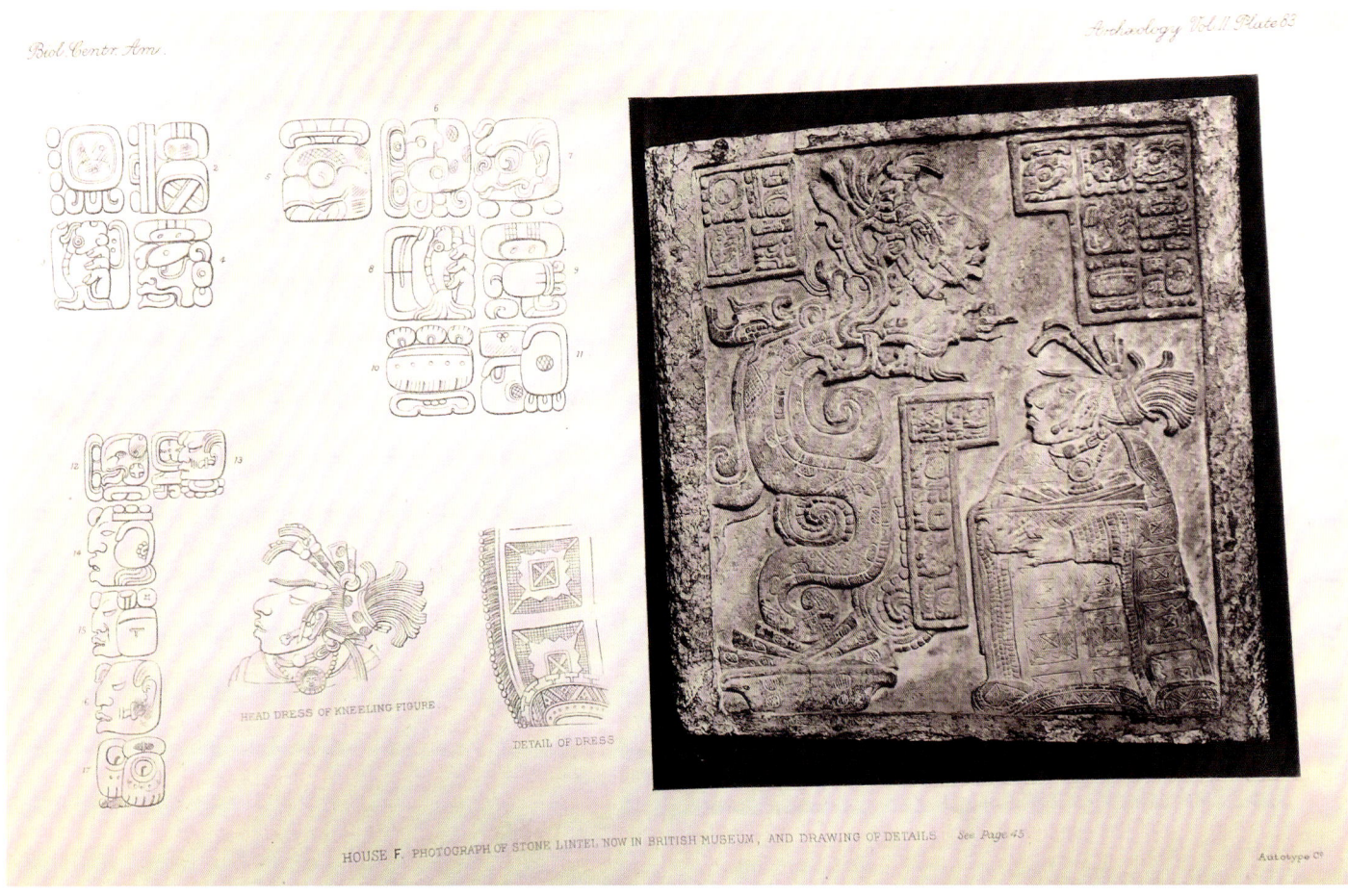

FIG. 85 Photographic plate of Lintel 15 from Yaxichilán in the *Biologia Centrali-Americana*, opposite a drawing of epigraphic and iconographic details by Annie Hunter.

FIG. 86 Cleared view of the Palace, taken from the Temple of the Inscriptions, Palenque.

Alfred Maudslay (1850–1931)

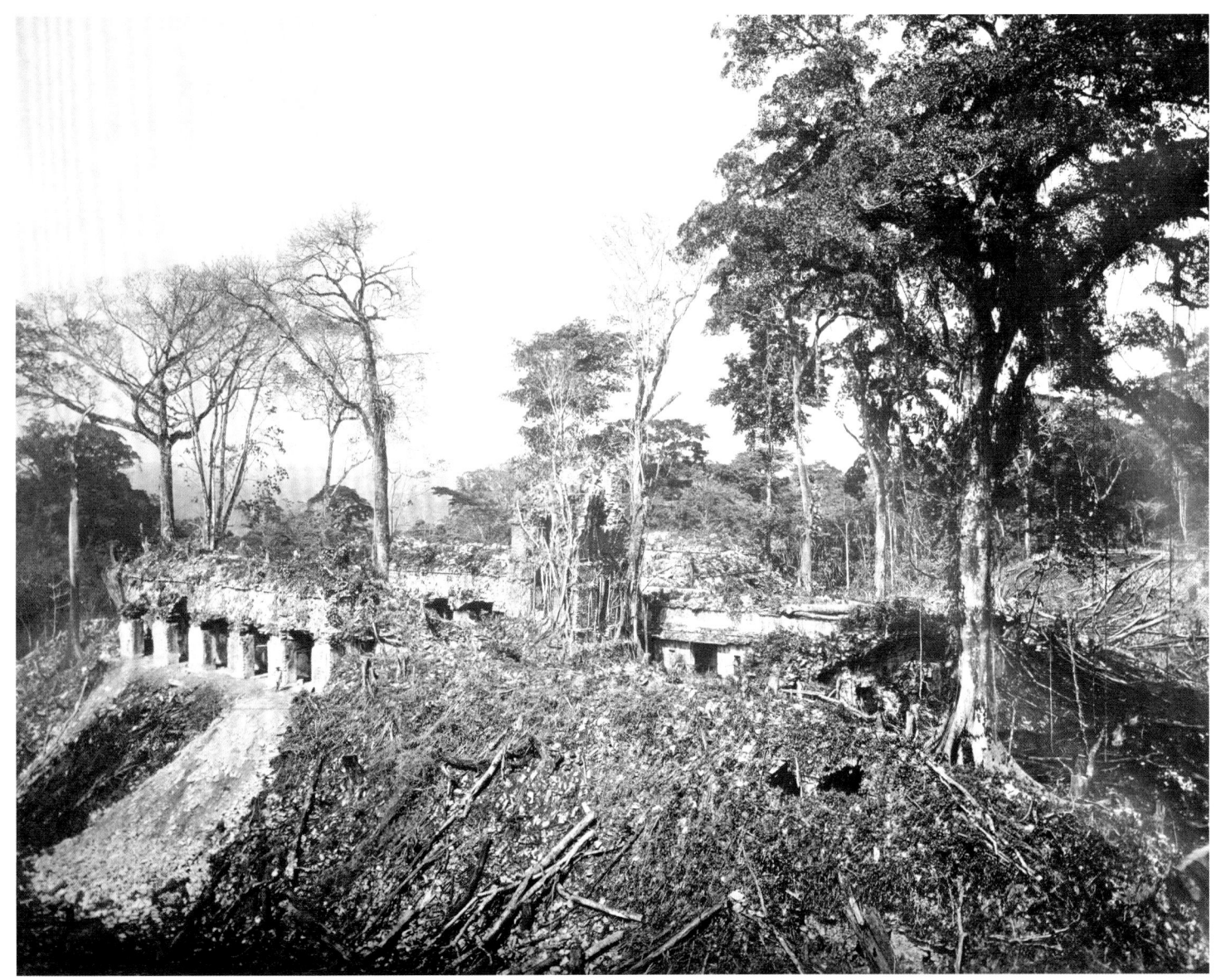

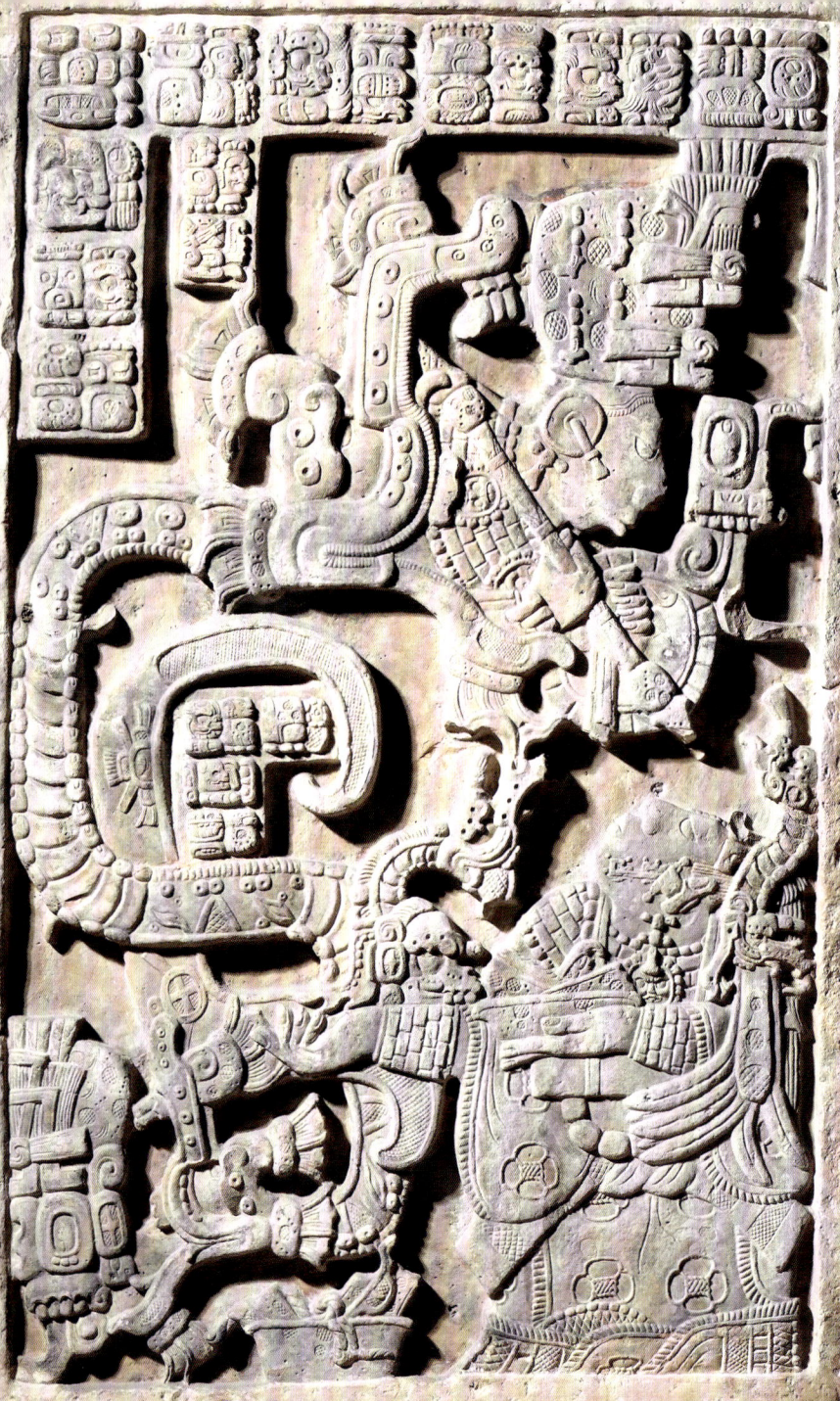

FIG. 87   Lintel 25 from Yaxchilán, in the British Museum, London.

Alfred Maudslay (1850–1931)

was fraught with difficulties, and he therefore began to supplement his photographs with accurate casts and to collaborate with illustrators such as Edwin J. Lambert, Adela Breton, and Annie G. Hunter. Hunter's drawings, which form the majority of those found in the *Biologia*, do not simply consist of faithful renderings: often they reconstruct some of the missing areas that are difficult to make out in the original field photographs. According to a letter she wrote to Charles P. Bowditch, who funded several important expeditions in Yucatán and in Central America, and had a keen interest in Maya epigraphy, the drawings were revised by her and Maudslay "over and over again."[3] Despite the hopes at the dawn of photography that the camera would bring objectivity that was impossible with illustration, Maudslay at once practiced the most evolved form of photographic art and heralded a return to the pre-eminent role of drawing in modern archaeology.

FIG. 88 Drawings of Lintels 24 and 25 by Annie Hunter in the *Biologia Centrali-Americana*.

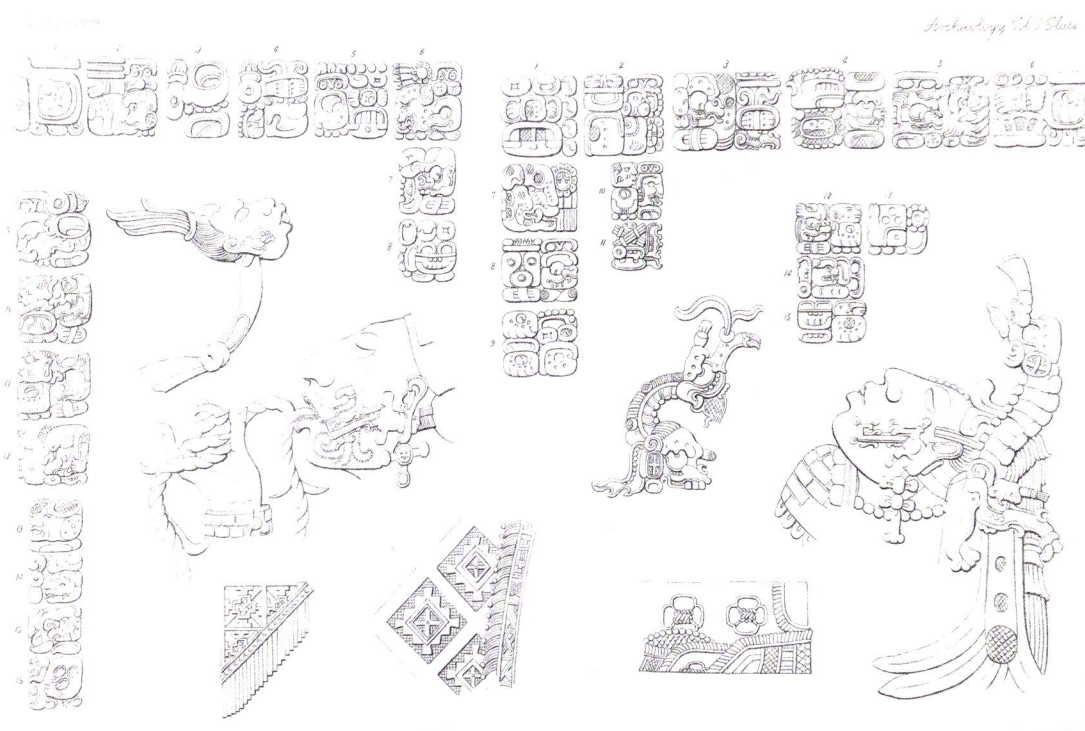

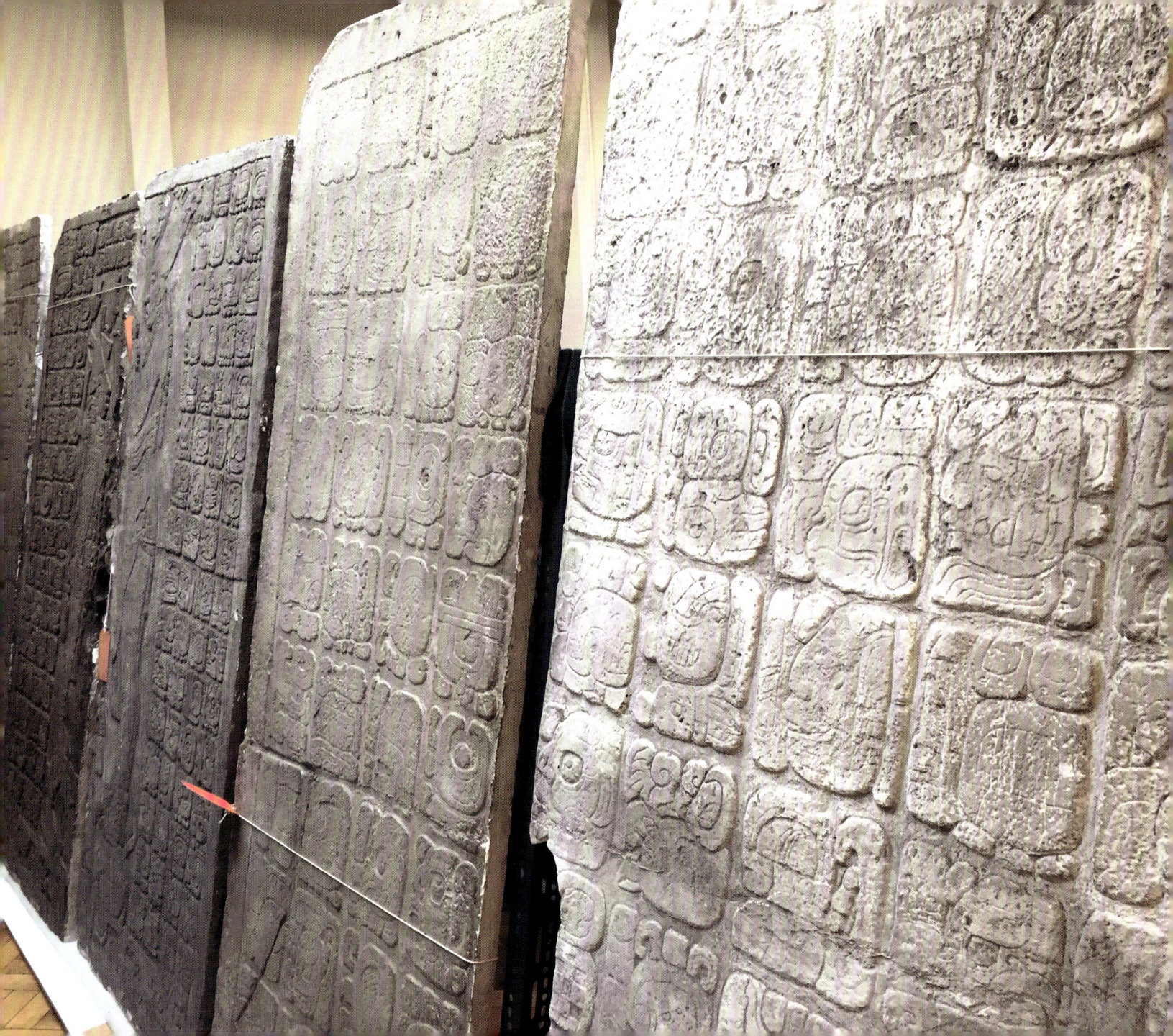

FIG. 89   A selection of Maudslay's casts in the British Museum, London.

To further facilitate accurate renderings, Maudslay not only made casts of many of the sculptures he documented in the field but also photographed the casts themselves. He found once back in England that the casts provided a more evenly colored surface and could be photographed using controlled lighting in a way that was impossible to do in the field. Many of the photographs and drawings that would make their way into the *Biologia* were of casts made using the methodology learned from Charnay.

Maudslay's work in mapping, photographing, and making the dozens of surviving casts offers a view of the sweeping monumentality of his vision. He was not one for theoretical reflection and personal anecdotes, and his journals provide little more than lists of supplies needed and bookkeeping required when undertaking archaeological exploration on a large scale.

In the end, Maudslay's work inaugurated a new era in Mesoamerican archaeology while leaving behind a striking photographic record of a disappearing world. Despite the monumentality of his expeditions, his photographs are more than mere documentation of fieldwork. Maudslay wanted to be remembered for his images, but he also wanted those images to be useful tools in the hands of linguists, scholars, and epigraphers who were at the time grappling with the unreadable Maya script. In this he succeeded admirably, documenting the grand sweep of the ruins of Central America and Mexico while at the same time providing images with such clean close-up views that even today they remain a critical reference in the field.

COPÁN

Stela N is "the most elaborately carved of all the monuments now standing at Copan, and is in fairly good preservation." Maudslay took molds of the hieroglyphs and a considerable number of photographs. The stela had also been drawn by Catherwood, and, since it had suffered damage in the meantime, Maudslay had to make use of Catherwood's drawings in the reconstructed drawings that appear in the *Biologia*.

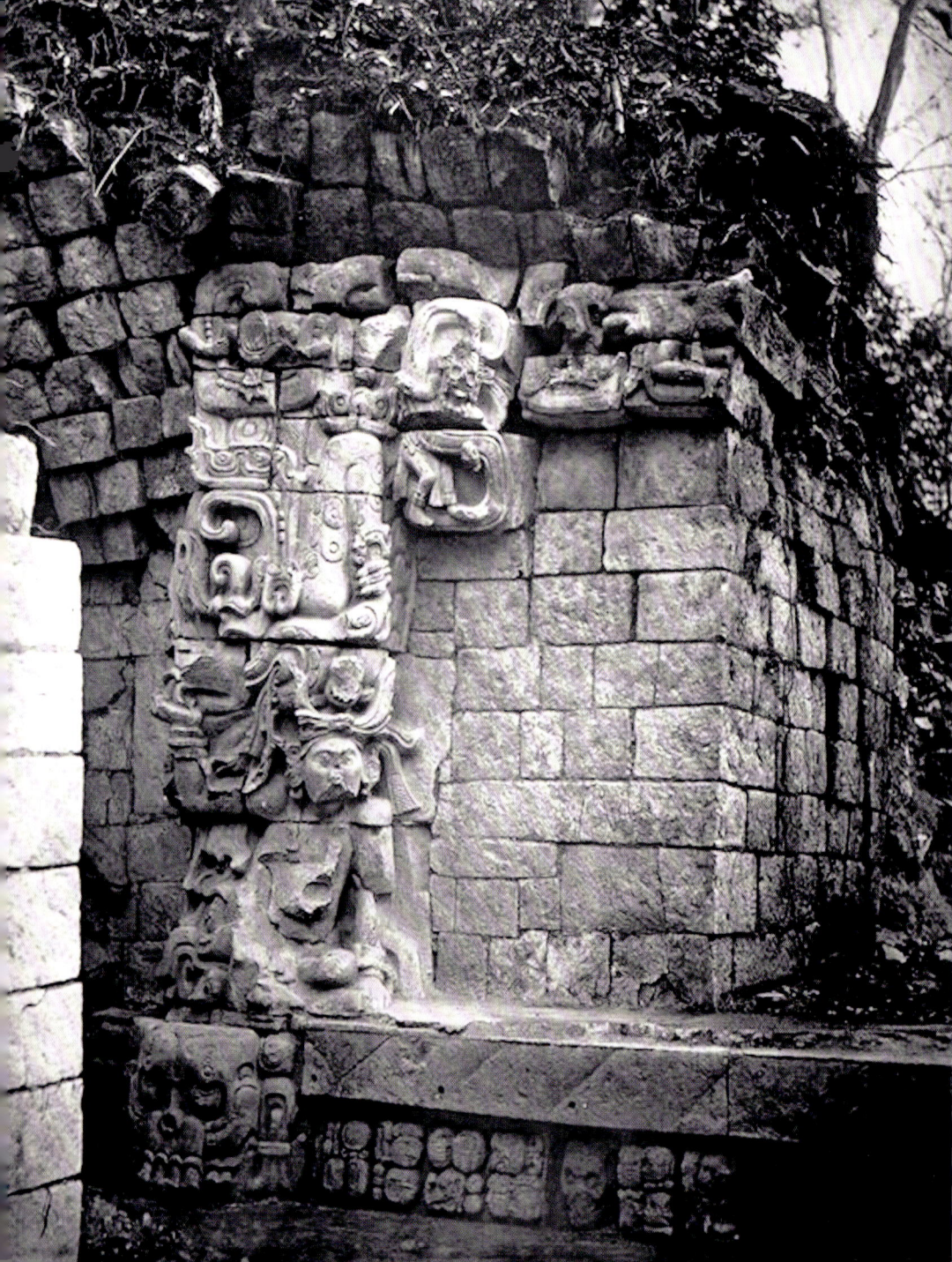

FIG. 90   West side of doorway leading to the inner chamber of the Temple, Copán.

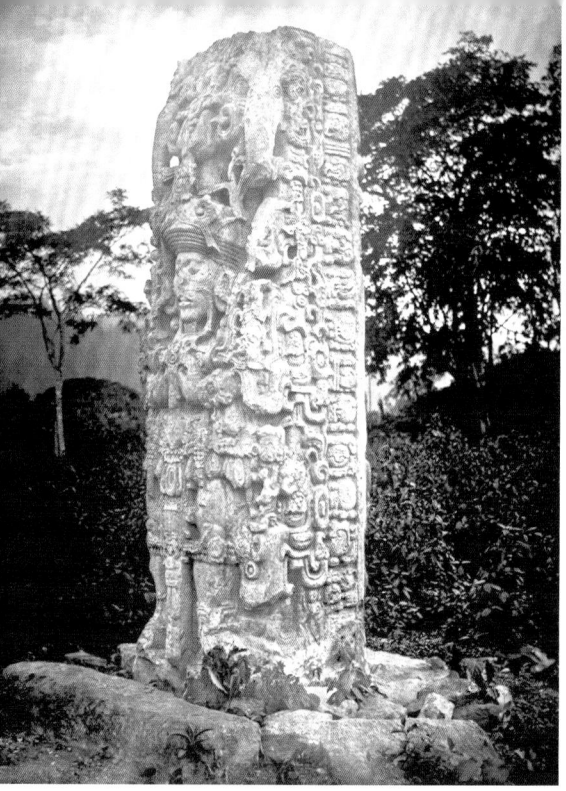

FIG. 91 Stela B, Copán. Maudslay's description of Stela B hearkens to some of the drawings done by the Comte de Waldeck and the elephants he saw in the hieroglyphs. Maudslay, however, was more circumspect: "The elephant-like appearance of these heads has been the subject of much discussion, but I fail to see any reason why the form may not have been taken from the head of a tapir, an animal still commonly found in the neighborhood. The exaggeration in the length of the nose or trunk is too common a feature in almost all the numerous grotesque heads found on these sculptures to call for any special comment in this case" (Maudslay, *Biologia Centrali-Americana*, p. 23).

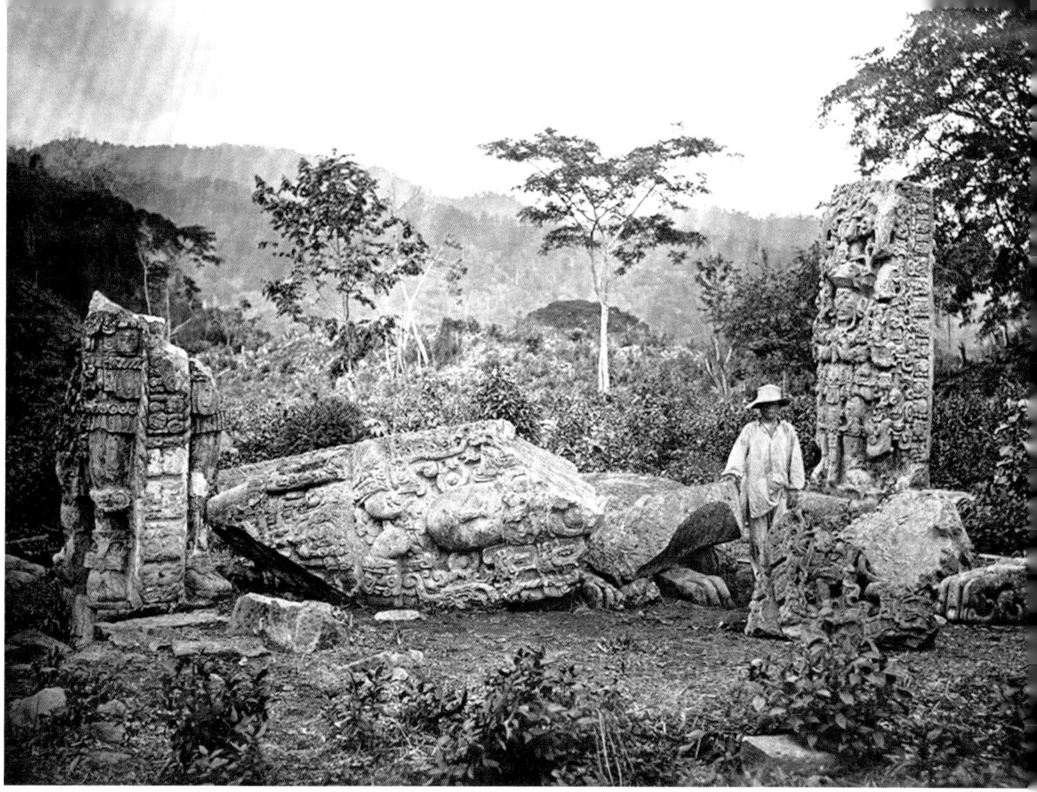

FIG. 92 East face of Stela C, Copán. The photograph of this stela gives little hint of the challenges that Maudslay faced in taking it. With the help of "pulleys and improvised shear-legs we were with difficulty able to raise the fallen portion so as to enable me to mould the glyphs on the underside and to obtain a photograph of the west side" (Maudslay, *Biologia*, p. 44).

Exposing the Maya

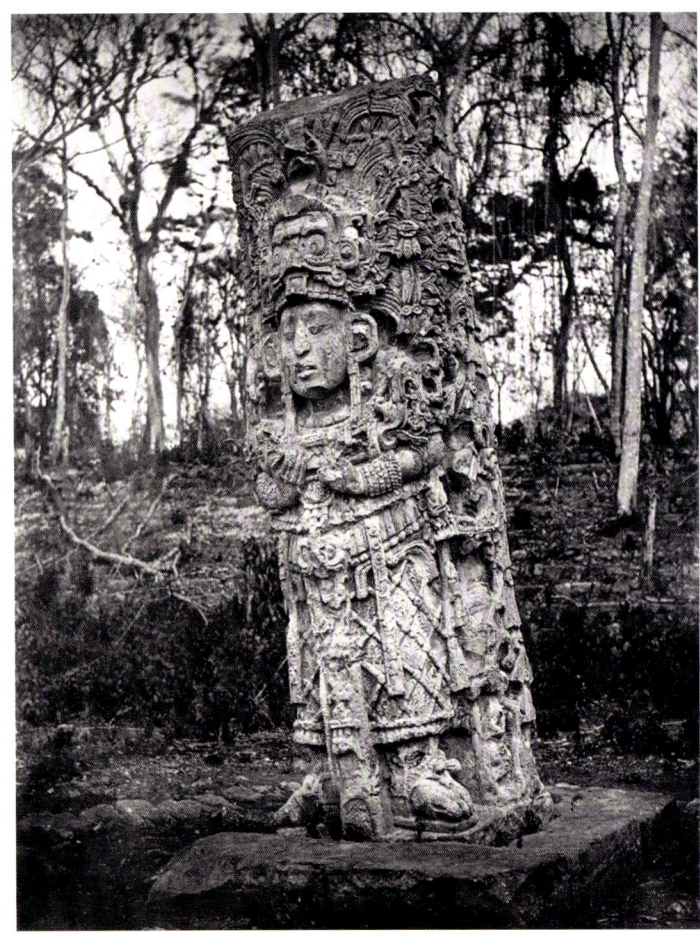

FIG. 93 Stela H, Copán. Maudslay was quite taken with this carving of the figure of a woman and the fact that the mode of dress, with a jaguar belt, was very much the same in many of the monuments. This carving is simpler, at least to his eye, with less ornate bracelets and simple sandals.

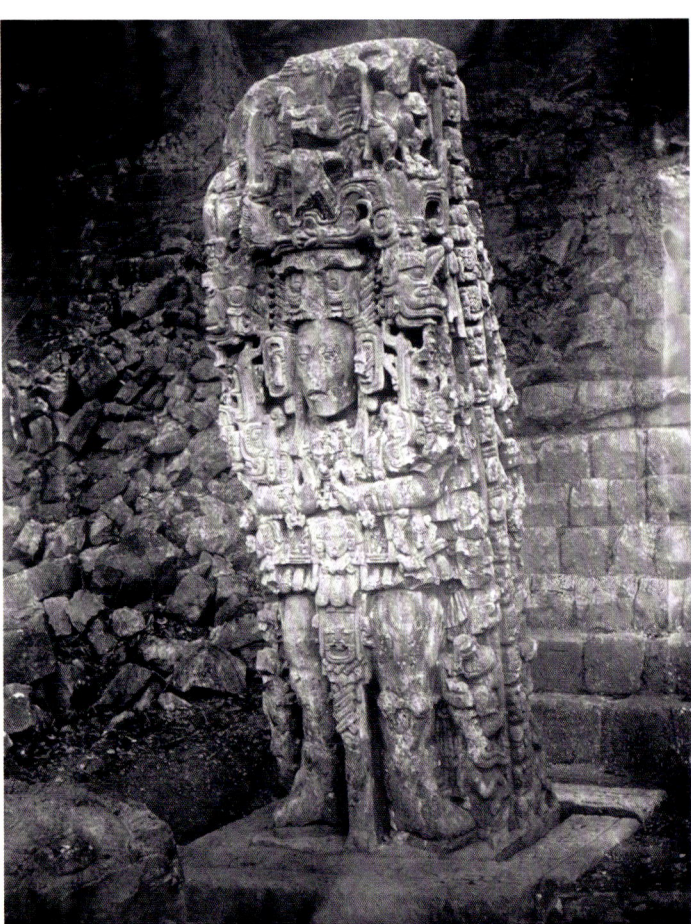

FIG. 94 North face of Stela N, Copán.

Alfred Maudslay (1850–1931)

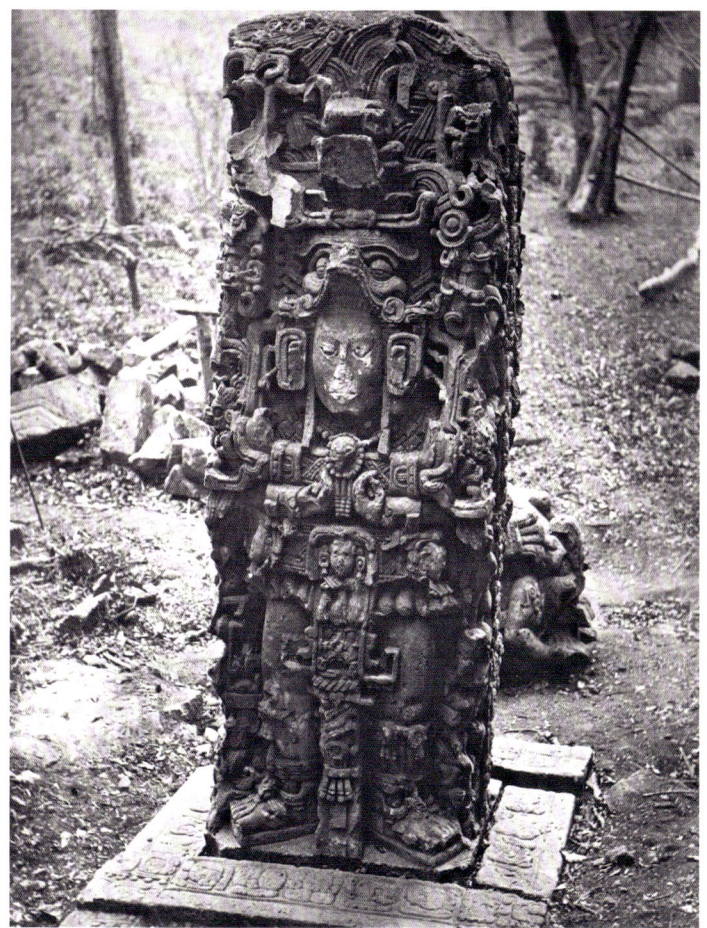

FIG. 95 South face of Stela N, Copán.

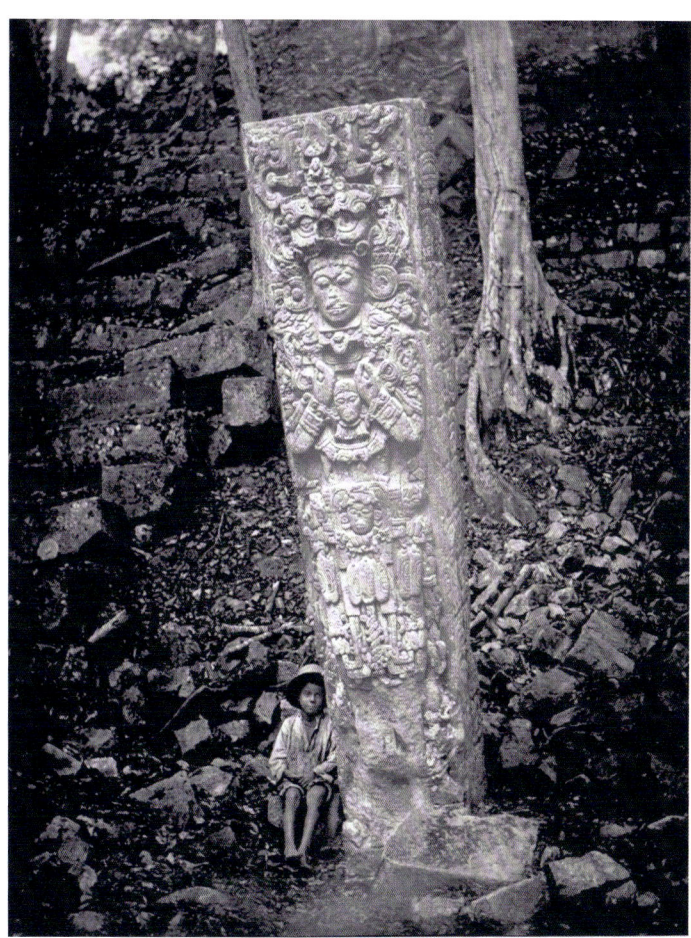

FIG. 96 West face of Stela P, Copán.

QUIRIGUÁ

The Great Turtle, as Maudslay named it, is a huge sculpture, which he notes must weigh nearly twenty tons. "It was not until the earth had been dug away from its base that the great hands or flippers could be seen, which proved the main design to be the representation of a great turtle."[4] The photograph depicts the molding of the turtle, which is more than seven feet high, 9 feet in length and 11 feet wide.

FIG. 97 East side of Monolithic Animal B, Quiriguá: "The drawing of this inscription has been a matter of the greatest difficulty, as the figures are so extraordinarily contorted and complicated" (Maudslay, *Biologia*, p. 9).

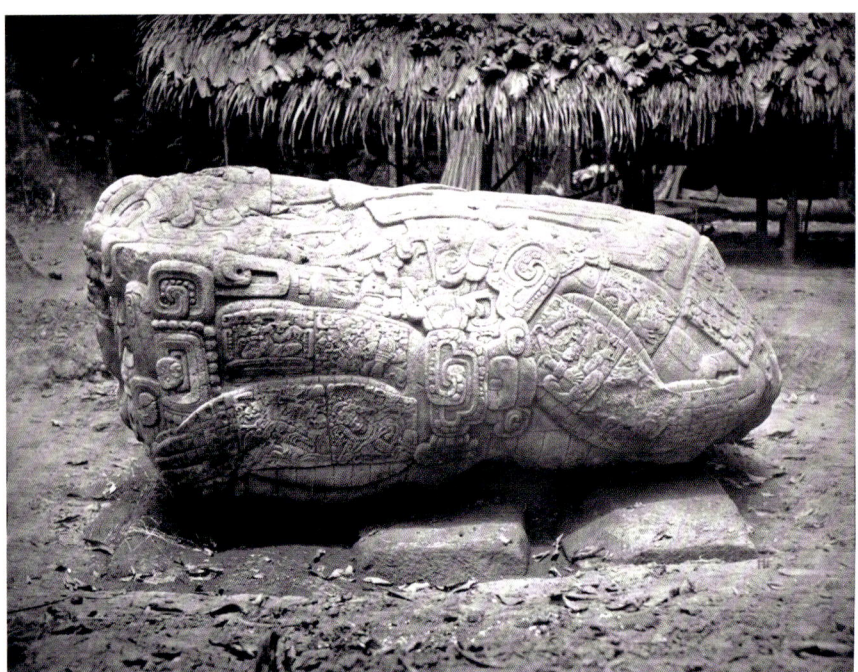

FIG. 98 North face of Stela D, Quiriguá.

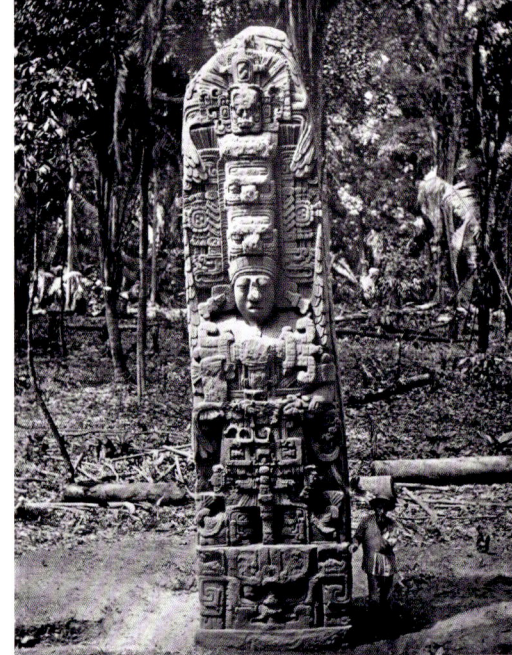

FIG. 99   Molding the Great Turtle, Quiriguá.

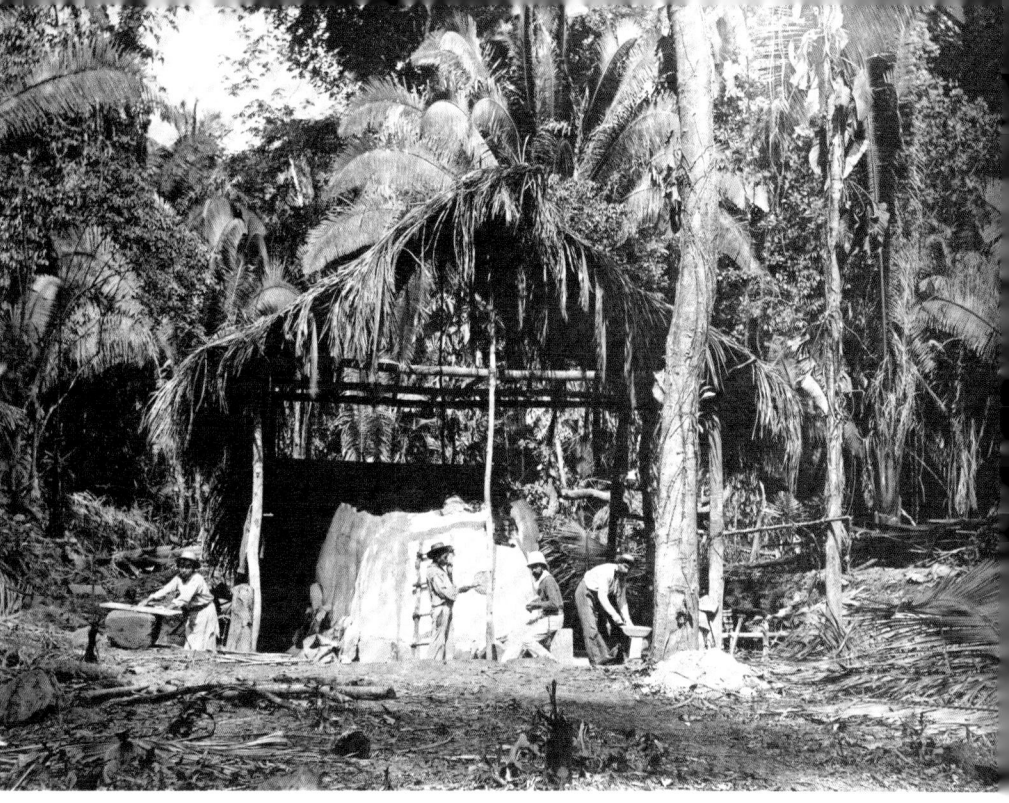

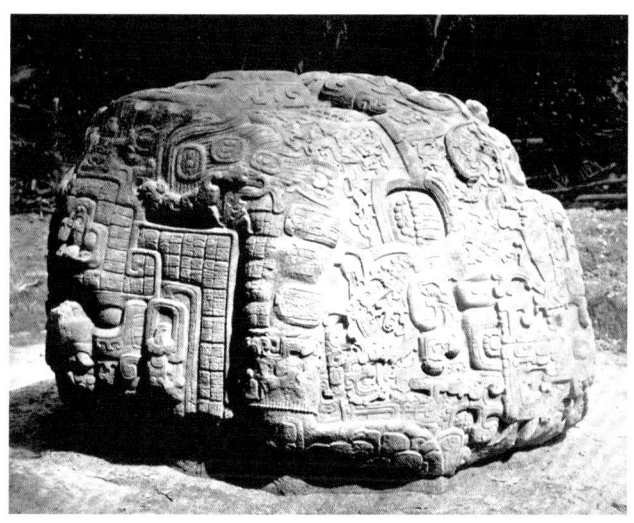

FIG. 100   South face and east side of the Great Turtle P, Quiriguá.

Exposing the Maya

FIG. 101 North face of the Great Turtle P, Quiriguá.

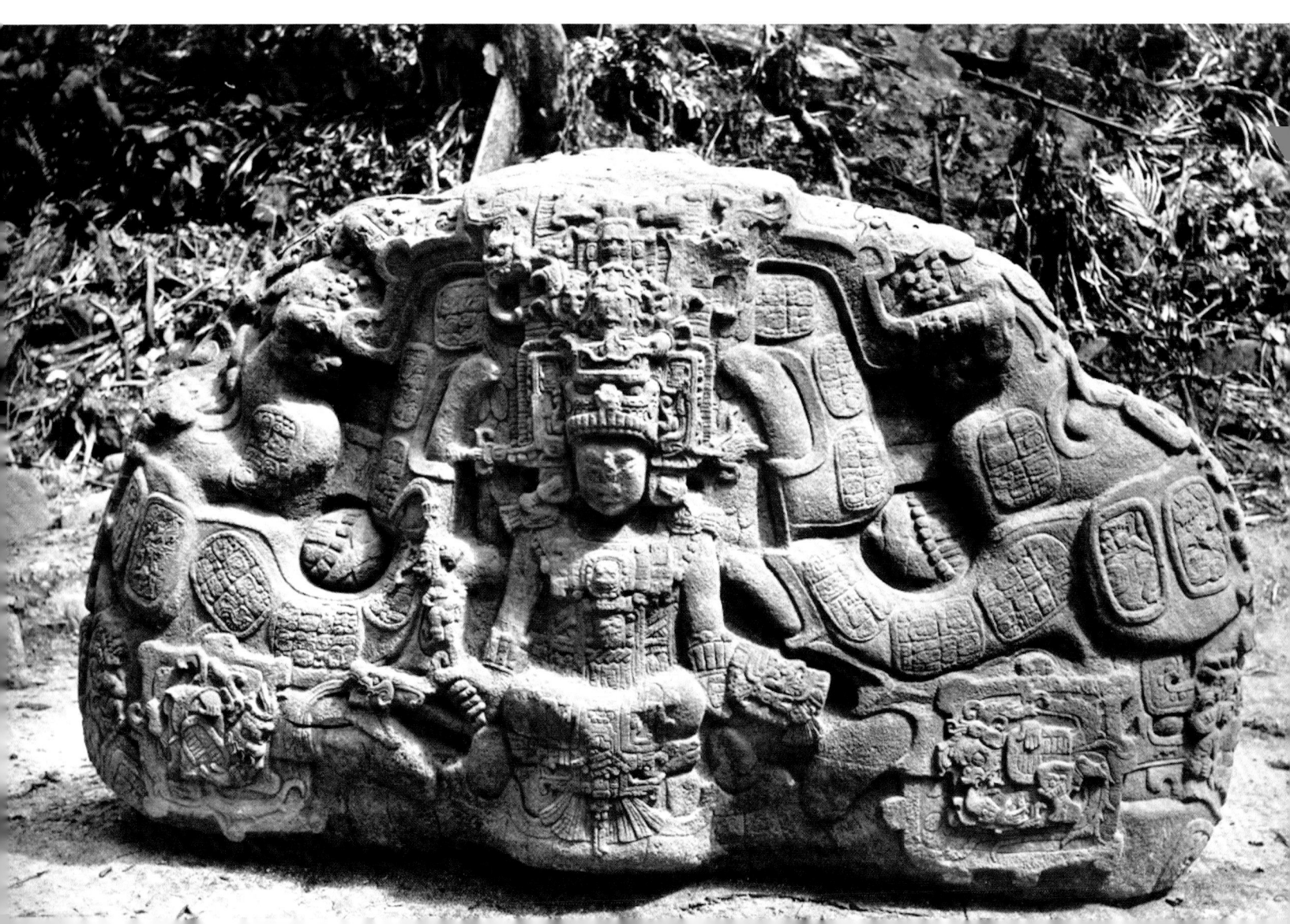

Alfred Maudslay (1850–1931)

CHICHÉN ITZÁ

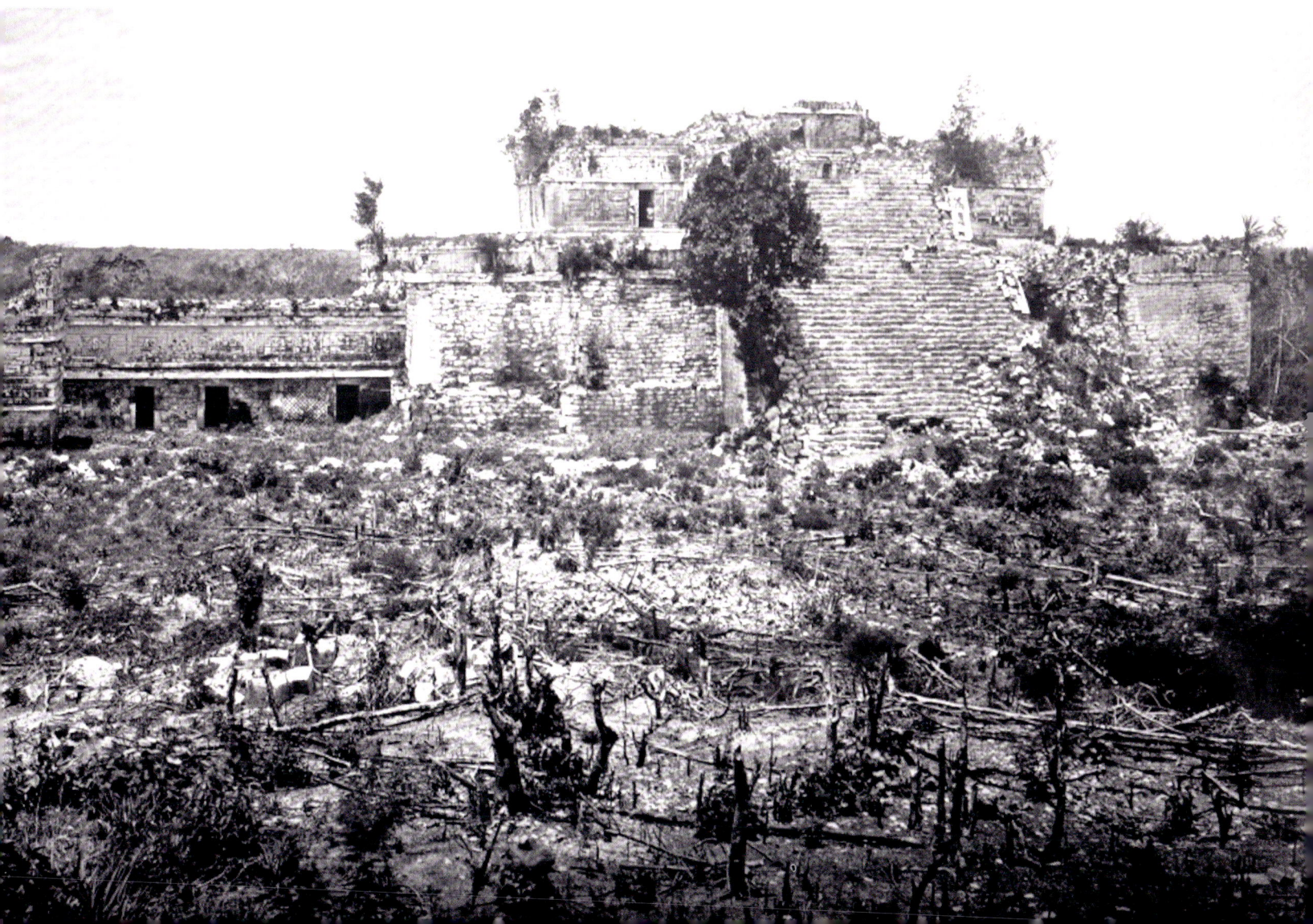

FIG. 102   North front of the Casa de Monjas, Chichén Itzá.

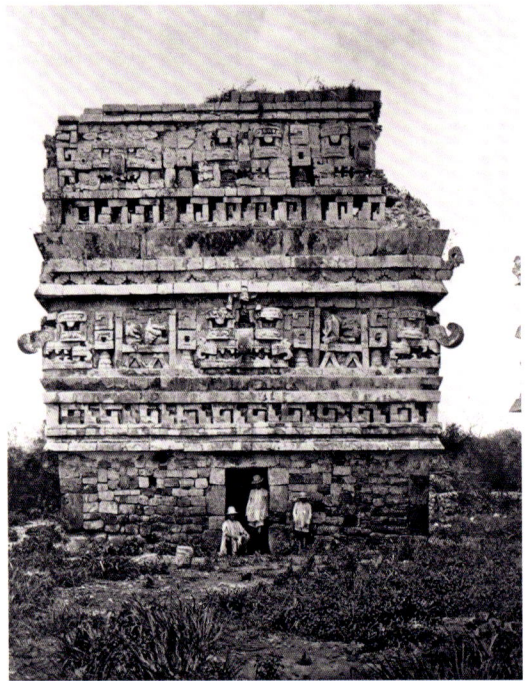

FIG. 103 Casa de Monjas, detached building from the west, Chichén Itzá.

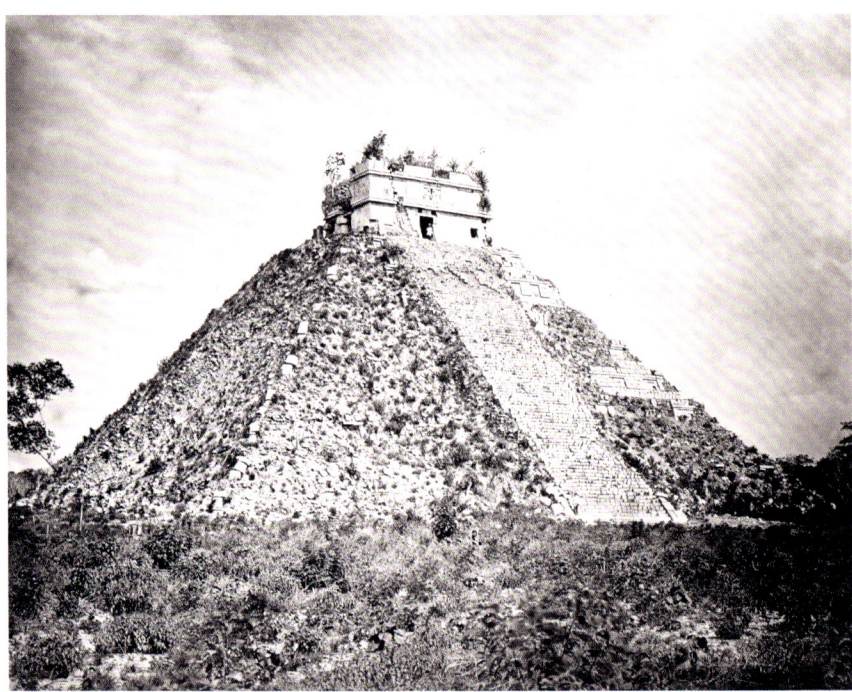

FIG. 104 El Castillo, looking southeast. Maudslay is at great pains to accurately measure the building's size, since "the large amount of fallen stone" prevents an accurate survey.

PALENQUE

"The sides of the foundation mound are so deeply covered with fallen stones and earth that there is difficulty in ascertaining their original shape." In order to accurately map and photograph the site, a great deal of work had to be done. Writing about his arrival at the Palace, Maudslay explains that he found "both the East and West Courts filled up almost completely to the level of the floors of the houses with broken masonry which had fallen from the surrounding buildings, and covered over with decaying trunks and a luxuriant vegetation."

FIG. 105 Southeast corner of the eastern court, the Palace, Palenque.

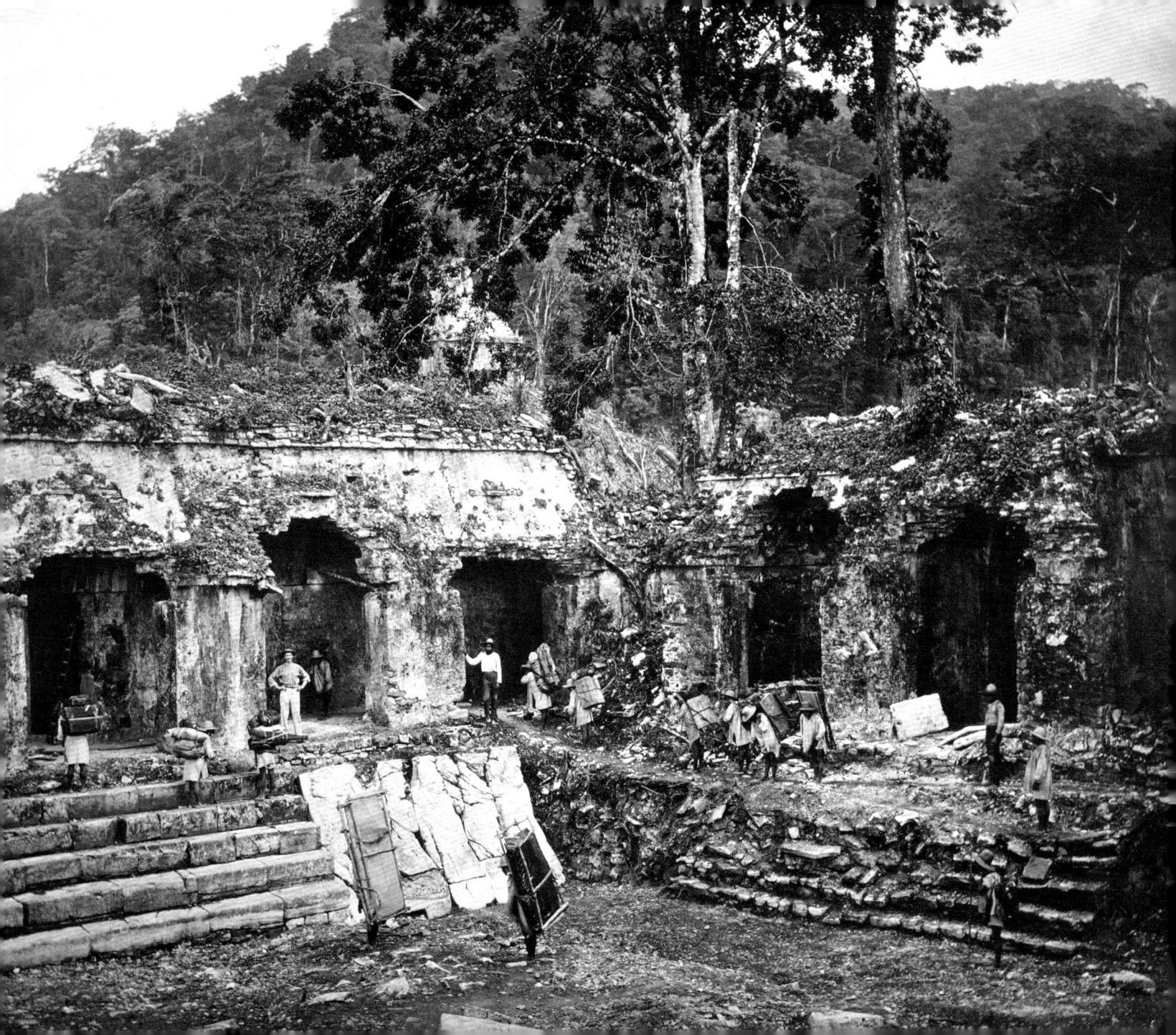

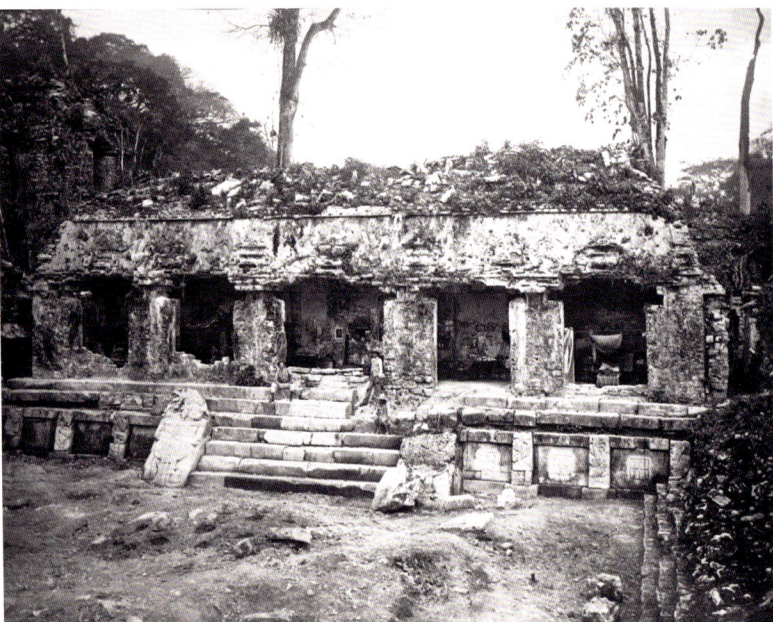

FIG. 106 East face of House C, the Palace, Palenque.

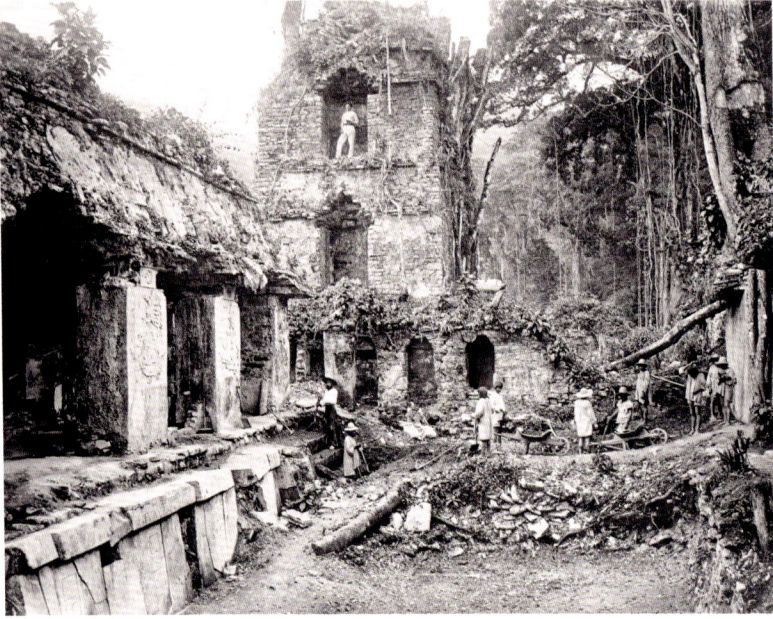

FIG. 107 Western court and tower, the Palace, Palenque, looking south, with Maudslay in the tower.

FIG. 108 House C and the tower, viewed from the western court, the Palace, Palenque.

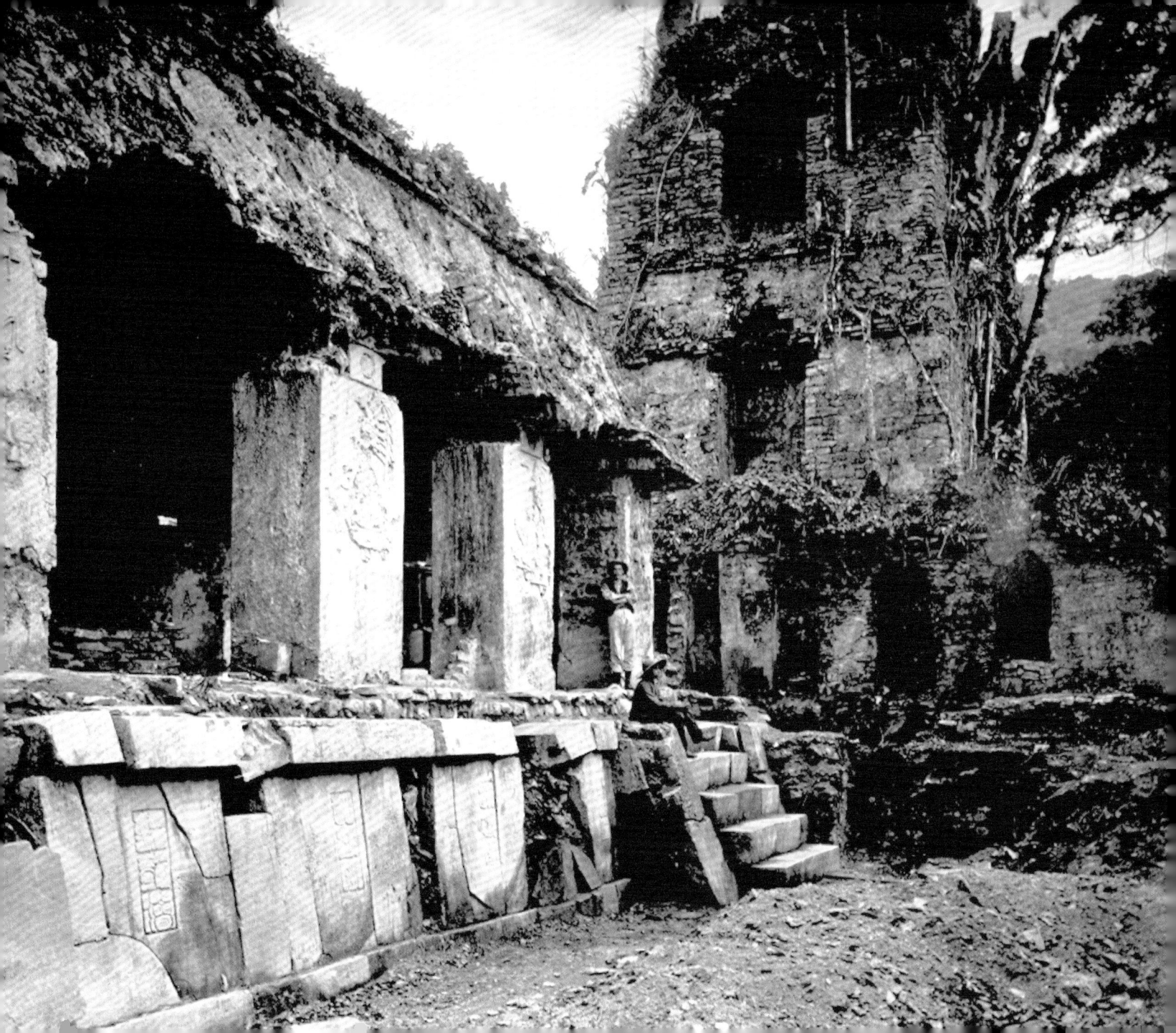

YAXCHILÁN

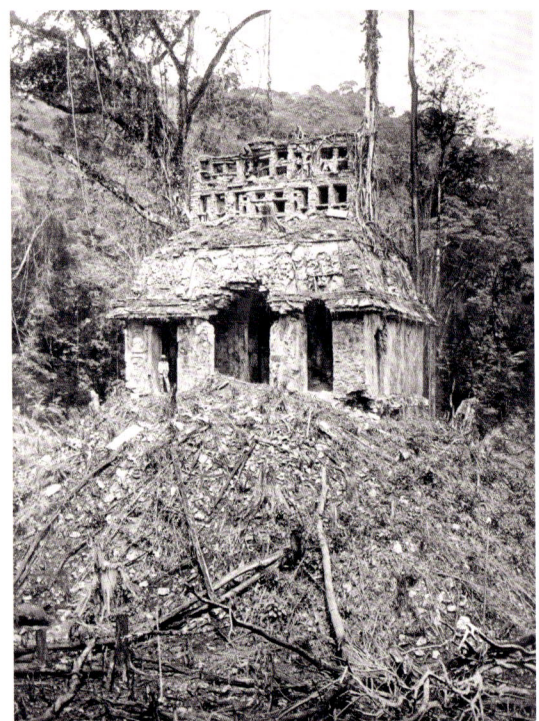

FIG. 109 Temple of the Sun, Palenque.

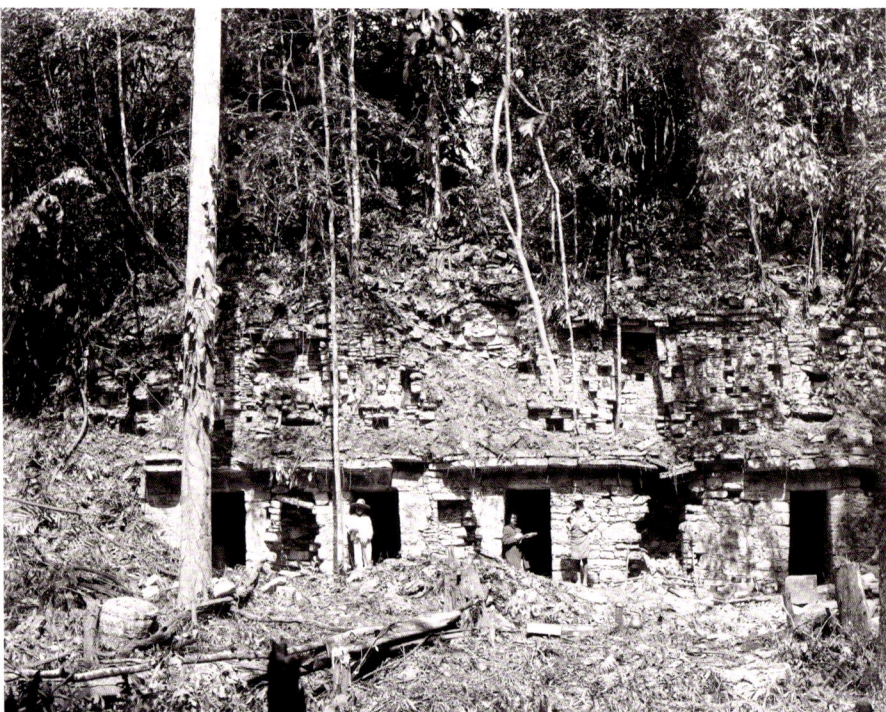

FIG. 110 Exterior view of House H, Yaxchilán. It was at Yaxchilán, called Menche in the *Biologia*, that Alfred Maudslay met Désiré Charnay and began supplementing his photographic documentation of the archaeological sites by making casts. It was also here that Maudslay came across a group of carved lintels that he removed and sent back to England, where they remain in the British Museum. Maudslay recounts his decision to take them in the *Biologia*, "In one of the half-ruined buildings we found a beautifully carved lintel fallen from its place and resting face downwards against the side of the doorway. This excellent example of Maya art I determined to carry home with me, and at once set my men to reduce the weight of the stone, which must have exceeded half a ton, cutting off the undecorated ends of the slab and reducing it in thickness" (Maudslay, *Biologia*, p. 42). Maudslay would several years later obtain "leave" from the Guatemalan government to remove many more lintels, which made their way along the Usumacinta River and, ultimately, onto the walls of the museum in Bloomsbury.

Alfred Maudslay (1850–1931)

FIG. 111 Lintel 15, Yaxchilán.

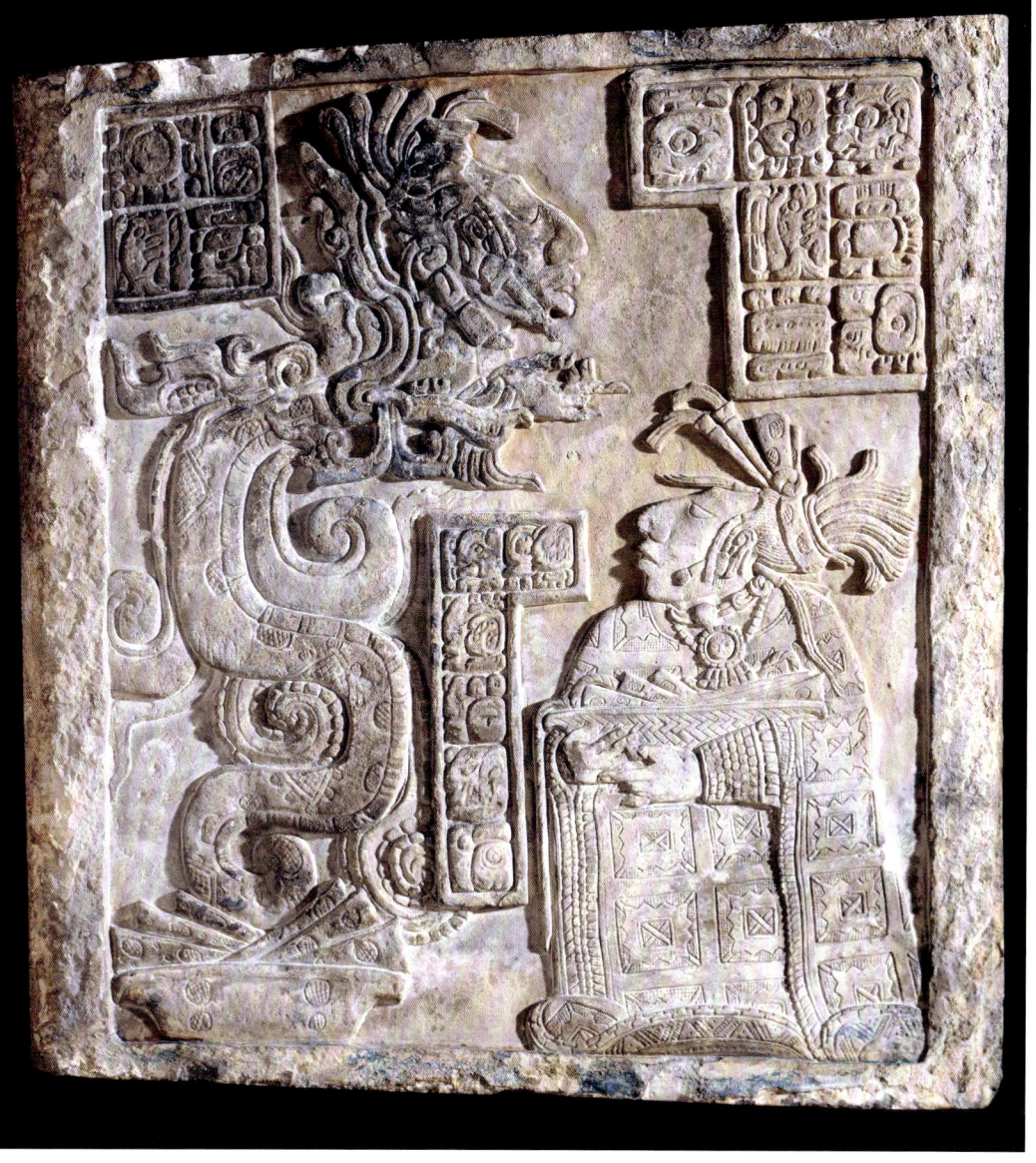

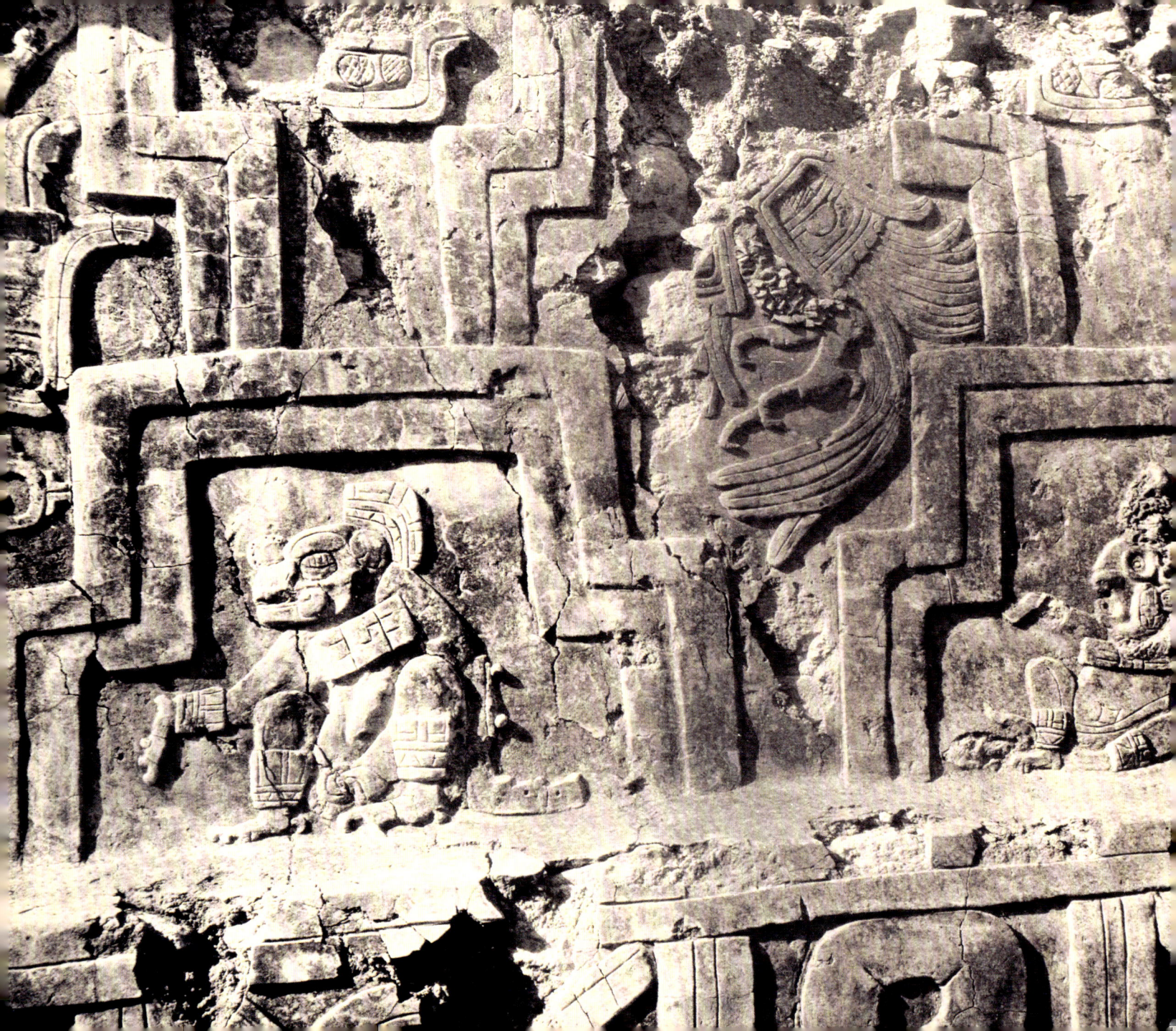

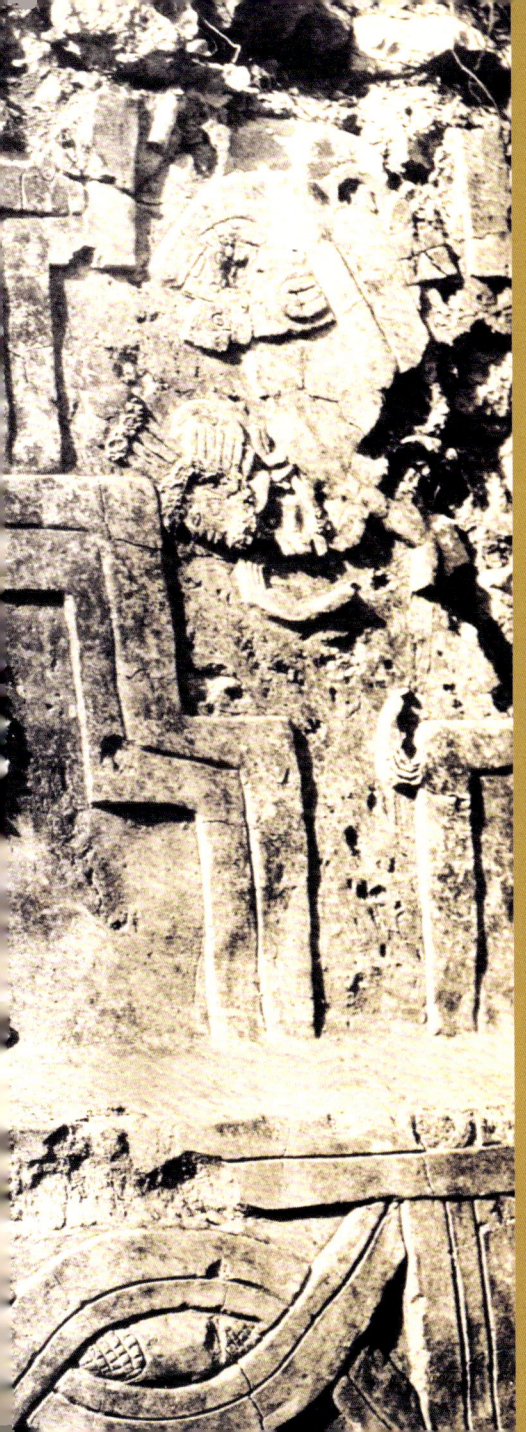

Adela Breton
(1849–1923)

Adela Breton is best known as a meticulous artist whose watercolors have preserved the colors and details of Mexican murals and frescoes that in most cases have not survived into the current age. Breton made a sudden, striking appearance in the world of Mesoamerican archaeology in 1894. We know little of her life before that date, other than that her family home was in Bath, in the west of England, that she had travelled to the Continent—most notably for her artistic training in Florence—and that she had dutifully cared for her aging parents until her widowed father's death in 1887 gave her the freedom and financial means to travel. By 1894 she had stepped onto the stage, traveling extensively throughout Mexico, with a particular focus on the western regions of the country—exploring, painting, drawing, and deepening her understanding of the ruins. At that time, she started working on frescoes that had been newly discovered at Teopancaxco, apparently at the behest of

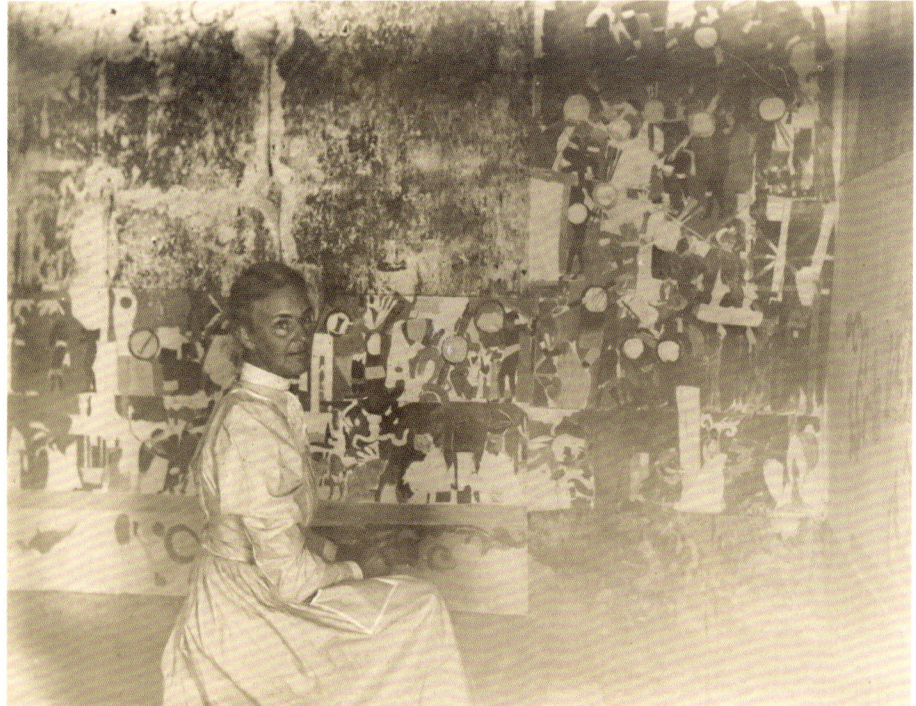

FIG. 112 Adela Breton in front of the temple mural in Chichén Itzá, Yucatán.

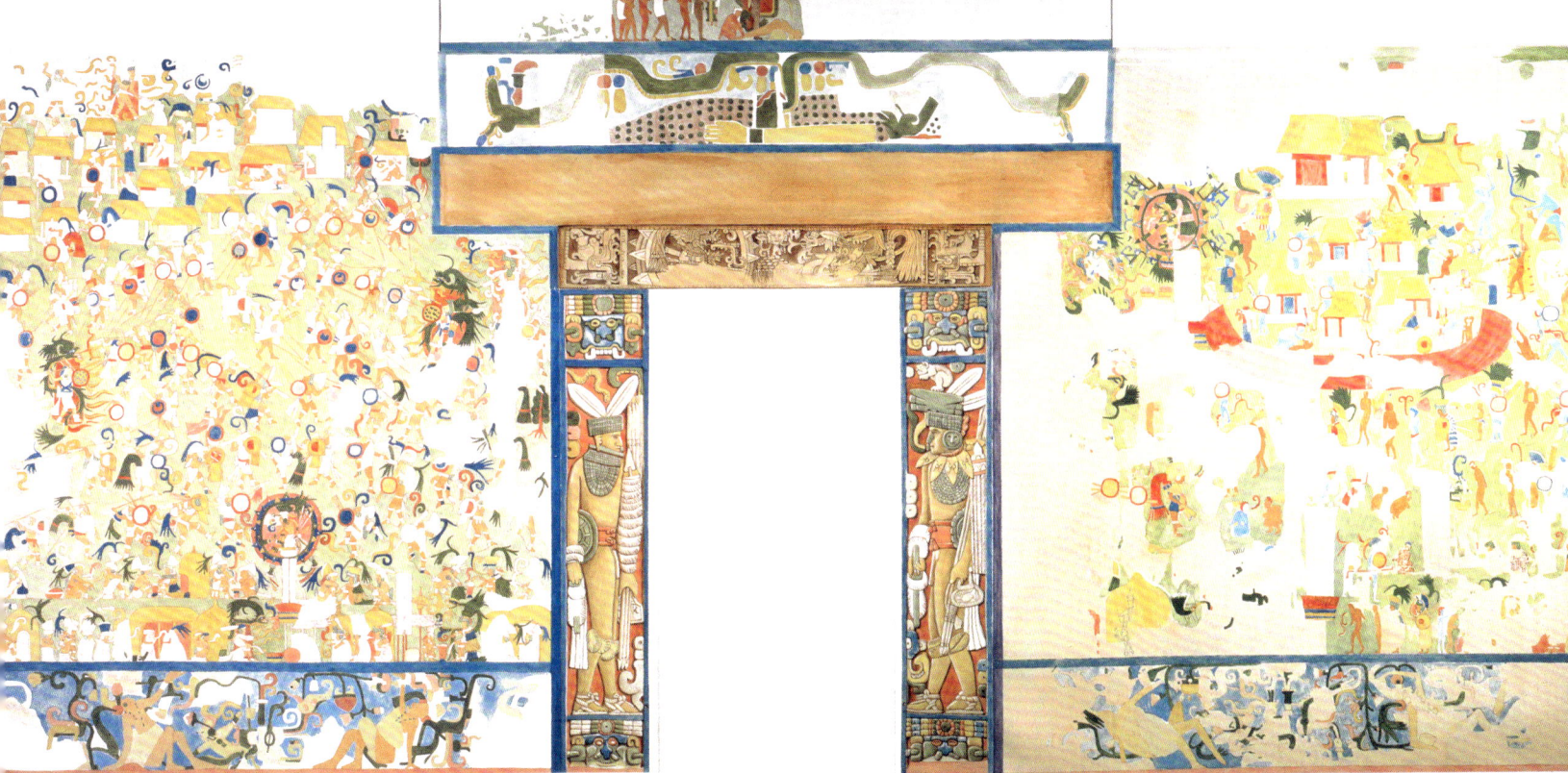

FIG. 113 Watercolor copy of the painting on the west wall of the inner (or 'painted') chamber of the Temple of the Jaguars, Chichén Itzá.

Alfred Maudslay. Thus, at the age of forty-five, she embarked on a new career, one in which she would be solicited by all the major actors in the field. By the time she came on the scene, Charnay, the Le Plongeons, Maler, and Maudslay had all preceded her to Chichén Itzá. Breton made her invaluable contribution there, creating images of the frescoes and murals at the site. Over several years she worked to rescue the wall paintings of Chichén "from oblivion, recording them before they disappeared entirely."[1]

Breton's work brought forth something that photography could not provide the scholars in the field. She copied fragile paintings that were poorly protected and could not be fully captured by photography, which was unable to render color or objects in dark spaces. She also came to believe that visualizing these ancient artefacts in their original color was key to understanding the culture that created them. Breton was a photographer in her own right, but one who used the medium purely as a tool for producing realistic reproductions of the work of earlier Mesoamerican artists in the form of illustrations. She also used her photographs, as well as those of others from the sites she visited, to provide accurate colors using the technique of hand-coloring photographic plates. Hers is a fascinating case study in how photography and illustration worked together to capture the fading remnants of this past civilization. But, unlike the earlier prophets of photography as the objective witness that faithfully reproduces reality, Breton's work makes evident that there were limits to the technology's ability to fully expose the vestiges of the past.

THE WALL PAINTINGS AT CHICHÉN ITZÁ[2]

Students of Central American archeology have scarcely as yet appreciated the important part that painting formerly played in the decorative art of the region. The first explorers were overwhelmed by the grandeur and strangeness of the ruins and were too fully occupied in making plans of the structures, and mould of the reliefs and monoliths, to have time for more than hasty notes of the colors of them. This was unfortunate, for where the buildings were covered with debris, when first excavated, the colours were often fresh, and exposure to the weather has since destroyed them.

From the remains still visible, it is evident that all the sculptured parts were coloured and that the colours were more or less symbolic. Those people *saw* in colour and light and shade. That is why mere outline copies of the sculptures, and casts set up in a light for which they were not intended, give a very inadequate idea of the actual effect. The color is also a great help towards understanding the subjects.

At Chichen Itza there was a remarkable development of Art; not only were the columns, door posts and interior walls of some of the buildings covered with coloured reliefs representing personages and events, but many chambers were entirely painted in fresco with historical scenes.

These wall paintings are of the highest interest, not only from the point of view of archeology but from that of Art. In color, drawing and design they can hold their own any where, although to a modern eye they may appear quaint and childlike as do those of the Early Italian school. As they are, unfortunately, much destroyed, they cannot be seen fairly in a hurried visit, but after studying them day by day, and when the light is good, one comes to feel a great admiration for artists who could as skillfully transfer the bright harmonious tints of their sunset skies to an intractable material like plaster.

Mr. Thompson,[3] Dr. L. Plongeon and Mr. Maudslay copied some portions of these paintings, but from various reasons their copies have not become known as they deserved, and it was at Mr. Maudslay's suggestion that I attempted the great task of copying the whole series.

The Casa de la Monjas[4] retains only a small part of its paintings, in a small upper chamber and in the vault of the large chamber on the same terrace. […] In Temple A. (or Temple of the Tigers) the walls of the outer chamber were painted, but owing to the roof having fallen in, they were exposed to the weather and only a few round shields are now left, showing that the subjects were battles as in the inner chamber. This latter has suffered from the local tourist who has written names all over it, and also from copyists who have outlined the figures in pencil, or worse still, with a red line which at first sight appears original until one sees that it crosses gaps in the plaster. Still, with care and patience something can be saved from the wreck which becomes each year more deplorable, now that the removal of the trees and plants which protected the exterior allows the tropic rains to pour down the walls.

The paintings were not the first decoration of the building. Traces of a previous coat can be seen here and there, showing a kind of diaper pattern in red and blue. But they were done a sufficiently long time before the place was abandoned for a crack in the plaster to have required mending and recolouring. There are also *graffiti* scratched in the plaster by ancient devotees.

METHOD. - There were certainly two artists employed, and their methods were different. One was a master who knew exactly what he meant to do, and did it in a calm methodical way, with certainty and swiftness of brush in the sweeping outlines. The other, more impetuous, dashed in figures just as they came into his head, after he had fixed the positions of the shields. These positions (at any rate on the south wall) are not haphazard, and it might be worth while for a mathematician or astronomer to study them. This artist understood how to place one tint over another to give a rich and glowing effect. He put in few outlines, and the greater part of his work is in dry colour which comes off easily, or peels away in patches. I attribute to him about half the work,—the north and south walls, and the middle and north end of the east wall.

Exposing the Maya

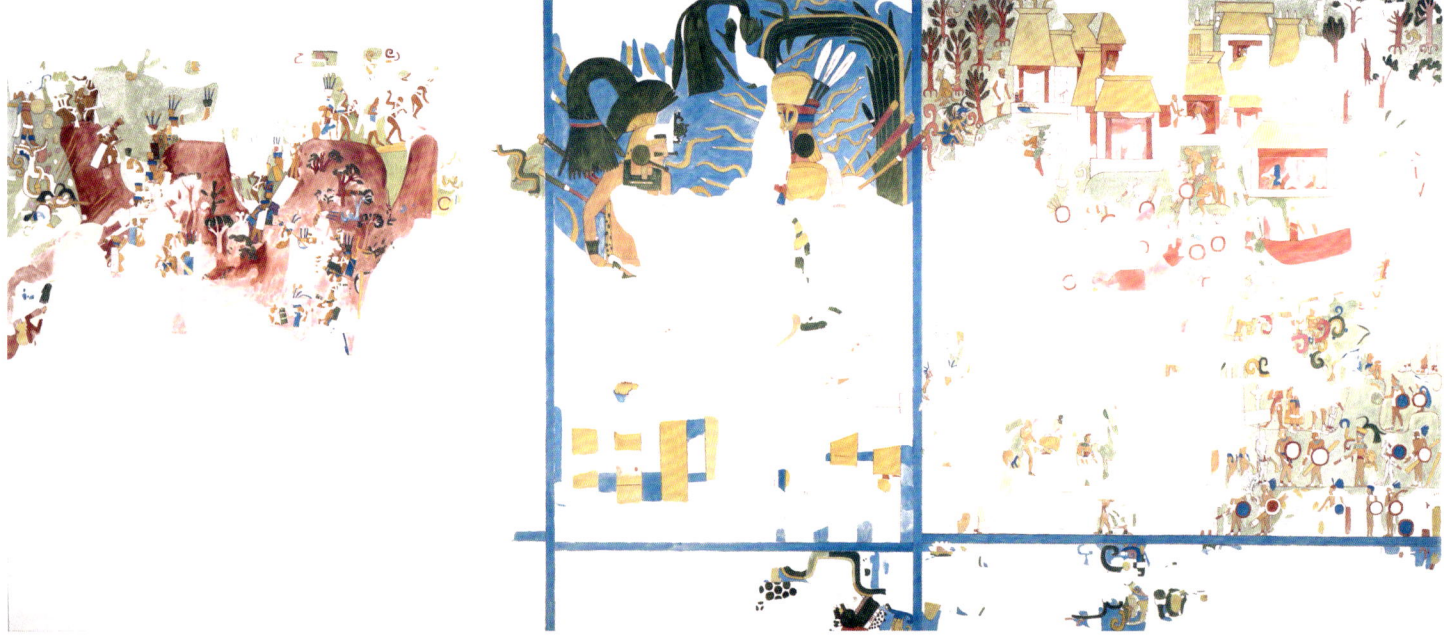

The other artist drew all his figures carefully in red outline on the damp plaster, and also, in true fresco fashion put on this chief masses of color while the plaster was damp. This helps to give the delightful varied effect of the tints, only enough colour being mixed for each day's work. Then the details were added in dry colours. Few of these are left, and the devices of the shields have been almost entirely obliterated by modern visitors to insert their own names.

COLOR USED. – Two reds, two blues, four greens, yellow, white, black, and a purplish tint, and various tones of flesh colour, were used, and although there is no attempt at shading, they are so skilfully contrasted that there is a strong effect of relief. One figure will be light against the ground and another dark. It is only when copying them that one can appreciate the art with which each colour is added to enhance the brilliance and harmony of the whole, as one does in copying Turner's best water colours. It will be understood that these copies give but a poor idea of the glow of soft warm color when the sun shines in through the narrow door on an

FIG. 114   Painting of the sculptured stone altar in the outer chamber, Temple of the Jaguars, Chichén Itzá.

afternoon in April or May. Very many of the figures are now mere vague patches of colour, and I have not tried to re-draw them or to do more than reproduce the present fragmentary appearance of the original.

DESCRIPTION. – The long walls of the east and west sides are each divided into three panels. On the west, there is one over the door and those on either side. We suppose that the series begins with the south-west panel, the first to the right on entering. Dr. Le Plongeon has described this in his book, *Queen Moo*.[5] The personages in feather mantles recall the statues which upheld the sculptured stone table in the outer chamber.

The south wall is particularly interesting as it shows the methods of attacking lofty places. There are three scaffold-towers on which are warriors, whilst others are climbing a great ladder made by notching a long tree-trunk. The personages floating in the air above the houses at the top of this panel will be observed. Part of the painting in the vault is left at this end, with the scene of a sacrifice, and some lean prisoners at one corner. Especially noteworthy are the high narrow white banner like Tibetan prayer-flags near the bottom of this wall.

The east wall has in its centre panel two life-sized personages, one the same as the central figure on the sculptured wall of Chamber E. (the lower Temple of the Tigers), the other, perhaps the hero laid out at the bottom of this panel, and also in the panel above the Lintel [sic] and in the border of the North Building of the Ball-Court. The great feathered serpent appears to be in reversed position with his head downwards, judging from the feathers. In the southern panel of this wall, which is very much destroyed, there are several animals and birds amongst the trees on the sides of the fortified villages. The northern panel has a series of hills with attacking and defending forces. Here the artist evidently gave a variety of trees and rocks in the landscape, but scarcely anything remains.

On the north wall there is a sun-disk in the centre at the top, and a number of perhaps mythical personages who look as if they had come out of some illuminated manuscript with their curious red backgrounds and flourishes. Here the green ground rises diagonally from the bottom to the top. The colours of the figures and the sky are peculiarly rich.

The north end of the west wall has an attack by blue-bodied warriors on a village defended by a fortification coloured red like that of the south east panel. This red object was at first called a canoe until Mr. Maudslay showed that all the houses were inside it, and then it was found that similar representations of defences were to be seen on the so-called slate "palettes" of ancient Egypt.

The border or dado round the lower part of the walls is somewhat similar to those of chamber E. and the North Building. It has personages whom one may perhaps call mythological, entwined with flowery "speeches." The small personage in both borders of the west wall is the same who occurs as a sort of Punchinello in many reliefs as at Palenque and Quirigua.

There is a great variety of types. Some warriors are very tall and athletic, especially those descending on the South wall, with red feather headdresses. Others are short and plump as in the south west panel. Some profiles have been preserved, though as a rule the shield is so held as almost to cover the face, and where it is visible, the eye has usually been destroyed. There are two good profiles on the Red Hills and some in the south-east panel, and the two lama-like persons on a roof in the corner of the south west panel. The flesh-tints vary from the pale yellow of the sun-disk personages and the women to the dark brown of the defenders of the Red Hills, and of the chiefs sitting before their hut-doors in the bottom row of the south wall.

The speeches have yet to be interpreted though one may suppose that the warriors cry "Victory or Death" when their speeches are a flourish of red and blue. A man at the top of the south west panel whose atlatl is held downwards as a sign of defeat, has a dejected-looking speech, somewhat like that of a man with bound arms in a Mont Alban relief.

Alice Le Plongeon: "Dr. Le Plongeon's Latest and Most Important Discoveries among the Ruined Cities of Yucatan"

In October and November 1875, the Le Plongeons had worked on clearing out what they called Casa del Tigre (House of the Tiger) and later the Chacmool Monument and that is now called the Upper Temple of the Jaguars. Alice Le Plongeon wrote of this excavation:

A thorough excavation brought to light a stone altar; the upper part, or table, consisted of two stones fifteen centimeters thick, that together were two meters ten centimeters square, or be it six feet ten inches. Most unhappily the roof, in falling, broke the table into fragments; nevertheless, as the piece remained in place, it is not difficult to see that it was sculptured in bas-relief, representing two men, one seated, the other standing. The edge of the table is also exquisitely carved, showing priests in various postures making offerings; of the parts least injured Dr. Le Plongeon made moulds. Smashed, even pulverized in some parts by the enormous stones, weighing hundreds of pounds, that fell on it, the table yet served to protect fifteen figures that supported it as caryatides. These were placed three abreast, five deep, with their arms upraised. They are eighty-five centimeters high, fifty centimeters wide at the top, and thirty-five at the base. Except in their position, there are not two alike in any respect. The outermost ones have their noses broken, but those within are perfect as if just from the master's hand. They are very interesting and important, showing, as they do, the features, ornaments, and dresses of those people, for the artists paid little attention to the body, bestowing the utmost skill and care on the face, ornaments, and dress. The heads are well shaped, disproving again the assertion of some writers that the Mayas deformed their skulls. [...]

All the caryatides have head dresses on which are chiseled with great delicacy various designs, some figuring mosaic work, that those people used to ornament their dresses, made of bone, shell, ivory and such substances, cut in various shapes, and painted with bright colors. Other headgears are covered with feathers, the lines exquisitely fine; and the back of each figure is sculptured to imitate a mantle of feathers, but in each the feathers are differently arranged. Their hair is cut short in front and combed straight, to come partly over the forehead; thus, we see that it is a very old fashion to *bang* the hair. The eyes are two-thirds natural size; some are decidedly feminine, and their dress seems to be that of women. The eyes are open, foreheads broad, noses correct in shape according to our present ideas of beauty, some quite small and fine; lips thin and firm. Some have the upper row of teeth visible, and they are small and even, not filed like a saw, so that fashion was evidently not compulsory, though some followed it, as we learn from the Chaacmol statue and others. All have ornaments in their noses, and some of them consist of two small disks, linked by a tiny straight bar. It is very possible that these links were made of some metallic substance. Besides the ornaments fastened on the nostrils, several have one hanging from the cartilage, down over the lips. As well as disfiguring a pretty face, it must have been most uncomfortable, and shows that people in those times made themselves the foolish slaves of fashion just as now.

Exposing the Maya

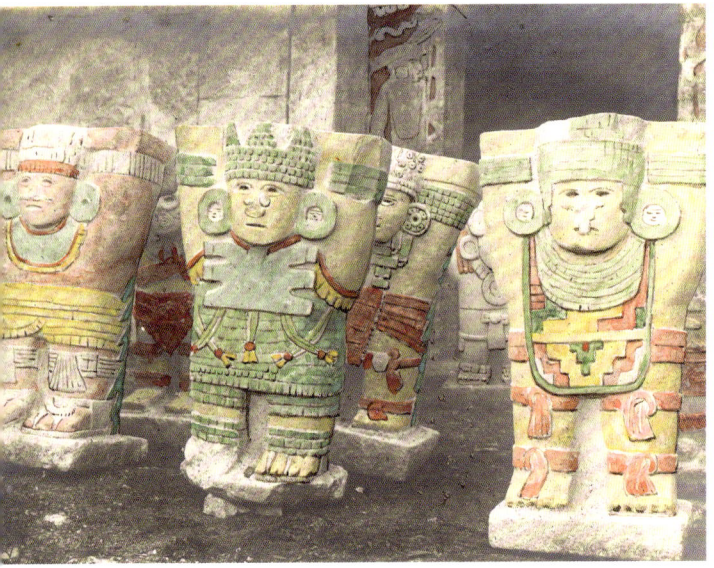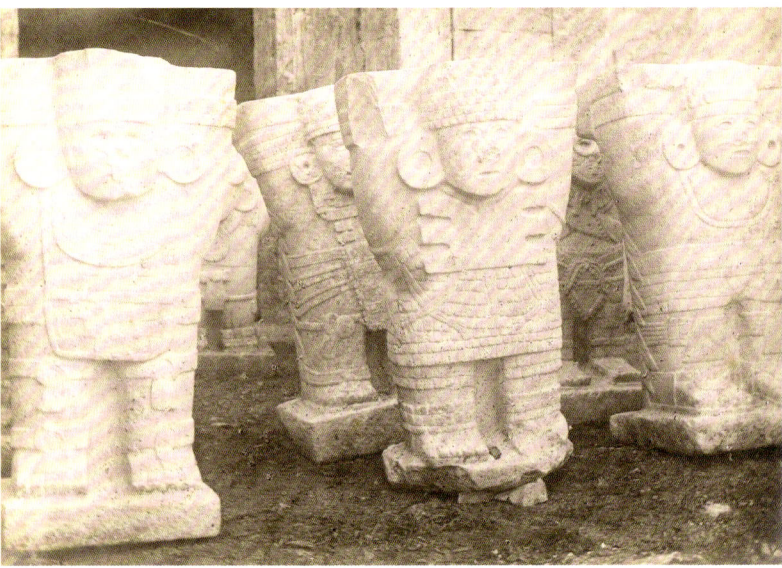

One face is so covered that the features can hardly be seen; two serpent heads face each other on the forehead and their bodies encircle the eyes; other snake bodies surround the mouth, the beads resting on the cheeks. [...] The toenails of these figures have fallen out; for the Maya artists made nails and eyes of shell for their statues, which were also painted in vivid colors. The feet are shod with sandals, each fastened with a different bow knot, or clasp. From their necks are suspended badges, necklaces, and other ornaments. One has an animal carved on the badge. Some have handsome waist belts, and three-cornered aprons, trimmed in diverse manners, especially with flat plaiting.[6]

FIG. 115   Retouched photograph of caryatids V, VI, IX, X, XIV and XV from Temple A, Chichén Itzá.

FIG. 116   Photograph of caryatids from Temple A, Chichén Itzá.

Chichén Itzá 1900 [Adela Breton]

When I came to Chichen in 1900 I saw a piece of engraved stone and asked Mr. Maudslay and Mr. E. Thompson, owner of the property in Chichen, of what it was part. They did not know about the existence of the altar, but, helped by the picture published in 'Queen Moo' I looked around and little by little gathered

Adela Breton (1849–1923)

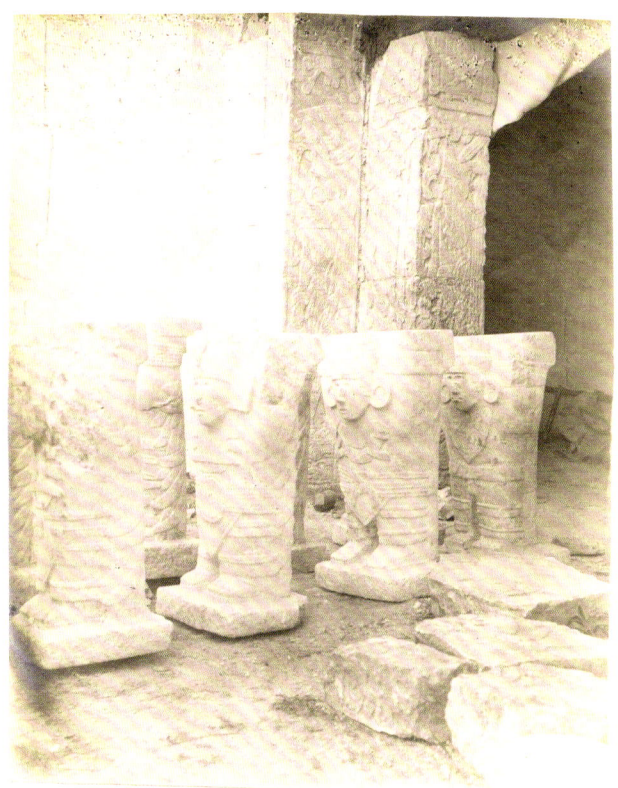

FIG. 117 Photograph of caryatids I, II, III, IV and VIII from Temple A, Chichén Itzá.

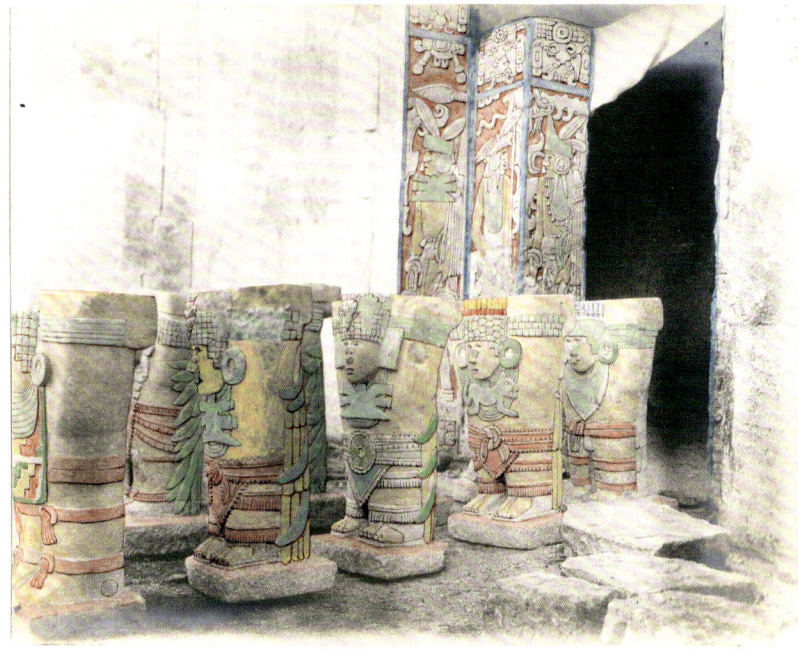

FIG. 118 Photograph retouched with watercolor of caryatids I, II, III, IV, V and IX from Temple A, Chichén Itzá.

enough pieces to reconstruct the altar table in part. [...] Once the table of the altar had been found, we had to look for the statues. I talked about them with [...] the Inspector of the ruins, and he noticed observantly that one of the stones in the floor seemed to be loose. He started digging with his labourers and there they found the fifteen statues, in good condition, having been very carefully buried by Dr. Le. P.[7]

Exposing the Maya

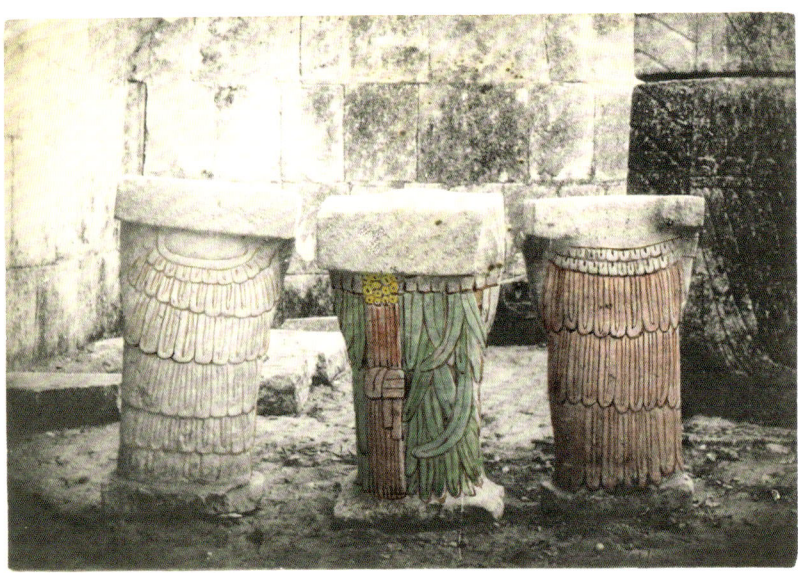

FIG. 119 Photograph retouched with watercolor of caryatids XI, XIII and XII from the outer chamber, Temple A, Chichén Itzá.

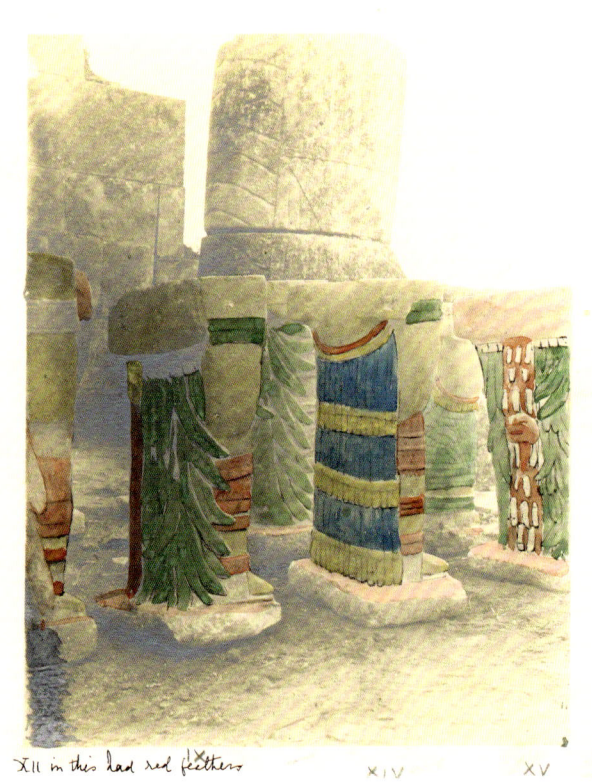

FIG. 120 Photograph retouched with watercolor of caryatids XV, XIV, IX and XII from the outer chamber, Temple A, Chichén Itzá.

Adela Breton (1849–1923)

FIG. 121 Watercolor of caryatid X, Chichén Itzá, showing front and back views.

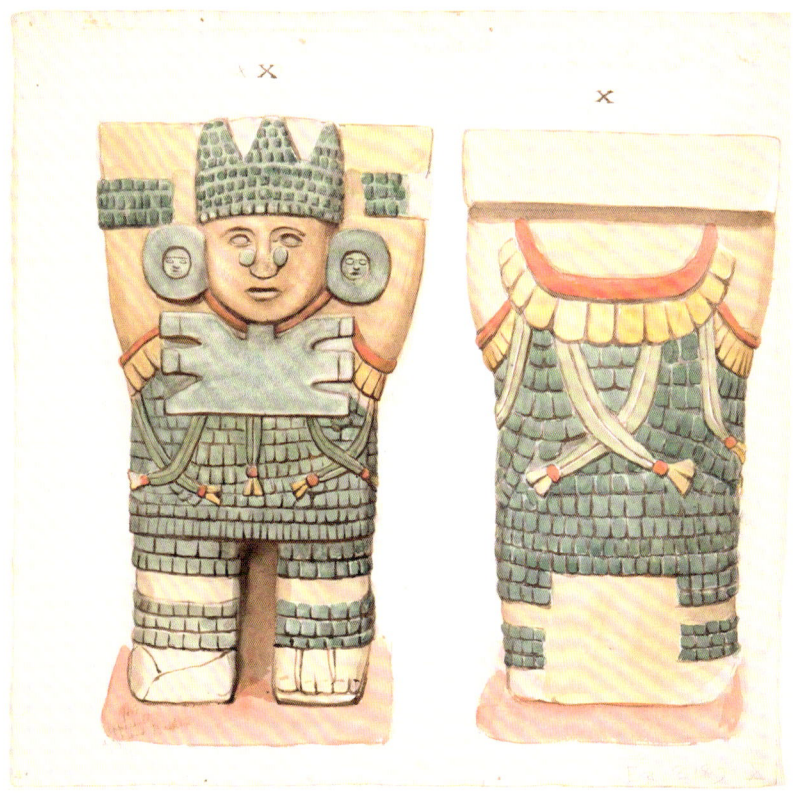

May 9th, 1903

> The Inspector suddenly appeared with 2 carts to carry off the statues & knowing how they would be knocked about I had to make drawings of them, which took a fortnight of hard work. They only took four at a time with an interval between. You have no idea how beautiful they are, if one brings oneself down to their level. I had to sit on the ground to do them. They are <u>most</u> interesting.
>
> Letter from Adela Breton to Alfred Tozzer (written in Cordoba, Mexico)[8]

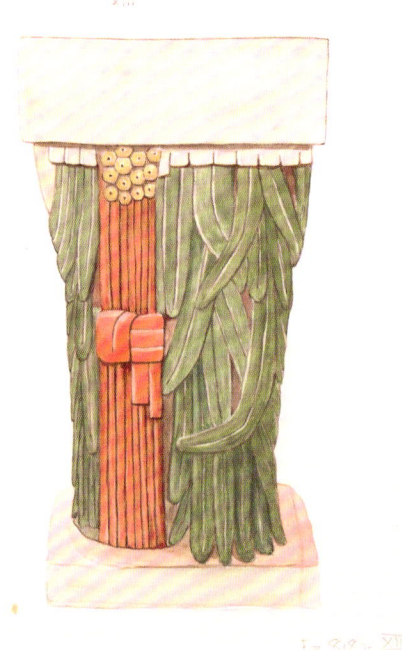 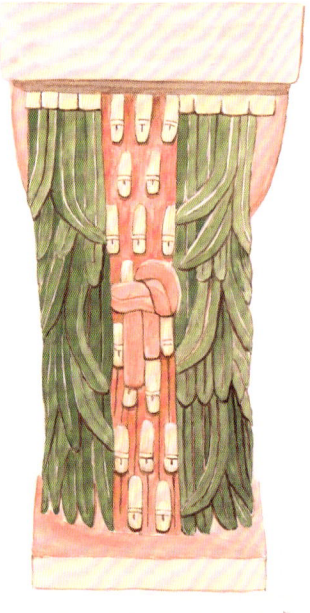

FIG. 122   Watercolor of caryatid XIII from the outer chamber, Temple A, Chichén Itzá, with a detailed view of the back.

FIG. 123   Watercolor of caryatid XV from the outer chamber, Temple A, Chichén Itzá, with a detailed view of the back.

December 20, 1905

> The important thing in colouring Yucatec things, is to keep what artists call the <u>tone</u>. That is the remarkable thing about those ancient painters,—their understanding of <u>tone</u> is wonderful, & this makes it so difficult to do justice to them in copies. Every tint must be in exact harmony [as to] its neighbours, <u>in tune</u>, like chords in music.
>
> Letter from Adela Breton to Alfred Tozzer[9]

Adela Breton (1849–1923)

ACANCEH

In 1906 residents quarrying for building materials at the archaeological site of Acanceh unearthed a wall two meters tall, with vividly colored stucco reliefs. Adela Breton happened to be in the Yucatán at the time the wall was uncovered, and she went to the site where she made sketches which she later elaborated with the help of photographs. It is obvious that she relied heavily on the photographs in her possession, but it is not clear whose photos she was using. They have been attributed to Mrs. Jennie James, who lived in Mérida and became friendly with Breton during her stays in Chichén Itzá.

> In Yucatan 200 ruins have now been catalogued, all of them buildings constructed of cut stone and with good architecture. But scarcely anything has been done in the way of scientific excavation of the innumerable mounds. Acanceh, a small town an hour south-west of Merida by train, possessed three or four ancient mounds about 40 feet high. One of these had been used as a quarry until a year ago, when the destroyers, having worked across the top, came upon the last remaining face of a building which was covered with painted reliefs in stucco. This is nearly at the top of the mound. At some period the reliefs had been whitewashed, the space in front filled with rough stones up to a few inches from the wall, and then earth and lime dust thrown in to make all solid. On removing this, a length of 40 feet of wall appeared, with a band of reliefs in panels, surmounted by a cornice with a symbolic design and another border below. Each of the twenty-one panels contains a symbolic bird or a quaint hybrid beast, done with the greatest skill in very high relief, and painted in colours on a red ground. The ruffled breasts of the birds are curiously given by means of quantities of chipped flakes of crystalline limestone which stand out from the cement.[10]

Breton published an article about the site and the frescoes in an article for *Man* entitled "Archaeology in Mexico." Although she did not detail her own work in that article, she wrote about it in a letter to William Henry Holmes: "I went to Yucatan for 2 months, & copied the important colored stucco reliefs found last year at Acanceh—40 feet long 21 panels in two rows, each containing a bird man, or beast, quite the most striking & artistic things (such brilliant coloring) we have had yet, with the exception of Herr Maler's stelae. There were also remains of frescoes & painted glyphs in a funeral chamber."[11] Her

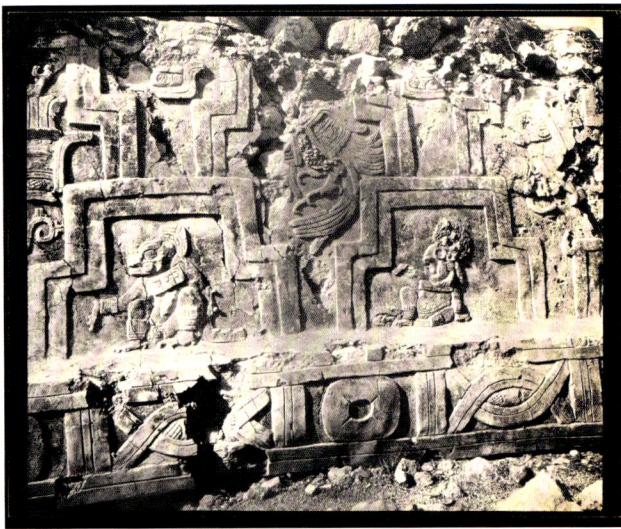

FIG. 124 Photograph of Acanceh by Teobert Maler.

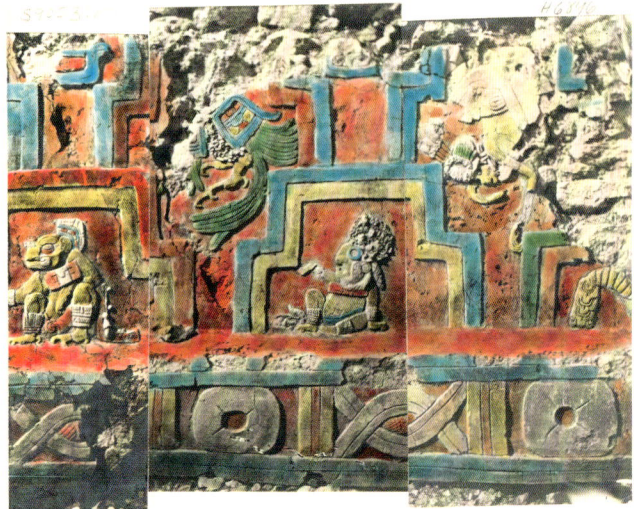

FIG. 125 Colored photograph of Acanceh by Breton.

watercolors at Acanceh, which she produced by working from sketches and photographs, show how she intertwined the visual media of the camera and the paintbrush to create works that are now the only remaining evidence of the colors that quickly vanished once they were exposed to the elements.[12]

FIG. 126 Full-scale copy of the stucco façade of the temple on the pyramid at Acanceh. Transparent and opaque watercolor and graphite on tracing cloth.

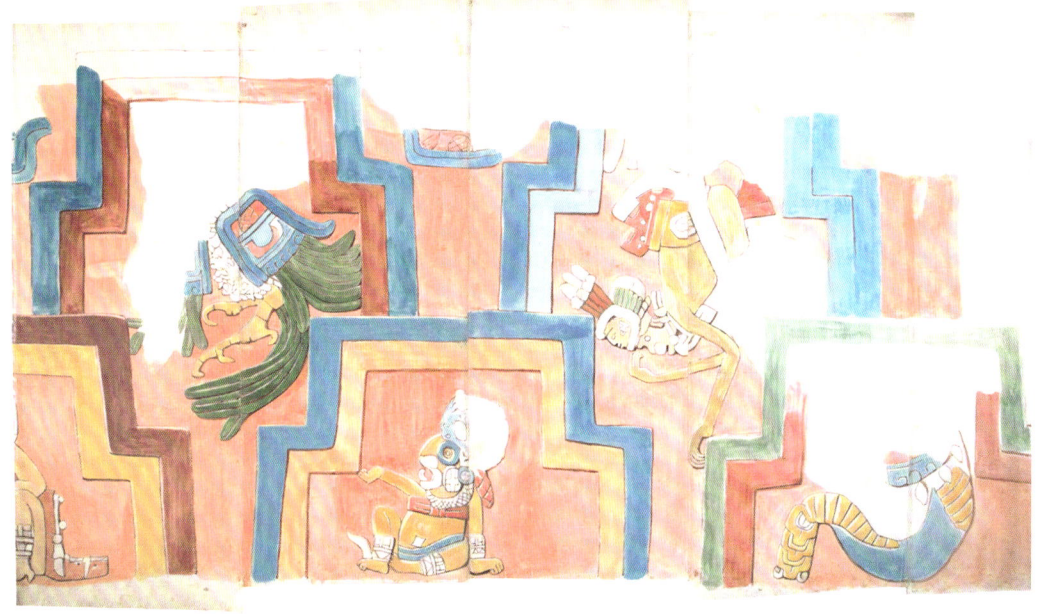

FIG. 127 Photograph of the Acanceh frieze by Teobert Maler.

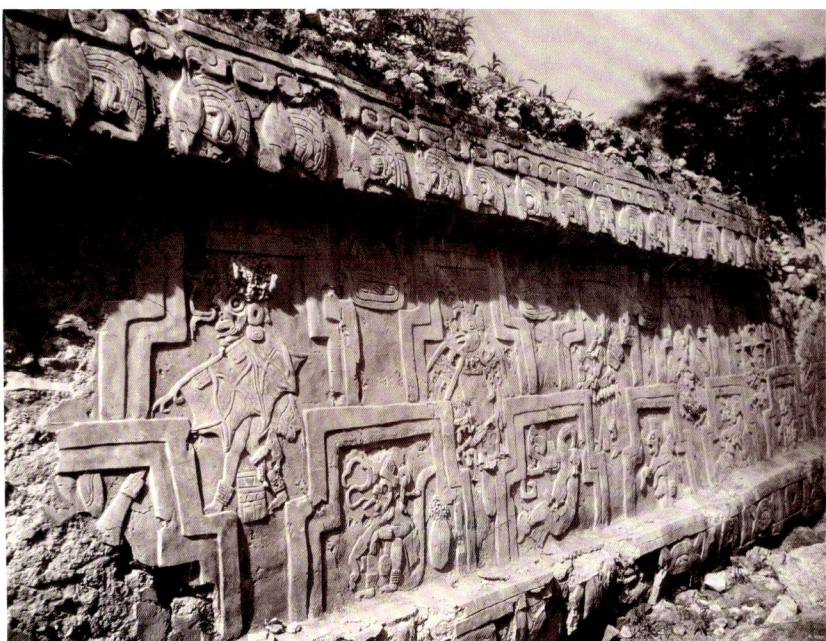

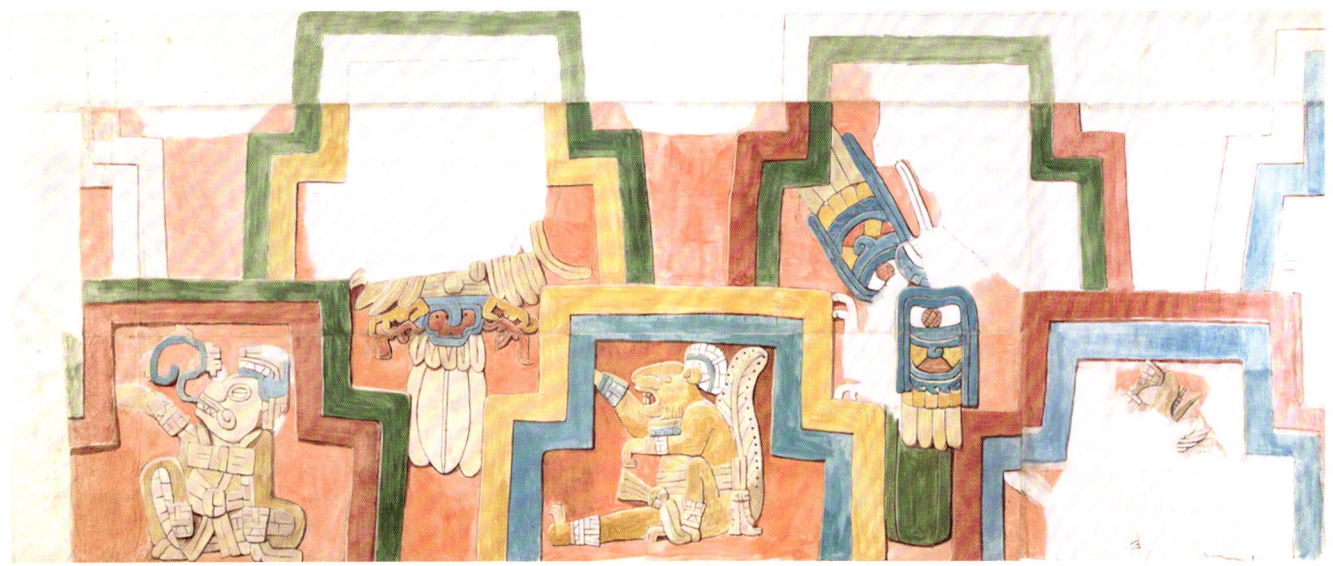

FIG. 128 Full-scale copy of the stucco façade of the temple on the pyramid at Acanceh. Transparent and opaque watercolor and graphite on tracing cloth.

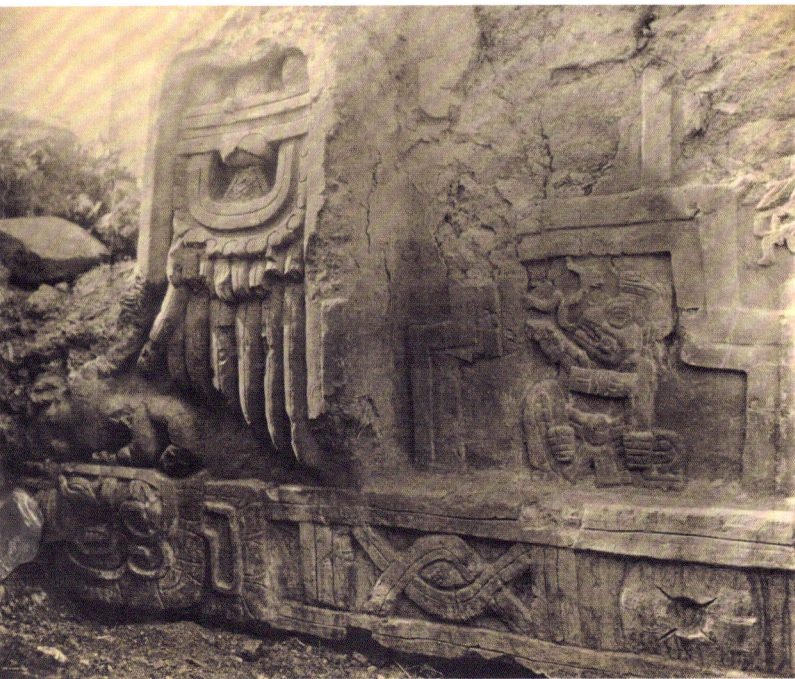

FIG. 129 Detail of the Acanceh frieze by Teobert Maler. A very similar photo is found in Breton's article in the journal *Man* from 1908, with the photo credited to her.

Adela Breton (1849–1923)

FIG. 130 Photograph of the same Acanceh stone relief seen in fig. 130 colored by Breton.

FIG. 131 Watercolor copy of the stucco façade of the temple on the pyramid at Acanceh. Also shown in figs. 129 and 130.

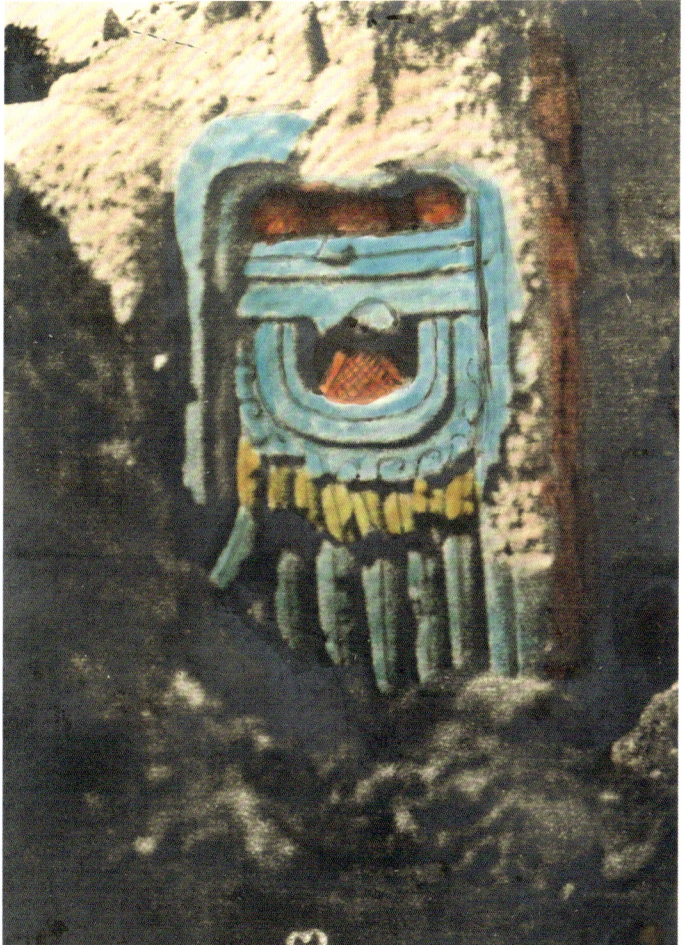
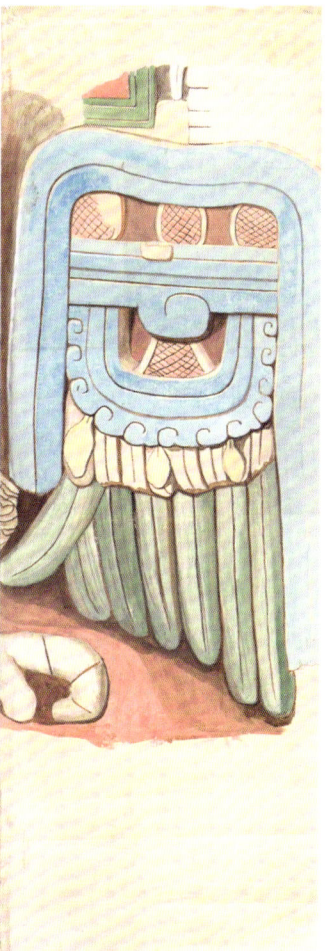

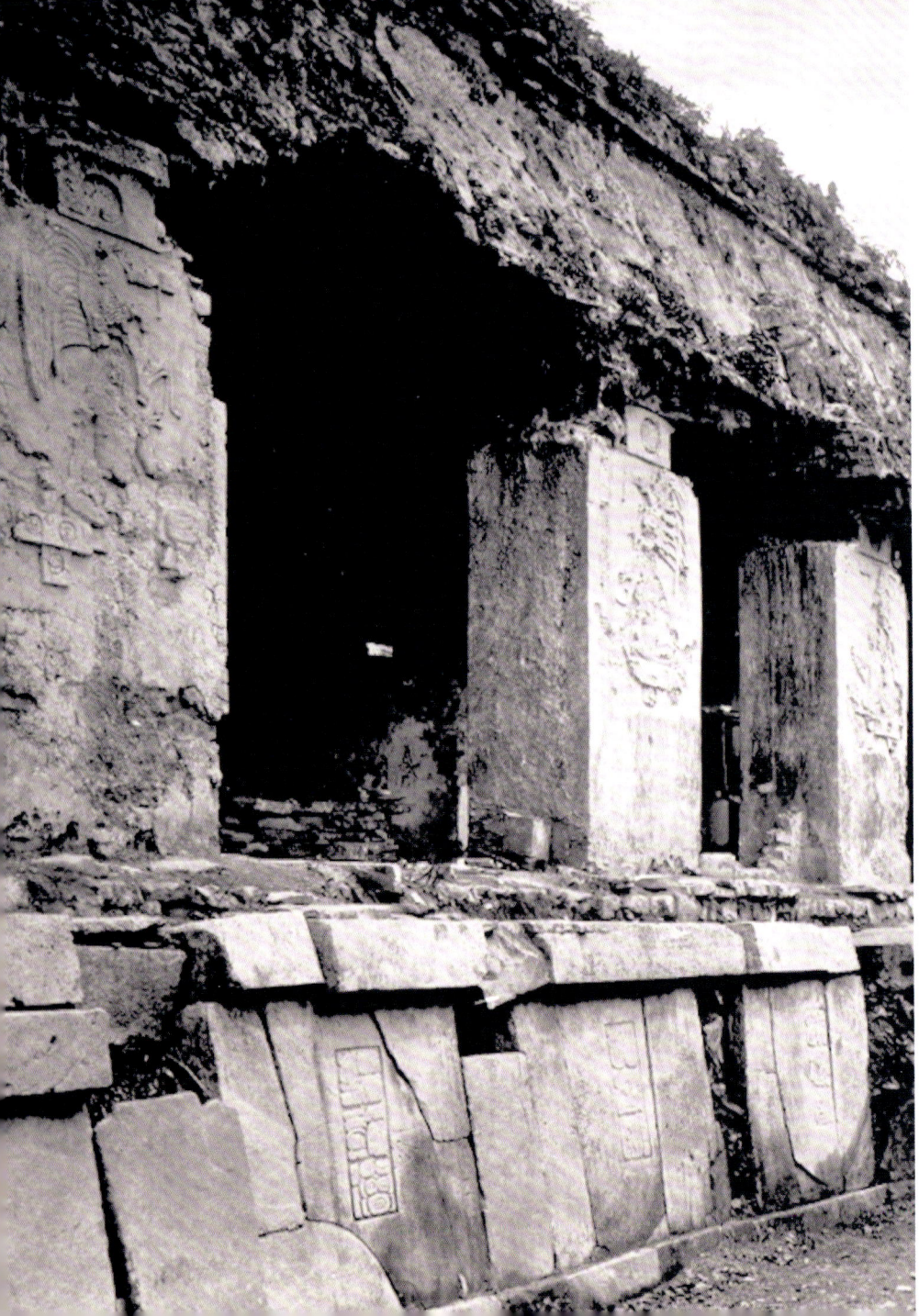

Notes

Introduction

1. John Ruskin, preface to *The Seven Lamps of Architecture*, 2nd ed. (London: Smith, Elder and Co., 1855), xv.
2. Keith F. Davis, *Désiré Charnay: Expeditionary Photographer* (Albuquerque: University of New Mexico Press, 1981), 5.
3. Sir John F. W. Herschel to William Henry Fox Talbot, May 9, 1839, cited in Beaumont Newhall, *The History of Photography from 1839 to the Present* (New York: The Museum of Modern Art, 1982), 23.
4. Barry Bergdoll, "A Matter of Time: Architects and Photographers in Second Empire France," in Malcolm Daniel, ed., *The Photographs of Édouard Baldus* (New York and Montreal: The Metropolitan Museum of Art and the Canadian Centre for Architecture, 1994), 105.
5. Ernest Lacan, *Esquisses photographiques à propos de l'Exposition universelle et de la guerre d'Orient* [1856], reprinted in André Rouillé, *La Photographie en France: textes & controverses. Une anthologie, 1816–1871* (Paris: Macula, 1989), 130.
6. Jules Janin's review of Maxime Du Camp's 1852 publication *Égypte, Nubie, Palestine et Syrie*, quoted in Rouillé, *La Photographie en France*, 124.
7. Paul Martellière, "De la photographie comme complément des études archéologiques," *Bulletin de la Société archéologique, scientifique et littéraire du vendômois*, vol. 13 (1879): 216.
8. Martellière, "De la photographie," 220.
9. Peter Martyr d'Anghiera, *Selections from Peter Martyr*, translated by Geoffrey Eatough, Repertorium Columbianum, Volume 5 (Turnhout, Belgium: Brepols, 1998), 71.
10. Leonardo López Luján, "The First Steps on a Long Journey; Archaeological Illustration in Eighteenth-Century New Spain," in Joanne Pillsbury, ed., *Past Presented: Archaeological Illustration and the Ancient*

Americas (Washington, DC: Dumbarton Oaks, 2012), 80.
11. López Luján, "First Steps," 79–80.
12. López Luján, "First Steps," 80.
13. Khristaan D. Villela, editor's notes for Antonio de León y Gama, "A Historical and Chronological Description of Two Stones, Which Were Found in 1790 in the Principal Square of Mexico during the Current Paving Project," in Khristaan D. Villela and Mary Ellen Miller, *The Aztec Calendar Stone* (Los Angeles: Getty Research Institute, 2010), 50.
14. López Luján, "First Steps," 88.
15. León y Gama, "Historical and Chronological Description," 58.
16. León y Gama, "Historical and Chronological Description," 58–59.
17. Michael D. Coe, *Breaking the Maya Code* (London and New York: Thames and Hudson, 2012), 74.
18. Gillett G. Griffin, "Early Travelers to Palenque," in Merle Greene Robertson, ed., *Primera Mesa Redonda de Palenque*, Part I: *A Conference on the Art, Iconography, and Dynastic History of Palenque, Palenque, Chiapas, Mexico. December 14–22, 1973* (Pebble Beach, CA: Robert Louis Stevenson School, 1974): http://www.mesoweb.com/pari/publications/RT01/EarlyTravelers.pdf, 10.
19. Coe, *Breaking the Maya Code*, 75. See also Griffin, "Early Travelers to Palenque," 10.
20. Griffin, "Early Travelers to Palenque," 10.
21. Quoted in Adam T. Sellen, "Nineteenth-Century Photographs of Archaeological Collections from Mexico," in Joanne Pillsbury, ed., *Past Presented: Archaeological Illustration and the Ancient Americas* (Washington, DC: Dumbarton Oaks, 2012), 212.
22. Coe, *Breaking the Maya Code*, 80.
23. Paul Edison, "Colonial Prospecting in Independent Mexico: Abbé Baradère's *Antiquités mexicaines* (1834–36)," *Proceedings of the Western Society for French History*, vol. 32 (2004): 195.
24. Ignacio Bernal, *A History of Mexican Archaeology: The Vanished Civilizations of Middle America* (London: Thames and Hudson, 1980), 100.
25. Bernal, *History of Mexican Archaeology*, 101.
26. Coe, *Breaking the Maya Code*, 77.
27. Bernal, *History of Mexican Archaeology*, 119.
28. Khristaan D. Villela, "Beyond Stephens and Catherwood: Ancient Mesoamerica as Public Entertainment in the Early Nineteenth Century," in Joanne Pillsbury, ed., *Past Presented: Archaeological Illustration and the Ancient Americas* (Washington, DC: Dumbarton Oaks, 2012), 159.
29. Villela, "Beyond Stephens and Catherwood," 159.
30. Bryan R. Just, "Printed Pictures of Maya Sculpture," in Joanne Pillsbury, ed., *Past Presented: Archaeological Illustration and the Ancient Americas* (Washington, DC: Dumbarton Oaks, 2012), 361.
31. Sellen, "Nineteenth-Century Photographs," 213; Janet E. Buerger, *French Daguerreotypes* (Chicago and London: University of Chicago Press, 1989), 34.
32. Sellen, "Nineteenth-Century Photographs," 213.
33. Just, "Printed Pictures," 363 Also on the collodion process, Newhall, *History of Photography*, 59–60.
34. Just, "Printed Pictures," 363.
35. Martellière, "De la photographie," 222.
36. See, for example, William H. Stiebing, *Uncovering the Past: A History of Archaeology* (Buffalo, NY: Prometheus Books, 1993).
37. Davis, *Désiré Charnay*, 9.
38. Quoted in Donald Malcolm Reid, *Whose Pharaohs? Archaeology, Museums, and Egyptian National Identity from Napoleon to World War I* (Berkeley: University of California Press, 2003): https://hdl-handle-net.proxy1.library.jhu.edu/2027/heb.90010, accessed February 21, 2021.
39. Désiré Charnay, *Cités et ruines américaines: Mitla, Palenqué, Izamal, Chichen-Itza, Uxmal* (Paris: Gide / A. Morel et Cie, 1862–63), 439.
40. Barbara W. Fash, "Visual Time Machines: Nineteenth-Century Photographs and Museum Re-Presentations in Maya Archaeology," in Sheila Bonde and Stephen Houston, eds., *Re-Presenting the Past: Archaeology through Text and Image* (Oxford and Oakville, CT: Oxbow Books, 2013), 91.

Désiré Charnay (1828–1915)

1. *Cités et ruines américaines: Mitla, Palenqué, Izamal, Chichen-Itza, Uxmal* (Paris: Gide / A. Morel et Cie, 1862–63). All quotes from Charnay in this chapter are taken from his travel narrative in volume 2 of *Cités*, and all translations are by Katia Sainson.
2. *Cités*, i.
3. *Cités*, i–ii.
4. The excerpts in this section are taken from Charnay's narrative relating to Mitla in *Cités*, 247–67.
5. According to Désiré van Monckhoven (*A Popular Treatise on Photography* [London: Virtue Brothers, 1863], 67): "There are two excellent varnishes suitable for the purpose—amber varnish and the white gum of Soehnee varnish. The amber varnish is thus prepared. A quantity of yellow amber broken into small pieces […] is placed in a bottle (¾ capacity). A mixture of equal parts of chloroform and

Notes

ether is now poured into the bottle [...] after some few days, the liquid contents of the bottle are poured upon a filter and the pale, yellow liquid which passes through is amber varnish." Monckhoven's treatises first appeared in French and in English in the late 1850s.
6. Charnay, *Cités*, 325. The excerpts in this section are taken from Charnay's narrative relating to Chichén Itzá in *Cités*, 323–47.
7. The excerpts in this section are taken from Charnay's narrative relating to Uxmal in *Cités*, 362–80.
8. The excerpts in this section are taken from Charnay's narrative relating to Palenque in *Cités*, 412–41.
9. The order of the paragraphs in this section was altered for cohesion: this paragraph from p. 431, next paragraph from 430, last paragraph from 441.

Augustus Le Plongeon (1826–1908) and Alice Le Plongeon (1851–1910)

1. Augustus Le Plongeon, "Archaeological Communication on Yucatan," *Proceedings of the American Antiquarian Society*, vol. 72 (1878): 69.
2. Alice Le Plongeon, "Ruined Uxmal," *New York World*, June 27, 1881, 1–2.
3. Letter from Augustus Le Plongeon to Charles P. Bowditch, December 13, 1902, Peabody Museum, Harvard University, Cambridge, MA. Cited in Lawrence Gustave Desmond, *Yucatán through Her Eyes: Alice Dixon Le Plongeon: Writer and Expeditionary Photographer* (Albuquerque: University of New Mexico Press, 2009), 26.
4. Alice Le Plongeon's diary 1873–1876, Getty Research Institute, 2004.M.18, entry for October 6, 1875. Le Plongeon's diaries have been edited and published in Desmond, *Yucatán through Her Eyes*. This entry appears on p. 99.
5. She is referring to Augustus Le Plongeon.
6. Allan Kardec is the nom de plume of Hippolyte Léon Denizard Rivail (1804–1869), the founder of Spiritism.
7. Alice Le Plongeon's diary, October 16, 1875 (Desmond, *Yucatán through Her Eyes*, 104–6).
8. Today called the Upper Temple of the Jaguars. The Le Plongeons later found the statues referred to as the "atlantes" or "caryatids" while excavating this structure. This is also the location of the large painted murals that would later be copied by Adela Breton.
9. Alice Le Plongeon's diary, October 18, 1875 (Desmond, *Yucatán through Her Eyes*, 108). Adela Breton would later work on copying these murals, succeeding in capturing color and images that it was not possible to photograph at that time.
10. Alice Le Plongeon's diary, October 24, 1875 (Desmond, *Yucatán through Her Eyes*, 112).
11. Alice Le Plongeon's diary, Sunday November 1, 1875 (Desmond, *Yucatán through Her Eyes*, 117).
12. Alice Le Plongeon's diary, November 3, 1875 (Desmond, *Yucatán through Her Eyes*, 118).
13. For more on the naming of this sculpture, see Desmond, *Yucatán through Her Eyes*, 117.
14. Perhaps *antenatus*: someone born before the establishment of the country, in other words pre-Columbian.
15. Alice Dixon Le Plongeon, letter to her parents Henry and Sophia Dixon dated December 26, 1875 and January 4, 1876, Getty Research Institute, 2004.M.18 ADLP Diary–Letters Sent Not in Diary; reproduced in Desmond, *Yucatán through Her Eyes*, 357. Desmond notes that the letter was written during the couple's stay in three villages in Yucatán: Pisté, Valladolid, and Motul.
16. Alice Le Plongeon, "Dr. Le Plongeon's Latest and Most Important Discoveries among the Ruined Cities of Yucatan," *Scientific American Supplement*, vol. 448, August 3, 1884, 7145.
17. *Yucatán through Her Eyes*, 171.
18. Le Plongeon, "Ruined Uxmal."
19. Alice Le Plongeon, "An Example of Patience for Photographers," *The Photographic Times and American Photographer*, vol. 14, no. 162 (n.s. no. 42) (1884): 302–4.

Teobert Maler (1842–1917)

1. Bryan R. Just, "Printed Pictures of Maya Sculpture," in Joanne Pillsbury, ed., *Past Presented: Archaeological Illustration and the Ancient Americas* (Washington, DC: Dumbarton Oaks, 2012), 372.
2. Ian Graham, "Exposing the Maya," *Archaeology*, vol. 43, no. 5 (September/October 1990): 43.
3. The excerpts in this section are taken from *Researches in the Central Portion of the Usumatsintla Valley: Report of Explorations for the Museum, 1898–1900*, Memoirs of the Peabody Museum of American Archaeology and Ethnology, Volume II, part 1 (Cambridge, MA: Peabody Museum, 1901). Throughout this chapter, Maler's texts are edited.
4. Maler, *Researches*, 1:43.
5. Maler, *Researches*, 1:45–46.
6. Maler, *Researches*, 1:49–50.
7. Maler, *Researches*, 1:54.
8. Maler, *Researches*, 1:59–60.
9. Maler, *Researches*, 1:62–74.
10. The excerpts in this section are taken from *Researches in the Central Portion of the Usumatsintla Valley: Report of Explorations*

Notes

for the Museum, 1898–1900, Memoirs of the Peabody Museum of American Archaeology and Ethnology, Volume II, part 2 (Cambridge, MA: Peabody Museum, 1903). Chapter XIII on Yaxchilan (pp. 104–97) mostly draws from experiences at the site in 1897 and 1899.

11. Maler, *Researches*, 2:108.
12. Maler, *Researches*, 2:110.
13. Maler, *Researches*, 2:113.
14. Yaxchilan was the site of a treasure-trove of carved stone low-relief lintels that originally framed the doorways of some of the site's major structures. Alfred Maudslay, who had visited the site in 1886, removed several lintels, which are currently found in the collections of the British Museum, London. These include, most notably, those taken from Structure 21 (lintels 15, 16, 17), Structure 23 (lintels 24, 25), and Structure 42 (lintel 41).
15. Maler, *Researches*, 2:189.
16. Maler, *Researches*, 2:118–19.
17. Maler, *Researches*, 2:126–28.
18. Maler, *Researches*, 2:131–32.
19. Maler, *Researches*, 2:133.
20. Maler, *Researches*, 2:144.
21. Maler, *Researches*, 2:145.
22. Maler, *Researches*, 2:147–48.
23. Maler, *Researches*, 2:151–52. As mentioned above, lintels 24 and 25 from Structure 23 were removed from the site by Alfred Maudslay and are in the collection of the British Museum.
24. Maler, *Researches*, 2:152–53.
25. Maler, *Researches*, 2:158.
26. Maler, *Researches*, 2:174–77.

Alfred Maudslay (1850–1931)

1. Many of the biographical details of Maudslay's life are taken from Ian Graham's *Alfred Maudslay and the Maya* (Norman: University of Oklahoma Press, 2002).
2. Bryan R. Just, "Printed Pictures of Maya Sculpture," in Joanne Pillsbury, ed., *Past Presented: Archaeological Illustration and the Ancient Americas* (Washington, DC: Dumbarton Oaks, 2012), 368.
3. A. G. Hunter to C. P. Bowditch, March 3, 1916, Archives of the Peabody Museum of Archaeology and Ethnology, Cambridge, MA. As quoted in Graham, *Alfred Maudslay*, 223.
4. A. P. Maudslay, *Biologia Centrali-Americana, Archaeology,* Volume V, Text Volume II, (London: R. H. Porter, 1901), 17.

Adela Breton (1849–1923)

1. Mary F. McVicker, *Adela Breton: A Victorian Artist amid Mexico's Ruins* (Albuquerque: University of New Mexico Press, 2005), 65.
2. Adela Breton, "The Wall Paintings at Chichen Itza," in *Congrès international des Américanistes: XVe session, tenue à Québec en 1906* [Proceedings] (Québec: Dussault & Proulx, imprimeurs, 1907), 2:165–9.
3. The archaeologist Edward H. Thompson owned the land on which the ruins of Chichén Itzá were located as well as the hacienda that abutted the site, although the ruins themselves were under the control of the Mexican authorities. At the time Adela Breton met him, he was associated with the Peabody Museum.
4. This is a reference to the Nuns' Palace.
5. Augustus Le Plongeon, *Queen Móo and the Egyptian Sphinx* (New York: Publ. by the author, 1896).
6. Alice Le Plongeon, "Dr. Le Plongeon's Latest and Most Important Discoveries among the Ruined Cities of Yucatan," in *Scientific American Supplement*, vol. 448, August 3, 1884, 7143–47.
7. Adela Breton manuscript, n.d., HF 7705, Bristol Museum & Art Gallery, cited in McVicker, *Adela Breton*, 80; also in S. Giles and J. Stewart, eds., *The Art of Ruins: Miss Adela Breton and the Temples of Mexico: Catalogue for an Exhibition, December 1989 to March 1990* (Bristol: City of Bristol Museum and Art Gallery, 1989). Breton photographed and drew several of the caryatids (or atlantes). McVicker writes: "Coloring photographs to convey a realistic sense of the objects was commonly done. This was a meticulous process, and applying color to the varying shades of grays resulted in subdued shades that could barely suggest the vividness of the original."
8. Tozzer Papers, Peabody Museum Archives, Harvard University, Cambridge, MA.
9. Tozzer Papers, Peabody Museum Archives, Harvard University, Cambridge, MA.
10. Adela Breton, "Archaeology in Mexico," *Man*, vol. 8 (1908): 36–37.
11. Adela Breton (from Mexico City) to William Henry Holmes, dated August 31, 1907, National Anthropological Archives, Smithsonian Institution, Washington, DC.
12. See McVicker, *Adela Breton*, 138; and Virginia E. Miller, "The Frieze of the Palace of the Stuccoes, Acanceh, Yucatan, Mexico," *Studies in Pre-Columbian Art and Archaeology*, no. 31 (1991): 1–72.

Bibliography

Archival sources

Désiré Charnay's photographic archives can be found at the **Musée du Quai Branly, Paris**. A great many of his photographs have been digitized and can be accessed through the museum's site: http://collections.quaibranly.fr.

Charnay's *Cités et ruines américaines: Mitla, Palenqué, Izamal, Chichen-Itza, Uxmal* (1861) has been digitized; the images are in the public domain and can be downloaded from the **Library of Congress**'s website.

The **Augustus and Alice Le Plongeon** archive of papers and photographs is housed in the library of the **Getty Research Institute, Los Angeles**. Original photographs can also be found in the collections of the **American Museum of Natural History, New York** (Division of Anthropology), and the **Peabody Museum of Archaeology and Ethnology, Cambridge, Massachusetts**.

Teobert Maler's negatives from his exploration of the Usumacinta Valley (including Chiapas) in Mexico and Guatemala in the period 1895–1905 are kept in the **Peabody Museum of Archaeology and Ethnology in Cambridge, Massachusetts**. The collection consists of glass-plate black-and-white negatives of Indigenous people, artifacts, and architectural elements and ruins. The Peabody also has a collection of photographs predating his work for the museum. The **Ibero-Amerikanisches Institut in Berlin**, Germany, and the **Instituto Nacional de Antropología e Historia (INAH) in Mexico City**, Mexico, also house collections of Maler's photographs, negatives, and glass plates. In addition to this, the Ibero-Amerikanisches Institut has other archival materials such as field notebooks and manuscript pages.

Alfred Maudslay's substantial photographic archive is found at the **British Museum, London**. The archive also contains manuscript materials such as field notebooks and journals.

Forty-one photographs from the *Biologia Centrali-Americana* in the collection of the **Brooklyn Museum, New York**, have been digitized.

Adela Breton's archives can be found at the **Bristol Museum & Art Gallery**, http://museums.bristol.gov.uk/list.php?keyword=adela+breton. The **Peabody Museum in Cambridge, Massachusetts**, and the **Penn Museum Archives** also hold letters, photographs, and watercolors by Breton.

Works cited

Adamson, David. *The Ruins of Time: Four and a Half Centuries of Conquest and Discovery among the Maya*. London: George Allen & Unwin, 1975.

Baudez, Claude. *Jean-Frédéric Waldeck, peintre: le premier explorateur des ruines mayas*. Paris: Hazan, 1993.

Berg, Keri. "The Imperialist Lens: Du Camp, Salzmann and Early French Photography." *Early Popular Visual Culture*, vol. 6, no. 1 (April 2008): 1–18.

Bergdoll, Barry. "A Matter of Time: Architects and Photographers in Second Empire France." In Malcolm Daniel, ed., *The Photographs of Edouard Baldus*. New York and Montreal: The Metropolitan Museum of Art and the Canadian Centre for Architecture, 1994.

Bohrer, Frederick N. "Photography and Archaeology: The Image as Object." In Sam Smiles and Stephanie Moser, *Envisioning the Past: Archaeology and the Image*, 180–91. Malden, MA: Blackwell, 2005.

Brasseur de Bourbourg, abbé. *Monuments anciens du Mexique: Palenqué et autres ruines de l'ancienne civilisation du Mexique: collection de vues, bas-reliefs, morceaux d'architecture, coupes, vases, terres cuites, cartes et plans, dessinés d'après nature et relevés par M. de Waldeck*. Paris: Arthus Bertrand, 1866.

Breton, Adela. "Archaeology in Mexico." *Man*, vol. 8 (1908): 34–37.

Breton, Adela. "The Wall Paintings at Chichen Itza." In *Congrès international des Américanistes: XVe session, tenue à Québec en 1906* [Proceedings], vol. 2, 165–69. Québec: Dussault & Proulx, imprimeurs, 1907.

Buerger, Janet E. *French Daguerreotypes*. Chicago and London: University of Chicago Press, 1989.

Bullock, William. *A description of the unique exhibition called Ancient Mexico, collected on the spot in 1823 by the assistance of the Mexican government, and now open for public inspection at the Egyptian Hall, Piccadilly*. London: Printed for the proprietor, 1824.

Catherwood, Frederick. *Views of Ancient Monuments in Central America, Chiapas and Yucatan*. New York: Bartlett and Welford, 1844.

Charnay, Désiré. *Cités et ruines américaines: Mitla, Palenqué, Izamal, Chichen-Itza, Uxmal, recueillis et photographiés par Désiré Charnay avec un texte par M. Viollet-le-Duc*. Paris: Gide / A. Morel et Cie, 1862–63. This was issued as a pair of volumes. The first volume was a folio-sized collection of forty-nine plates (forty-seven photographic prints and two photolithographs). The second volume, which contained Charnay's travel narrative—entitled "Le Mexique: 1858–1861: souvenirs et impressions de voyage"—was accompanied by an introductory essay by Eugène Viollet-le-Duc, the architect and leader of the preservationist movement in France, whose mission was to document, photograph, preserve, and restore the ancient monuments of France.

Cyphers, Ann. "Mesoamerica." In Paul Bahn, ed. *The History of Archaeology: An Introduction*. Abingdon and New York: Routledge, 2014.

Davis, Keith F. *Désiré Charnay: Expeditionary Photographer*. Albuquerque: University of New Mexico Press, 1981.

Debroise, Olivier. *Mexican Suite: A History of Photography in Mexico*. Austin: University of Texas Press, 2001.

Desmond, Lawrence Gustave, and Phyllis Mauch Messenger. *A Dream of Maya: Augustus and Alice Le Plongeon in Nineteenth-Century Yucatan*. Albuquerque: University of New Mexico Press, 1988.

Desmond, Lawrence Gustave. *Yucatán through Her Eyes: Alice Dixon Le Plongeon, Writer and Expeditionary Photographer*. Albuquerque: University of Mexico Press, 2009.

Edison, Paul. "Colonial Prospecting in Independent Mexico: Abbé Baradère's *Antiquités mexicaines (1834–36)*." *Proceedings of the Western Society for French History*, vol. 32 (2004): 195–215.

Edwards, Elizabeth. *The Camera as Historian: Amateur Photographers and Historical Imagination, 1885–1918*. Durham: Duke University Press, 2012.

Fash, Barbara W. "Visual Time Machines: Nineteenth-Century Photographs and Museum Re-Presentations in Maya Archaeology." In Sheila Bonde and Stephen Houston, eds. *Re-Presenting the Past: Archaeology through Text and Image*, 91–113. Oxford and Oakville, CT: Oxbow Books, 2013.

Feyler, Gabrielle. "Contribution à l'histoire des origines de la photographie archéologique: 1839–1880." *Mélanges de l'École française de Rome. Antiquité*, vol. 99, no. 2 (1987): 1019–47.

Giles, S., and J. Stewart, eds. *The Art of Ruins: Miss Adela Breton and the Temples of Mexico: Catalogue for an exhibition, December 1989 to March 1990*. Bristol: City of Bristol Museum and Art Gallery, 1989.

Graham, Ian. "Exposing the Maya." *Archaeology*, vol. 43, no. 5 (September/October 1990): 36–43.

Graham, Ian. *Alfred Maudslay and the Maya*. Norman: University of Oklahoma Press, 2002.

Just, Bryan R. "Printed Pictures of Maya Sculpture." In Joanne Pillsbury, ed., *Past Presented: Archaeological Illustration and the Ancient Americas*, 356–84. Washington, DC: Dumbarton Oaks, 2012.

León y Gama, Antonio de. "A Historical and Chronological Description of Two Stones, Which Were Found in 1790 in the Principal Square of Mexico during the Current Paving Project." In Khristaan D. Villela and Mary Ellen Miller, *The Aztec Calendar Stone*, 50–80. Los Angeles: Getty Research Institute, 2010.

López Luján, Leonardo. "The First Steps on a Long Journey: Archaeological Illustration in Eighteenth-Century New Spain." In Joanne Pillsbury, ed. *Past Presented: Archaeological Illustration and the Ancient Americas*, 69–105. Washington, DC: Dumbarton Oaks, 2012.

Le Plongeon, Alice. Diary 1873–1876, 2004.M.18 [manuscript]. Getty Research Institute, Los Angeles.

Le Plongeon, Alice. "Ruined Uxmal." *New York World*, June 27, 1881, 1–2.

Le Plongeon, Alice. "An Example of Patience for Photographers." *The Photographic Times and American Photographer*, vol. 14, no. 162 (n.s. no. 42) (1884): 302–4.

Le Plongeon, Alice. "Dr. Le Plongeon's Latest and Most Important Discoveries among the Ruined Cities of Yucatan." *Scientific American Supplement*, vol. 448, August 3, 1884, 7143–47.

Le Plongeon, Augustus. "Archaeological Communication on Yucatan." *Proceedings of the American Antiquarian Society*, vol. 72 (1878): 65–75.

Le Plongeon, Augustus. *Queen Móo and the Egyptian Sphinx*. New York: Publ. by the author, 1896.

Bibliography

Maler, Teobert. *Researches in the Central Portion of the Usumatsintla Valley: Report of Explorations for the Museum, 1898–1900*, Memoirs of the Peabody Museum of American Archaeology and Ethnology, Volume II, parts 1 and 2. Cambridge, MA: Peabody Museum, 1901–3.

Martellière, Paul. "De la photographie comme complément des études archéologiques." *Bulletin de la Société archéologique, scientifique et littéraire du vendômois*, vol. 13 (1879): 215–23.

Maudslay, Alfred P. *Biologia Centrali-Americana, or Contributions to the Knowledge of the Fauna and Flora of Mexico and Central America*, vols. 55–59, *Archaeology*, with appendix by J. T. Goodman. London: R. H. Porter and Dulau, 1889–1902.

McVicker, Mary F. *Adela Breton: A Victorian Artist amid Mexico's Ruins*. Albuquerque: University of New Mexico Press, 2005.

Miller, Virginia E. "The Frieze of the Palace of the Stuccoes, Acanceh, Yucatan, Mexico." *Studies in Pre-Columbian Art and Archaeology*, no. 31 (1991): i–iii, v, vii, 1–72.

Monckhoven, Désiré van. *A Popular Treatise on Photography*. London: Virtue Brothers, 1863.

Mondenard, Anne de. *La Mission héliographique: cinq photographes parcourent la France en 1851*. Paris: MONUM, 2002.

The Remarkable Miss Breton: Artist, Archaeologist, Traveller. Bath: Bath Royal Literary & Scientific Institution, 2017.

Rouillé, André. *La Photographie en France: textes & controverses. Une anthologie, 1816–1871*. Paris: Macula, 1989.

Sellen, Adam T. "Nineteenth-Century Photographs of Archaeological Collections from Mexico." In Joanne Pillsbury, ed. *Past Presented: Archaeological Illustration and the Ancient Americas*, 207–29. Washington, DC: Dumbarton Oaks, 2012.

Stephens, John L. *Incidents of Travel in Yucatan*. New York: Harper & Brothers, 1843.

Stiebing, William H. *Uncovering the Past: A History of Archaeology*. Buffalo, NY: Prometheus Books, 1993.

Timby, Kim. "Colour Photography and Stereoscopy: Parallel Histories." *History of Photography*, vol. 29, no. 2 (2005): 183–96.

Trutat, Eugène. *La photographie appliquée à l'archéologie: reproduction des monuments, œuvres d'art, mobilier, inscriptions, manuscrits*. Paris: Gauthier-Villars, 1879.

Villela, Khristaan D. "Beyond Stephens and Catherwood: Ancient Mesoamerica as Public Entertainment in the Early Nineteenth Century." In Joanne Pillsbury, ed. *Past Presented: Archaeological Illustration and the Ancient Americas*, 143–71.Washington, DC: Dumbarton Oaks, 2012.

"Le Yucatán est ailleurs." Expéditions photographiques (1857–1886) de Désiré Charnay. Arles and Paris: Actes Sud and Musée du Quai Branly, 2007.

Index

Page numbers in *italics* refer to illustrations and their captions

Acanceh: reliefs and wall paintings *4*, *146*, 161–62, *162*, *163*, *164–65*
Aglio, Agostino
   Ancient Mexico exhibition, London (engraving) *17*
   The Antiquities of Mexico (illustrations) 16
Agüera, Francisco 12
Almendáriz, Ricardo 14
Alzate y Ramírez, José Antonio: *Descripción de las antiguedades de Xochicalco* 12, *13*, 18
Ancient Mexico exhibition (1824), Egyptian Hall, Piccadilly, London *17*
Arago, François 9, 10, 11, 24
archaeological expeditions 11
   exploitation of ancient sites 26, 75, 88
   funding 25, 30, 88
   see also under named photographers
archaeological illustrations 16, 18
   camera lucida, use of 21
   disadvantages compared to photography 10–11, 129
   drawings 12, *13*, 15, *18*, *19*, *20–21*, 22 *see also* Breton, Adela; Hunter, Annie G.
   engravings 11, 12, *13*, *17*, 22, 56
   lithographs 11, 14–15
archaeological photography
   advantages over illustrations 10–11, 129
   development of 9, 10, 11, 24, 26–27, 88
   see also under named photographers
archaeology, development of 10, 25, 64
Aztecs 11, 22, 24, 30
   Coatlicue (mother goddess) 12, *14*
   Sun Stone (Calendar Stone) *8*, 12, *15*, *16*, *17*, 22, *22*, 24

Baldus, Édouard 10
Baradère, Jean-Henri: *Antiquités mexicaines* 16, *17*, 18
Blackwell, Maude A. 69
Bowditch, Charles P. 67, 129
Brasseur de Bourbourg, Abbé Charles Étienne 25
   Monuments anciens du Mexique 18, *19*
Breton, Adela 24, 148, *148*
   archaeological expeditions 24, 25, 148
   documentation of fragile artifacts 26, 148, 149, 162
   paintings and drawings 148, 160, 161
      Acanceh: reliefs *4*, 161–62, *162*, *163*, *164*, *165*
      Chichén Itzá
         Nuns' Palace (Casa de Monjas) 151, 169n.4
         Upper Temple of the Jaguars
            "caryatids" found by Le Plongeons 76, 155–56, *157*, *157*, *159*, *160*
            "painted" chamber *148*, *149*
            stone altar *152*, 154–55
            wall paintings *148*, 149, *149*, 150–54, 168n.8, 168n.9
      for Maudslay 129, 148–49, 151
      Teopancaxco: frescoes and murals 148–49
   as a photographer 149, 162
      hand-coloring plates 149–50, *162*, *165*
   writing 150–54, 156–57, 159, 161, *164*
British Museum, London 26, *128*, *130*, *144*, 169n.14, 169n.23
Bullock, William: *Ancient Mexico* exhibition (1924) *17*

Caldéron, José Antonio 14
calotypes 9
Castañeda, José Luciano 15–16
Catherwood, Frederick 56
   camera lucida, use of 21
   daguerreotypes 22
   illustrations
      "Broken Idol at Copan" from *Views of Ancient Monuments ...* *20*, 21–22
      "Casa del Gobernador, Uxmal" from *Incidents of Travel in Yucatan* (Stephens) *20–21*
      Views of Ancient Monuments in Central America ... 20
Chacmool *see under* Le Plongeon, Alice and Augustus
Charles IV, king of Spain 16
Charnay, Désiré 24, 30–31, *31*, 48, 56
   archaeological expeditions 24, 30, 31–36, 42, 45–46, 48–50, 56–57, 61
   exploitation of ancient sites 26, 88
   funding 25, 30, 97
   meeting with Maudslay 125, *144*
   plaster casts of sculpted reliefs 61, 125, 131
   archaeological photographs 24, 30–31, 32, *33*, 46, 48–49
      Chichén Itzá 149
         Ball Court with tiger bas-relief *46*
         Chichan-Chob (Prison) *47*
         Nuns' Palace (Casa de Monjas) *43–45*
      Izamal: Kabul pyramid with self-portrait *31*
      Mexico City: Calendar Stone *16*
      Mitla
         Fourth Palace *33*, 36, *40–41*
         Great Palace *34–35*, *37*, *38*
         Priest's House *33*
         Second Palace *39*
      Palenque
         Palace Complex 59, *60–61*
         Stone of the Cross 57, *58*, 59
      Uxmal 53
         Governor's Palace 49–50, 54, *54*, *55*
         Nuns' Palace 48, *49*, 50, *51–53*
            Serpent Façade *52–53*
      Yaxchilán 97
   photographic equipment and processes 30, 45, 48–50, 54, 59, 65
      collodion (wet-plate) 24, 30, 32, 36, 42, 48, 50, 54, 56, 59, 61, 167n.5
      darkrooms 24, 45, 48, 49–50, 59
   publications
      Cités et ruines américaines ... 16, 30, *33*, *37*, *39*, *43*, *44*, *47*, *49*, *50*, *51–53*, *54–55*, 61
      Les Anciennes villes du Nouveau Monde 97
Chiapas, Mexico *see* Palenque; Yaxchilán
Chichén Itzá, Yucatán 26, 42, 45–46, 65, 149, 169n.3
   Ball Court with tiger bas-relief *46*
   Chichan-Chob (Prison) *47*
   El Castillo *140*

Index

south portico with bearded man bas-relief 70, 71
"High Priest Cay" statue 76, 76–77
Lower Temple of the Jaguars: bas-reliefs 62, 67, 68
Nuns' Palace (Casa de Monjas) 43–45, 69, 70, 123, 139, 140, 169n.4
    wall paintings 151
Temple A see Upper Temple of the Jaguars below
Temple of the Eagles and Jaguars: platform 72, 73
Temple of the Tigers (Casa del Tigre) see Upper Temple of the Jaguars below
Upper Temple of the Jaguars 70, 71, 154
    caryatids 76, 155–56, 156, 157, 157–59, 159, 160, 168n.8
    "painted" chamber 148, 149
    stone altar with bas-reliefs 152, 154–55, 156–57
    wall paintings 69, 73, 148, 149, 149, 150–54, 168n.8, 168n.9
Coatlicue (Aztec mother goddess) 12, 14
collodion (wet-plate) photography 9, 24, 25, 30
    varnishes 36, 167n.5
    see also under Charnay, Désiré; Le Plongeon, Alice and Augustus
Copán
    doorway to inner chamber of Temple 132
    statues 20
    stelae 131, 133–35

daguerreotypes 9, 10, 22, 22, 23, 24, 30
Darwin, Charles: *On the Origin of Species* 122
Del Río, Don Antonio 14
    Description of the Ruins of An Ancient City 14–15
Dresden Codex 11
dry-plate photography 9, 25, 125, 1215
Du Camp, Maxime 11, 22
Dupaix, Guillermo 15–16

Friedrichsthal, Emanuel von:
    daguerreotypes 24
    figure from Mayapan 23
Frith, Francis 11

Girault de Prangey, Joseph-Philibert 11
Godman, F. Ducane: *Biologia Centrali-Americana* (with Salvin) 122, 125
Gonzales, Agustin 56, 57
Gros, Jean-Baptiste-Louis, Baron 11, 22
Humboldt, Alexander von 11, 18, 22, 24
    Vue des Cordillères (Views of the Cordilleras) 11, 12, 18, 19, 56
Hunter, Annie G.: archaeological drawings in *Biologia Centrali-Americana* 126, 129, 129

Izamal, Yucatán 42

Kabul pyramid (with Charnay) 31

James, Mrs. Jennie 161
Janin, Jules 12
Jiménez, José María 98, 103

Kardec, Allan (Hippolyte Rivail) 71, 168n.5
Kingsborough, Edward King, Viscount 22
    The Antiquities of Mexico 16, 56

Lacan, Ernest 10
Lambert, Edwin J. 129
Le Plongeon, Alice and Augustus 24, 65, 70, 72, 78, 79, 84
    archaeological expeditions 64, 66, 76, 77, 78–79, 81–82
    exploitation of ancient sites 26, 75, 88
    theories about Mayan civilization 64, 65
    archaeological photographs 26, 64, 65, 69, 73, 80–81, 82–83, 85
        Chichén Itzá 149
        El Castillo: south portico with bearded man bas-relief 70, 71
        "High Priest Cay" statue 76, 76–77
        Lower Temple of the Jaguars (bas-reliefs) 62, 67, 68
        Nuns' Palace (Casa de Monjas) 69, 70
        Temple of the Eagles and Jaguars: platform 72, 73
        Temple of the Tigers (Casa del Tigre) see Upper Temple of the Jaguars below
        Upper Temple of the Jaguars ("Chacmool Monument") 70, 71, 73, 168n.8
        caryatids 76, 155–56, 156, 157, 157–59, 159, 160, 168n.8
        stone altar with bas-reliefs 152, 154–55, 156–57
        wall paintings 69, 73, 148, 149, 149, 151, 153, 168n.8, 168n.9
        Uxmal 77, 83
        Chenes Temple, Pyramid of the Magician 82, 83, 84
        Governor's Palace (Casa del Gobernador) 77–78, 78, 79, 80
        Sanctuary 85
        West Building, Nunnery Quadrangle 81
    Chacmool and Queen Moó story 64, 72
    "Funeral Monument" 71
    "statue" 26, 72, 73, 74–75
    photographic equipment and processes 65–66, 71, 73, 78, 80–81, 82, 85
        collodion (wet-plate) 73, 80, 81
        stereography 65–66, 67, 67, 68, 70, 75, 79
    publications
        diaries and articles (Alice) 64, 67, 69, 70, 71, 73, 76–77, 78–83, 85, 154–56
        letters (Alice) 74–75, 168n.15
        Queen Moo and the Egyptian Sphinx 64, 153, 156
Léon y Gama, Antonio de 12, 14
    Descripción histórica y cronológica de las dos piedras 12, 14, 15
Lorenzana, Cardinal: *Historia de la Nueva España* 12
Lorillard, Pierre 25, 97
Lottin de Laval, Victor 125
La Lumière magazine 10

Maler, Teobert 24, 88
    archaeological expeditions 24, 88, 89–90, 92, 95, 97, 98
    funding 25, 88, 92
    archaeological photographs 26, 88–89, 90, 92, 97
        Acanceh: reliefs 146, 162, 163, 164, 165
        Piedras Negras 89, 89

Index

lintels *93*, 93-94
stelae *90*, 90-92, *91*, *94*, 94-95, 98
Yaxchilán
lintels 97-98, *99*, 99-100, *104*, 105-6, *107*, *112*, 113-15
The Red Temple on the Shore (El Tiemplo de la Ribera) *101*
stelae *86*, 98, 100, *102*, 102-3, 105, 106, *107*, 108-13, *109*, 115-19, *116-17*
Structure 19 ("The Labyrinth") *96*, 97
Structure 33 *2*, *116*
Structure 40 *116*
photographic equipment and processes 88
night photography 88, 97, 98
Researches in the Central Portion of the Usumatsintla Valley 88-89, 90-95, 97-98, 99-119
Marquez, Pietro: *Due antichi monumenti di architettura messicana* 12, *13*, 18
Martellière, Paul 11
Martyr d'Anghiera, Peter: *The Decades of the New World* 11-12
Maudslay, Alfred 24, 88, 122, *123*, 142
archaeological expeditions 24, 122, 125
exploitation of ancient sites 26, 88, 97, *144*, 169n.14, 169n.23
funding 25, 125
meeting with Charnay 125, *144*
plaster casts of sculpted reliefs 26, *120*, 125, 129, *130*, 131, *133*, 136, *137*, *144*
archaeological photographs 26, 122, 125, 129, 131, 140, 144
Chichén Itzá
El Castillo *140*
Nuns' Palace (Casa de Monjas) *123*, *139*, *140*
with self-portrait *123*
wall paintings 151, 153-54
Copán
doorway to inner chamber of Temple *132*
stelae 131, *133-35*
Palenque *140*
Palace Complex *127*, 140
House C *142*, *143*
southeast corner of eastern court *141*
Western court and tower *142*, *143*
Temple of the Sun *144*
Quiriguá
stelae *136*
"The Great Turtle" 136, *136*, *137*, *138*
role in deciphering Mayan hieroglyphs 125, 131
Yaxchilán 97
House H *144*
lintels 97, *126*, *128*, *145*
removed and sent to British Museum 26, 97, *128*, *144*, 169n.14, 169n.23
photographic equipment and processes
dry-plate 125
publications
Archaeology for *Biologia Centrali-Americana* (Godman and Salvin) 97, 122, 125, *126*, 129, *129*, 131, *133*, *136*, *144*
notebooks *124*, 125
Maya 24
early exploration 11
gods 25, *55*, 90, 91-92, 94-95, 100, 103, 105, 110, 119
hieroglyphs 10, 11-12, 15, *18*, 24-25, *50*, *55*, 59, 113, 122, 125, 131, *133*, 161
deciphering 12, 25, 125, 131
interpretation 19, 56, 64, 113, *133*
on lintels 93-94, 100, 106, 114-15
on stelae 90, 91-92, 95, 103, 105, 108, 110, 113, 115, 118, 119
theorized connection to other civilizations 25, 64, 65
see also named cities
Menché *see* Yaxchilán
Mérida, Yucatán 42, 45, 66, 161
Mexico
archaeological excavations 12, 18, 26, 75, 161
expeditions 11, 15, 18, 19, 24, 30, 88, 148
War of Reform (1857-60) 31, 36
Mexico City
Coatlicue sculpture 12, *14*
Sun Stone (Calendar Stone) 12
illustrations *8*, *15*, *17*
photographs *2*, *16*, *22*, 24
Mission Héliographique (1851) 10
Mitla, Oaxaca 18, *33*, 36
Fourth Palace *33*, 36, *40-41*
Great Palace *34-35*, *37*, *38*
Priest's House *33*
Second Palace *39*
Monckhoven, Désiré van: *A Popular Treatise on Photography* 36, 167n.5

Oaxaca 31, *32 see also* Mitla

Palenque, Chiapas 19, 56-57, 59, 92, 140
excavations 14-15
Palace Complex 18, 59, *60-61*, *127*, 140
House C *142*, *143*
southeast corner of eastern court *141*
Western court and tower *142*, *143*
Stone of the Cross 57, *58*, 59
Temple of Inscriptions: glyphs 10, *18*, 19, 56
Temple of the Cross: panels 19
Temple of the Sun *144*
wall paintings 154
Peabody Museum, Harvard, Massachusetts 25, 88, 92, 169n.3
photography
advantages over illustration 10-11, 24-25, 30-31, 129
development of 9-10, 25, 30
disadvantages 24, 30, 32, 36, 42, 73
see also archaeological photography; types of photographic process
Piedras Negras, Coahuila 88-89
lintels *93*, 93-94
plan *89*
stelae *90*, 90-92, *91*, *94*, 94-95, 98
Prélier, Louis: Calendar Stone (daguerreotype) *22*

Quiriguá, Izabal
"The Great Turtle" 136, *136*, *137*, *138*
wall paintings 154

Rivail, Hippolyte Léon Denizard (Allan Kardec) 71, 168n.5
Romantic movement 21

Index

Salvin, Osbert: *Biologia Centrali-Americana* (with Godman) 122, 125
Salzmann, Auguste 11, 22
Squier, E. G. 64
Stephens, John Lloyd. 22
  Incidents of Travel in Central America ... 21
  Incidents of Travel in Yucatan 20–21, 21
stereography 25, 65–66, 67, *67*, *68*, *70*, *75*, *79*
"the Sublime and the Picturesque" 21

Talbot, William Henry Fox 9
Thompson, Edward H. 151, 156, 169n.3
Tozzer, Alfred 159, 160

Usumatsintla (Usumacinta) River, Mexico 89, 95, 97, *144*
Uxmal, Yucatán 19, 48, *53*, 65, 66
  Chenes Temple, Pyramid of the Magician *82*, *83*, *84*
  Governor's Palace (Casa del Gobernador) *20–21*, 49–50, 54, *54*, *55*, 77–80, *78*, *79*, *80*
  Nuns' Palace *28*, 48, *49*, *50*, *51–53*
    Serpent Façade *52–53*
  Sanctuary 85
  West Building, Nunnery Quadrangle *81*

Verninac Saint-Maur, Raymond de 26
  Voyage de Luxor 26

Waldeck, Jean Frederic Maximilien, Comte de 15, 19, 22, 24, *133*
  illustrations
    Monuments anciens du Mexique (Brasseur de Bourbourg)
      glyphs from Temple of Inscriptions, Palenque *18*, 19, 56
      panels from Temple of the Cross, Palenque 19
  publications
    Voyage pittoresque et archéologique dans la province d'Yucatan ... 19
wet-plate photography *see* collodion
Wollaston, William Hyde 21

Xochicalco 12, *13*, 18
  Temple of the Feathered Serpent 12

Yaxchilán, Chiapas 26, 92, 95, 97
  House H *144*
  lintels
    drawings by Hunter *126*, *129*
    photographs by Maler 97–98, *99*, 99–100, *104*, 105–6, *107*, *112*, 113–15
    photographs by Maudslay 97, *126*, *128*, *145*
    removed by Maudslay 26, 97, *128*, *144*, 169n.14, 169n.23
  The Red Temple on the Shore (El Tiemplo de la Ribera) *101*
  stelae *86*, 98, 100, *102*, 102–3, 105, 106, *107*, 108–13, *109*, 115–19, *116–17*
  Structure 19 ("The Labyrinth") *96*, 97
  Structure 33 *2*, *116*
  Structure 40 *116*
Yucatán 22, 24, 64, 66, 81 *see also* Chichén Itzá; Izamal; Mérida; Uxmal

Photo Credits

Österreichische Nationalbibliothek, Vienna
Figure: 14

George Eastman House, International Museum of Photography, Rochester, NY
Figure: 13

Getty Research Institute, Los Angeles
Figures: 42, 43, 44, 45, 46, 47, 48, 49, 50, 51, 52, 53, 55, 56, 58, 59, 60, 61, 62, 63, 64

Musée du Quai Branly, Paris
Figure: 15

Library of Congress, Washington, DC
Figures: 1, 2, 3, 4, 5, 6, 7, 8, 9, 10, 11, 12, 16, 17, 18, 19, 20, 21, 22, 23, 24, 25, 26, 27, 28, 29, 30, 31, 32, 33, 34, 35, 36, 37, 38, 39, 40, 41, 83, 85, 86, 88

Peabody Museum of Archaeology of Ethnology, Harvard University, Cambridge, MA
Figures: 54, 57, 65, 66, 67, 68, 73, 76, 82, 112, 113, 114, 125, 127, 130

Brooklyn Museum, New York
Figures: 90, 91, 92, 93, 94, 95, 96, 97, 98, 99, 100, 101, 102, 103, 104, 105, 106, 107, 108, 109

Bristol Museum & Art Gallery, Bristol, UK
Figures: 115, 116, 117, 118, 119, 120, 121, 122, 123, 124, 126, 128, 131

Ibero-Amerikanisches Institut, Berlin
Figures: 69, 70, 71, 72, 74, 75, 77, 78, 79, 80, 81, 129

British Museum, London
Figures: 84, 87, 110, 111

Authors
Figure: 89

Chapter 3: *The System of Real Numbers* 283
Chapter 4: *The System of Complex Numbers and the Quaternions* ..291
Chapter 5: *The Fundamental Theorem of Algebra* 297
Chapter 6: *Set Theory* 299
Chapter 7: *Logic* 313
Chapter 8: *Functional Analysis* 323
Chapter 9: *Topology* 345
Chapter 10: *Functions of Real Variables* 357
Chapter 11: *Abstract Algebra* 367
Chapter 12: *Categories and Functors* 379
Chapter 13: *Recent Discoveries and Achievements* 385
Chapter 14: *Language* 401
Appendix I: *The Fast Fourier Transform (FFT)* 405
Appendix II: *Historical Roots and Basic Notions in the Theory of Distributions* by L. Schwartz............................411
Appendix III: *The Theory of Wavelets* 425
CURRICULUM VITAE 431
BIBLIOGRAPHY 433
CHRONOLOGICAL TABLE 437
NAME INDEX 447
SUBJECT INDEX 451